SOCIALIST OPPOSITION IN EASTERN EUROPE

Jiri Pelikan

SOCIALIST OPPOSITION
IN
EASTERN EUROPE
the Czechoslovak example

Translated by Marian Sling and V. & R. Tosek

Allison & Busby, London

First published in Great Britain 1976
by Allison and Busby Limited
6a Noel Street, London, W1V 3RB

ISBN 0 85031 182 9 (hardback)
ISBN 0 85031 183 7 (paperback)

Set in 10 pt Times and printed by
Villiers Publications Ltd, Ingestre Road, London NW5 1UL

CONTENTS

New Questions

The shock and indignation caused by the invasion of Czechoslovakia on 20 August 1968, the protest against the occupation of the country by the armies of the five Warsaw Pact states and the cruel end of the Prague Spring, lasted just over a year. Although none of those who protested at the time have modified their original position of repudiation, there is an increasingly predominant view that August 1968 "is a thing of the past", and that this "traffic accident" (Michel Debré) must not get in the way of the highly promising rapprochement and co-operation between East and West, which is based on recognition of the current political status quo; a status quo which emerges as a continuation or acknowledgement of the unofficial agreements reached in Yalta in 1945. Even though protests are heard from time to time, notably whenever repression is used in occupied Czechoslovakia, the stream of parliamentarians, ministers and above all businessmen with Moscow as their destination, interrupted for a short time, has soon begun to flow once more. Political and economic agreements, official communiqués and statements are devised to create the impression that 1968 and the military intervention in Czechoslovakia never took place. Many representatives of the Right and of the Left, despite different terminologies, soon agreed that the Czechoslovak experiment of 1968 had been an attractive episode but doomed to failure right from the start, and that it must not jeopardise the balance in Europe and throughout the world, which is based on a division of spheres of influence between the two superpowers.

Yet barely eighteen months had passed before these exponents of *realpolitik* were once again faced with dramatic events in Eastern Europe — this time in Poland. The workers' revolt on the Baltic coast in the winter of 1970-71, and the subsequent change of leadership in Poland, once again shattered illusions about the "stable situation" in Eastern Europe. Yet all the experts and commentators who, as late as November 1970 (in connection with the signing of an agreement between Poland and the Federal Republic of Germany, an undeniable diplomatic success), had been predicting not just stability but a further strengthening of Gomulka's

7

power, very soon found their feet in the new situation: the entire conflict was blamed on Gomulka's stubbornness, and from this it could be deduced that the "new leadership" would set the accidentally derailed train back on its tracks.

No sooner had the excitement about Poland died down than signs of resistance and opposition appeared in the very heart of the "socialist camp", in the Soviet Union, to general astonishment. What had for a long time been regarded as untypical symptoms of dissatisfaction on the part of a handful of intellectuals, gradually proved to be the tip of an iceberg whose concealed layers sheltered a host of explosive problems. The world public became acquainted with names such as Sakharov, Solzhenitsyn, Grigorenko, Bukovsky, Zhores and Roy Medvedev, Chalidze, Litvinov, Yesenin-Volpin, Plyushch, Yakir and Krasin, Daniel and Sinyavsky, Maksimov, Nekrasov and others; but many more remained unknown. Gradually it became evident that these were no isolated cases; there followed the mass movement of the Jewish population for immigration to Israel, demands for equality in the Ukraine, in the Baltic states, in the Caucasus and Central Asia, the civil rights movement, the revival of religious groups as well as of Russian nationalism and of conservative Slavophilism. There are differing views about these opposition movements: some exaggerate them, others underrate them, but no one can close his eyes any longer to this many-sided and (in more ways than one) contradictory movement which is changing the political map of the USSR.

Signs of unrest and of intellectual ferment have appeared even in countries which were long ago "normalised". They include the trial of the young Hungarian poet and sociologist Haraszti, the expulsion of Andras Hegedus and other members of the "Budapest School" from the Party in 1973 (following student demonstrations which put forward the slogan "all power to the workers' councils", a slogan unheard of anywhere in Eastern Europe), and the position adopted by the "opposition communists" Havemann and Bietmann in the GDR. The elimination of the *Praxis* review and its group of Marxist philosophers and of other so-called "liberals" and "left-wing radicals" in Yugoslavia comes into this same category.

But in occupied Czechoslovakia above all, new voices began to make themselves heard: not just progressive intellectuals and exponents of the "Prague Spring" who refuse to accept "reality", but — for the first time in the post-war history of Eastern Europe — a *socialist opposition* which has come forward with statements,

8

leaflets, newspapers, programmes and various actions. Despite efforts by the occupation régime to silence these voices by means of political trials and reprisals, they continue to be heard even from behind prison bars, and are finding their way into the world at large.

All these phenomena have drawn the attention of the public in the West to the issue of political opposition in Eastern Europe and give rise to several new questions, which await an answer.

Did these opposition forces emerge by accident or were they even brought to life by "foreign subversion", as official East European propaganda would have it; or are they, on the contrary, the result of a crisis of the system which prevails in the USSR and in the East European countries?

Do these phenomena point to a gradual democratisation of the system, or to a return to the repressive methods of Stalinism?

Are they concomitant phenomena of "international détente" or can they, on the contrary, become a victim of this détente?

Which social forces in their respective countries do they represent?

What is their programme and what are the practical possibilities of implementing it and of exerting a genuine influence on social developments there?

But above all: can there be a socialist opposition in a country in which the Communist Party wields power, and what are its possibilities and prospects?

The Historical Roots of the Socialist Opposition

In order to illustrate this question with a concrete example, it is necessary to go back to the history of the socialist opposition in Czechoslovakia, to its initial demonstrations against the deformation of socialism, against its bureaucratic-centralist, étatist, police-state, authoritarian structures. It is important to remember that it has always differed from the anti-communist opposition on the Right, which existed since the party came to power in 1948 and whose members originally came from banned political groupings. They were later joined by those who were disillusioned with the everyday practices of a certain type of socialism, with the injustices committed in the name of socialism (especially the trials and purges carried out between 1949 and 1954), with forced collectivisation in the countryside, with the servile attitude of the leadership towards the Soviet Union — in brief, with all the measures which resulted in an identification of socialism with a police régime. There can be no doubt that socialism improved the living conditions of the workers with regard to social security, the health service, culture and education; but it also deprived them of the traditional rights for which generations of Czech and Slovak working-class people had fought: freedom of speech, freedom of assembly, the right to strike, independent trade unions, free elections, national sovereignty etc.

In Czechoslovakia, which had been a remarkably progressive democratic state between 1918 and 1948 (with the exception of the 1939-45 Nazi occupation), these infringements were particularly resented. And yet opposition after this period was essentially not directed against the socialist system as such, which by and large was accepted by the majority of the population, but rather against all its deformations: notably against the contradictions between socialist principles and their constant violation. The consciousness-forming process proceeded extremely slowly and unevenly, creating uneasiness and moral crises. In particular the younger generation of Party members, who had offered all their energy and talent to building a socialist society, gradually discovered these contradictions — at first sceptically then despairingly, and finally with a determination to eliminate them. And that is precisely where we must look first and foremost for the origins of the opposition and for its socialist-orientated protagonists.

Repression first hit the non-communist opposition, which admittedly did not merely defend the right to its own existence and freedom. It already foresaw at that time the consequences stemming from the Communist Party's position of monopoly power. Soon afterwards repression was shifted to the ranks of the Communist Party as well; it reached its climax in the big "show trial" of the General Secretary of the CPCz, Rudolf Slansky.

The big political trials in 1949-53 and the repression in general were not directed at a true opposition within the Communist Party, even though the defendants were condemned on the charge of attempting to topple the party leadership and of wanting to seize power as agents of "titoism", "trotskyism", "revisionism", "nationalism", "cosmopolitanism", but above all "zionism". Stalin and, under his influence, Klement Gottwald intended to use these political trials to *nip every possibility of an independent road to socialism in the bud. That is how they succeeded in establishing the Soviet model,* as well as the domination of the CPSU within the international communist movement. Slansky, Clementis, Geminder, Sling, Frank, Frejka, André Simone and the other accused who were to be executed did not oppose the Stalin and Gottwald line: they condoned the fight against Yugoslav revisionism, they backed the pro-Soviet orientation and accepted the USSR as a model. They became the victims not because of their views and deeds but because of a suspicion that one day they might oppose the Soviet Union's role as the sole centre, the pivot of world socialism.

Some landed in the dock because they were too well-versed in the history of the Comintern and the Party, others because during the war they had sought refuge in capitalist countries, thus widening their knowledge of the world and their horizons, others again because they maintained too many contacts in international circles, which allegedly divorced them from the "national reality". On the other hand, repression was meted out equally to people whose roots in the Czech or Slovak nation were too deep — after all, they could well turn into organisers of a nationalist revolt. Those who had fought in Spain or on other anti-fascist fronts did not accept the thesis that the Soviet Army alone had brought liberation. In short, they were all suspected of being potential tools of hypothetical deviations, since they had demonstrated a certain measure of independent thinking.

11

Stalin intended to forestall any risk of allowing the emergence of another Tito. That is why he replaced all communists who by their past, by their knowledge of Marxism and their capabilities in tackling particular tasks appeared to constitute a threat to mediocre officials, to irresolute and obedient apparatchiks, who were isolated from the masses but were well-disciplined. These subordinate officials were tied down by gratitude: they had been given a job which they did not deserve and in which they would never have remained without the support of "big brother".

This was the case with Antonin Novotny who, following direct intervention from the CPSU with the Czechoslovak leaders, made his way to the top of the Party leadership following Gottwald and Zapotocky. The CPCz leadership had already chosen the veteran communist Viliam Siroky as candidate for the Presidency of the Republic when Voroshilov arrived in Prague on orders from the CPSU, and enforced Novotny's election. Novotny was given the task of concluding the process of transforming the Communist Party — the only one in Central Europe able to look back on a long tradition of legality and able to rely on the support of broad sections of the population as well as on many intellectuals — into a willing tool of the CPSU and Soviet policy. Over a certain period the political trials acted as a deterrent, so that all opposition within the party could be stifled. After February 1948 all political activity outside the Communist Party was impossible. Attempts to revive political groups branded as illegal were drastically obstructed by the police, which instigated proceedings against tens of thousands of Czechs and Slovaks who ended up in prisons or forced labour camps. It was hardly possible to justify this repression by the need to protect the socialist state against the activities of enemies at home and abroad. In most cases the charges were sheer fabrications designed to create a prophylactic state of terror and fear; the victims were innocent and had fought by the side of the communists during the war so that socialism should one day become a reality. Czechoslovak communists — and the author was one of them — cannot be released from their responsibility for all this; they became aware of the extent and disastrous consequences of this tragedy only much later, at a time when the repressive machinery turned against themselves and brought in its wake the demoralisation of the entire movement.

Hence one of the first steps in opposition to the bureaucratic régime was to expose the full truth about the 1949-53 political trials, to rehabilitate the victims, both communists and non-communists, and to get rid once and for all of this cancerous evil of the past. One of the lessons which we drew from our confrontation with this period was that *freedom is indivisible, and every form of oppression in the end turns against those who have accepted it as a means of solving political and ideological controversies.* One of the first decisions of the Prague Spring was, therefore, the establishment of a commission of investigation; it was to work on the revision of the political trials and the rehabilitation of all who had become their victims between 1949 and 1954. The report of the Piller commission was the first official analysis of the oppressive mechanisms to appear in the socialist countries. In addition, it submitted a bill providing for the rehabilitation of all unjustly sentenced persons.*

At that time there was no political opposition in the true sense of the word outside the Communist Party, but rather latent discontent which took on various manifestations including outbreaks of popular anger in 1953, following the currency reform which adversely affected the people's living standards. There were local uprisings, in Pilsen for example, where the police and army were called in. The régime had banned any public expression of opposition; it thus inevitably lost contact with the population and had to set up a vast network of police agents and informers if it wanted to have an idea of their true feelings.

Any kind of political activity could only be conducted via the Communist Party which had a monopoly of all matters concerning political and economic life, culture, science, sports and, indeed, the private lives of citizens. This helps to explain how the membership of the Party rose after February 1948. Some people tried to get the help of the Party, without whose consent no one could hold any kind of public office, to gain personal advantages; others were compelled to join. Finally, a section of the young generation saw in the Party a way of translating their political ideals into reality.

At first the domination of the Party could be asserted only by force; later it was considered inevitable — right up to the 20th Congress of the CPSU. However, attempts by the Novotny leadership to conceal from Party members and from the population the true extent of the crimes committed during the Stalin era unleashed a wave of strong protest among communists. No practical consequences were drawn by the leadership from all that had happened

---

* cf. Pelikan, *The Czechoslovak Political Trials 1950-1954,* Macdonald & Co., London 1971.

— the impression was created that these had been nothing more than individual errors and had nothing in common with the personality cult, which Czechoslovakia was said to have been spared. At meetings where excerpts from the well-known Khrushchev speech were read out, party lecturers were asked embarrassing questions which they were unable to answer. Demands began to be heard for the rehabilitation of the victims of political trials, for the search for Czechoslovakia's own road to socialism, for creative Marxist thinking, for freedom of discussion within the Party. Many Party organisations asked for a special Congress to examine the application of the decisions of the CPSU in all spheres. Although the Party statutes make provisions for such a possibility (provided one-third of all branches demand the convocation of such a congress), the Party leadership sensed the danger, and after some brief hesitation decided to launch a counter-attack. The brutal reaction to these first manifestations of opposition ended with the expulsion of many communists. The same threat hung over many branches if they refused to withdraw their demand.

Even though this first opposition wave was stifled it did leave something behind. Party members with critical faculties realised that it was possible to break out of the ghetto in which they had voiced their doubts to no avail. For the first time an internal discussion took place in Party branches, new ideas were put forward, the members began to think about the content of everything which the Party was passing down merely to be rubber-stamped. A breach had been opened in the monolithic structure of the Party, and it could no longer be healed.

This first phase was followed by a period of slow and gradual formation of an opposition within the Party. This was by no means a conscious, organised process. After all, the very idea of an opposition was reprehensible — not just in the eyes of the leadership but also for the protesters themselves, who wanted to remain loyal Party members. Their objections and doubts were to be kept within the limits of constructive criticism. Meanwhile differences of opinion were voiced with increasing frequency, even though official quarters did their best to conceal them or to present them as sporadic occurrences. This tension was increased even further by reports from communists sentenced in the 1949-53 trials and suddenly released without rehabilitation. Unrest spread among students, journalists, writers and scientists in Slovakia, particularly after the Twenty-Second Congress of the CPSU and the Congress of the CPCz in 1962. Khrushchev's repeated attacks on Stalinism

14

strengthened the critical trends within the CPCz. At the Twelfth Party Congress a special commission of the Central Committee was formed, headed by Drahomir Kolder, which was to investigate once more the problem of political trials and rehabilitation.

The report of the commission submitted to the Central Committee session in April 1963 caused an immense stir in the Party and throughout the country, even though every attempt had been made to keep it secret and even though Novotny greatly restricted the political scope of its work. Despite its shortcomings the report clearly unveiled the mechanisms of the 1949-53 political trials, the falsifications used as a pretext, the part played by Soviet advisers as well as the role of Stalin and of the CPSU in these trials, which had cost dozens of members of the Czechoslovak leadership their lives and thousands of citizens their freedom.

Since the report also raised the question of personal responsibility, Novotny decided — in order to save his own skin — to sacrifice a number of his supporters in leading positions and to offer these posts to new people. He thus tried to pose as one of the champions of rehabilitation and as a reformer.

A new wind was now sweeping through the country. When reading today some of the newspapers of 1963 one realises that the first shots of the Prague Spring took place then within the Party and were already affecting cultural life, certain spheres of the economy, youth organisations and the press.

While the Czechoslovak leadership was still wavering between liberalism and orthodoxy, Moscow reacted harshly. It demanded that an end should be put to the whole fuss about the trials, that a stop should be put to irresponsible discussions, that ideological discipline and strict censorship should be restored, and that all "liberal" elements should be eliminated. Although this time the initiative for this about-turn came from Moscow, where Novotny's "indulgence" was criticised, the dogmatists in Prague soon resumed control over the Party. In order to justify the purges Novotny exposed an alleged plot by NATO intelligence services, which were said to have worked out a plan in Munich for subversive activities on three fronts: in the cultural sphere, on the Slovak question and on the generation conflict. Whoever should henceforth dare to criticise in any one of these three sectors — the régime's weak spots — could automatically be accused of complicity in the conspiracy. This made these problems taboo and barred them from discussion.

But it was no longer possible to prevent the various opposition currents from drawing closer together. They consolidated their position inside the Party, which they henceforth regarded as a platform for the dissemination of ideas for renewal.

This development was encouraged by the economic and political crisis throughout the country, which compelled Novotny to accept and even support certain new ideas. For example, groups of economists, lawyers, sociologists, psychologists and historians got together to analyse and prepare reform projects. The most important of these groups was formed around Professor Ota Sik. In 1963 and 1964 it drew up a plan for economic reform which was endorsed by the Central Committee in 1965. Notwithstanding their limited character these measures became the touchstone for a struggle between the progressive elements, who insisted on their application, and the Party and State apparatus, which tried hard to obstruct them from the moment it suspected that its power monopoly might be in jeopardy. Two further centres of new ideas were formed: a commission at the Institute for Political Law and Political Science headed by Zdenek Mlynar drew up a study on "the development of the political system in a socialist society"; another one, made up of several members of the Academy of Sciences under Radovan Richta, dealt with the repercussions of the scientific and technical revolution on the socialist system. The method of mixed commissions and teamwork enabled experts in various spheres to maintain contacts and thus created personal relations which were to play an important role in paving the way for the events in 1968.

While the Party leadership tolerated and even encouraged nonconformist discussions in scientific institutes, it became most intolerant the moment the discussions and the whole atmosphere of doubt and objections reached the population at large and particularly the young people. The students were the first to criticise the social stagnation, and pressed for more freedom to organise. The Conference of Prague Students in 1965 proposed a reform of the state-controlled youth organisation. The organisation was to be independent of the Party, and capable of representing the specific interests of various sections of the younger generation. The Party turned the proposal down. Its authors, including Jiri Müller (who was to be arrested in 1971), refused to give in and were subsequently expelled from the organisation and sent down from university. But the Party leadership was no longer in a position to restore calm and order. The agitation continued, reaching its height on 31 October 1967 with a street demonstration of Prague students for which massive police deployments were made. These repressive measures were among the factors which accelerated the 1967 crisis. In addition, discontent and the awareness of crisis were particularly widespread among artists and were expressed primarily in literature, on the stage and in films. A large number of works which condemned the vestiges of Stalinism and the deformation of socialist principles became instruments of a political struggle which was fought on two fronts: first of all among the mass of the people who saw in them an expression of their aspirations and hopes, and secondly in the leading group, which declared merciless war on all cultural workers. The culmination of this conflict was the Fourth Writers' Congress in June 1967. It turned into a political forum and contributed to a fundamental differentiation within the ranks of the Party while simultaneously encouraging opposition.

In a socialist state the conflict between authority, which has censorship and all the other means of pressure at its disposal, and socialist culture is a factor which needs to be analysed more attentively if one wants to study the problems raised by the opposition in those countries. It is not, as certain Western intellectuals and politicians assume, the struggle of a numerically small intellectual élite for the preservation of "its own" freedom of opinion and "its own" material and political privileges in order to step into the shoes of the working class and the state machinery. Official propaganda seeks to reduce the role of the opposition to this alone. It is true that in the socialist countries writers — and artists in general — are in a privileged position in relation to the rest of the population, above all from a purely material point of view. Furthermore, they enjoy greater freedom of expression, they are able to travel, establish contacts and so on. But if they question the power of the authorities then this is not in order to multiply the privileges which they are accorded in return for a conformist or at least an apolitical, neutral position. Quite the contrary, in doing so they risk losing them and being reduced to silence. If intellectuals, artists and scientists in a country such as Czechoslovakia offer their talents to building socialism, they do this because they are prompted by a need to reflect the wishes and aspirations of a population with whom they have close ties. And this is true even more when discontent cannot be expressed through normal political channels. Consequently, the cultural scene becomes a forum which expresses militant slogans for freedom and a return to the socialist ideal. That is the answer to the Western

17

observers who want to know why intellectuals and more particularly writers (who enjoy immense prestige in the East European countries) take an interest in political affairs and why such importance must be attached to their persecution. It explains likewise why *each and every socialist opposition working for the democratisation of the system in which it is developing considers the demand for greater freedom of expression indispensable* — though the Left in the West frequently regards it as a liberal and outmoded watchword. It can hardly be assumed that workers and peasants will manage their affairs properly if they have no access to sources of information concerning state matters and if this information is reserved exclusively for an élite of high-ranking officials. This does not mean that there will be no "élitist" endeavours, no exaggerations of any sort; these are the results of long years of suppression of free discussion. But these tendencies are neither typical nor decisive.

Among the acute tensions which emerged between 1965 and 1967, the Slovak question was one. It was the outcome of a policy in which the majority of 9.4 million Czechs asserted their economic and numerical superiority over the 4.2 million Slovaks. Novotny's policy drove the entire Slovak minority into an alliance with the Czech opposition. All the patriotic forces — ranging from communists such as Dubcek, Novomesky, Husak down to conservatives such as Bilak, Salgovic, Janik and even to nationalist anti-communists — formed a common front against Novotny's policy and the centralism emanating from Prague. This Slovak opposition was directed primarily against the person of Novotny, and demanded the recognition of equality for the Slovaks within the Republic. Its aim was not to change the system as a whole. In contrast to Czech opposition it attached only secondary importance to democratisation. Since it formed an important monolithic block in the Central Committee — about one-third — it played a decisive role in ousting Novotny in January 1968.

Later, however, this opposition slowed down to a considerable degree the democratisation process in Slovakia and throughout the whole country. It is no coincidence that the Slovak Party Congress at the end of August 1968 became Husak's first platform for an attack against the Extraordinary Congress of the Party which had been held in secret at Prague-Vysocany on 22 August 1968. Neither is it a coincidence that the Slovak leadership — admittedly with a few honourable exceptions — was the first to place itself in the service of the Soviet occupying power and the policy of "normalisation" and thus contributed decisively to Dubcek's overthrow.

Discontent, contradictions and controversies occurred equally *within the leadership*, among Party members and in the Central Committee. But what they lacked was a common platform, which could not be worked out for many reasons: surveillance by the secret service, mutual mistrust, personal differences and divergent interests. Nevertheless, certain common demands began to emerge: democratisation of internal Party life, restriction of the absolute power of the Presidium of the Central Committee, criticism of the personal style of leadership by First Secretary Novotny, greater control of the rank and file over the Party machine, strengthening of relations between the Party and the people. There was general agreement that Novotny constituted the major obstacle to the fulfilment of these demands since he held the two highest offices in Party and state: that of First Secretary and of President of the Republic. This resulted in a unanimous proposal by all the opposition forces that henceforth such an accumulation of offices must be prohibited. Novotny found himself in a difficult situation since he was confronted by resistance from the majority in the Presidium and from dogmatists and Stalinists who reproached him for his "liberalism", for certain ideological concessions such as the economic reform, for his tolerance in the cultural domain, and for the partial rehabilitation of the show trial victims. It was Brezhnev who delivered the *coup de grâce* when in December 1967 he refused to continue supporting Novotny and thus punished him for the position he had adopted at the time of Khrushchev's overthrow.

As soon as the Central Committee had decided on the separation of the highest offices on 5 January 1968 and had elected Dubcek First Secretary of the Party, the fragile union between Novotny's opponents split into three main trends. The "progressives" regarded this as merely a first step, and refused to be satisfied with a mere change of persons. They pressed for structural changes which would replace the bureaucratic-centralist model by a socialist democratic society, which would take proper account of the country's peculiarities — a demand which Dubcek gave the popular name of "socialism with a human face". Then there were the "centrists", who also wanted certain reforms but only those which did not affect the Party's monopoly position and which did not alter the structures of society. What they wanted was merely an improvement of the system. Finally came the "conservatives" who wanted no reforms whatsoever but, on the contrary, a strengthening of discipline, of existing structures and of the Party's monopoly.

19

For them the crisis was simply the result of a liberal policy and of a lack of tough leadership in implementing decisions which should not have been called in question in the first place.

Towards a Rebirth of Socialism

There are three reasons why the new leadership under Dubcek at first showed some hesitation following the plenary session in January 1968: first of all it had no clear, well-considered programme; secondly, there were differences among those who had supported it; and finally, it was not really as new as all that, since it consisted mostly of members of the old leadership. Novotny himself remained a member of the Presidium and President of the Republic. But prior to the change in power it had been impossible, for the reasons mentioned earlier, to draw up any sort of common programme, and the blame for this must not be placed on Dubcek and his supporters. It was in fact symptomatic of the authoritarian system that first of all the opposition was prevented from working out a political alternative, and that when it was not in a position to come forward with an immediate programme it was accused of incompetence.

Thus a programme had to be drafted which was guided solely by the requirements and the urgency of the moment, and which had all the shortcomings inherent in such a project. The progressives were afraid that the conservatives would hinder democratisation. After all, they still held all the key positions in the Party and state machinery. In order to avoid this pitfall the people were mobilised to bring pressure to bear on Dubcek and the leadership to accelerate structural reforms. The conservatives, on the other hand, resisted reforms which they considered too radical and also applied pressure on Dubcek, which made the population impatient. The centrists, in turn, searched for compromises. That is precisely how the first political programme of the "new course", the Action Programme of the CPCz, came into being; it was unanimously adopted by the Central Committee on 5 April 1968. (Two years later the same Central Committee, but without Dubcek and his supporters, declared it to be revisionist and annulled it.) Despite its many shortcomings, the programme was one of the most constructive ever to have been drawn up in a socialist country. The Soviet leadership immediately declared it heretical and condemned it.

Even though the Dubcek team in fact had to work against time and under constant pressure from outside, and was faced with thousands of concrete tasks in all spheres, it made an effort right from the start to engage in programmed studies. Dozens of groups and commissions worked on reform projects and plans, especially in preparation for the Fourteenth Extraordinary Party Congress which was convened for 9 September 1968, and which had the urgent task of drawing up a Party programme. The CPCz had for a long time been without an official programme. Novotny had always rejected the elaboration of one under the pretext that the programme of the CPSU applied equally for the Czechoslovak Party.

Not for decades had there been in Czechoslovakia as impassioned and vast a debate among Marxist theoreticians, as many newly published books and studies, as many theoretical proposals and practical projects as during the period between January and August 1968.

While the projects and documents worked out for the Fourteenth Party Congress represent a highly interesting platform, a long-term programme would have been drawn up later against the background of a re-established political stability. The eight-month period, full of dramatic events, is too short to blame the leadership for not coming forward with a complete and perfect programme. This does not mean that Dubcek and his comrades cannot be reproached for not having chosen more clear-cut tactics and for not having implemented all the given directives with the necessary determination. The protagonists of the Prague Spring were fully aware of these weaknesses. One must not forget that after January 1968 everyone in Czechoslovakia was anxious to be involved in public affairs, that little attention was given to a division of tasks among those responsible for practical work and the theoreticians who were to analyse developments and take new stock. Everyone wanted to be directly involved and, above all, to act.

Such an attitude might be classed as "spontaneous", "anarchic" or "chaotic". Seen from a distance, such an assessment is not without justification. But it was precisely this that gave the process its constructive, revolutionary character. How could it have been otherwise in a movement which was no longer prepared to be controlled from above and which rejected the regimentation that had until then decided what the people were or were not capable of accomplishing by virtue of their "degree of maturity"? It appears that every movement in the socialist countries which is pregnant with the seeds of renewal must experience such an atmos-

22

phere, even if different situations bring with them local peculiarities. It is unfortunately predictable that in countries with even
more authoritarian régimes and without Czechoslovakia's democratic traditions, such a process of transformation would create
far more dramatic and confused situations. *Following the Soviet
invasion and the subsequent repression Czechoslovakia too will
in the future find it hard to carry out new changes in the same
atmosphere of tolerance and national conciliation as that which
prevailed in 1968.* To foreign observers who regret that Dubcek and
his associates did not have the entire process well in hand and that
they did not act like Ceaucescu, Kadar and Tito, one can only say
that this might have helped Dubcek to remain in power and carry
out some reforms but that it would have meant the end of the
Prague Spring — the symbol of a spontaneous popular movement,
the expression of the aspirations and endeavours of a people to
share responsibility for the decisions affecting their future.

It would take too long to analyse the process which took place
in 1968. We shall, therefore, confine ourselves to describing the
major trends which made a decisive contribution to the formation
of a socialist opposition after the Soviet invasion.

The "progressive" group adopted the most determined attitude
towards the occupation and normalisation. The "conservative"
group, on the other hand, provided the first collaborators and later
the leading men around Husak whose own position is a problem
in itself: at first a supporter of Dubcek, he later changed sides. The
centrists were divided: some tried to come to terms with the
"conservatives" and joined the personalities in opposition only
when the latter were expelled from the Party — or they completely
withdrew from politics. The demarcation line between these various
trends was not always as clear-cut in the spring of 1968, and
outside pressures helped to level out certain differences, and to
promote the search for compromises which in the last analysis
did not satisfy anyone. Dubcek himself made quite sure that no
one should end up in a situation from which there would be no
way out, and in doing so he revealed a great deal of tact — a
position which earned him countless disappointments when people
whom he had trusted in spite of their political views stabbed him
in the back. The progressives under no circumstances wanted to
use their power to condemn the "conservatives" and all other
adversaries to silence or to a sterile opposition as had been the case
in the past. They preferred to come forward with concrete measures
which were to guarantee the possibility of a constant exchange of

23

opinions and of a democratic dialogue, both at Party level and outside, in its relations with the trade unions or with other political groupings whose autonomy was respected. That is how a combination of representative parliamentary and direct democracy was to become possible, as practised by workers' councils and through self-management by citizens at all levels. The draft of new Party statutes provided for respect for all currents inside the Party whereby a minority could make its position prevail and become a majority, while other provisions were there to safeguard the unity of the Party and its ability to act — fundamental elements of democratic discipline, which demands of a minority that it accept the majority decision.

This draft represented the greatest heresy in the eyes of Czechoslovak and Soviet dogmatists, since it once more raised the anathema of freedom of expression for dissenting tendencies and questioned the centralised structure of the Party. The Soviet reaction was so harsh that even the centrists withdrew their support of the draft, although at this juncture this paradoxically helped the position of the Stalinists. The progressives realised very well that differences of opinion inside the Party were necessary and inevitable. That is why they wanted clear and unequivocal rules for democratic procedure. These prospects were completely destroyed by the Soviet intervention. The conservatives had no scruples on the question of freedom of expression for minorities; they first of all condemned such trends to silence and later simply expelled them from the Party and from political life.

From Invasion to "Normalisation"

The pronounced split within the ranks of the Party only came to the fore at the time of the invasion, but even then not immediately. The practically unanimous reaction of the people and of Party members prevented those who approved of the invasion and had even paved the way for it from declaring this in public. This went so far that following the fiasco of a so-called "revolutionary worker and peasant government" all the plotters, headed by Alois Indra and Bilak, gave their sanctimonious assurance that they had had no idea of what was happening and that they regarded the Soviet intervention as a "great tragedy". It took them two years to pluck up courage and dare to admit at the December 1970 session of the Central Committee that they were the ones who had called in the Soviet armed forces — since they had seen no other solution. They thus admitted their weakness and their complete isolation from the people.

Immediately after the invasion a certain degree of unity continued among the Dubcek supporters, the progressives and radicals and even certain conservatives. Proof of this was the collective leadership made up of Dubcek, Svoboda, Smrkovsky and Cernik. At first the main part was played by the radicals who had emerged from the progressive trend. They had discerned the true impact of the intervention straight away and they rejected the interpretation given by those who wanted to present the whole thing as a mere misunderstanding. They also drew the proper conclusions: there was only one possibility to counter it and that was the mobilisation of the masses in active but unarmed resistance. Contrary to the intentions of the pro-Soviet and conservative elements and even the wavering centrists, they proposed to convene the delegates to the Fourteenth Party Congress in Prague for 22 August. The decision of the 1,290 delegates at the CKD factory at Vysocany to declare themselves an Emergency Party Congress was to be of tremendous importance not just at the time but also for the future. In fact, this marked the formation of a *New Communist Party* without any kind of intervention from the machinery, under the auspices of the working class of this Prague suburb with its revolutionary traditions: it was the point of departure for a socialist opposition which was to make its appearance only two years later.

The purpose of this Fourteenth Party Congress was not to bring about a split within the Party, and no decision to this effect was ever taken. It represented an absolute majority of Party members and expressed the desire to maintain unity by proposing the appropriate conditions for co-operation with all those who remained outside this trend. The fatal split did not take place until their return from Moscow when Dubcek and the entire leadership with the exception of Kriegel accepted the conditions contained in the Soviet ultimatum, i.e. to declare the Fourteenth Party Congress null and void. Even though this compromise went against Dubcek's grain he accepted it for diplomatic reasons, in order to salvage what could still be salvaged (what he achieved was that eighty of the delegates to the Fourteenth Party Congress were co-opted as new members of the Central Committee); the Soviets were not satisfied with the compromise and instead came forward with further demands. It could not save the unity of the Party, nor permit the policy inaugurated in January 1968 to continue. The Fourteenth Party Congress was declared invalid, without any concessions. There was no promise — as anticipated — that it would be postponed to a later date. It was never convened, and the majority of its delegates were expelled from the Party. Power returned to the hands of the old Central Committee, which had a majority of conservatives. The newly co-opted members were again in a minority. Not for long, of course, because in less than a year most of them were expelled as well. This in fact was nothing short of complete capitulation, even though it did not look like that at first. Dubcek and certain progressives regarded this as the only possible solution and as a positive compromise which made it possible to save some aspects of the reform programme.

But there were quite a few who opposed such a solution: one of them was Jaroslav Sabata at the Central Committee meeting on 31 August 1968. Dubcek and his supporters, however, had such authority in the Party and among the population at the time that there was no chance for anyone to enforce a different point of view without being accused of treason.

The documents of that time, notably the speeches and articles by Sabata, Smrkovsky, Bartosek, Kosik and others, show that the progressives never ceased to propose "an alternative". They maintained that the problem was not being confronted correctly: either

26

the Moscow diktat had to be accepted or else the country was to be placed under the direct running of a foreign power. The participants in the Moscow negotiations confirmed that in the course of the "talks" Brezhnev had threatened a massacre of the population as a kind of sacrifice for expiation. Yet reality was entirely different. True, the USSR had occupied the country, but it remained wholly isolated from the population. World public opinion showed utter contempt for the Soviet Union, which found itself in a kind of political quarantine. It did not succeed in setting up a government made up of quislings; both the lawful government and the Party and Parliament continued to pursue the policy mapped out by Dubcek. Internationally, Brezhnev suffered a severe blow: the majority of communist parties dissociated themselves from the CPSU and condemned the intervention with a vehemence unparalleled in the history of the communist movement. World public opinion adopted the same stance, including a number of old friends of the Soviet Union. The parts had been reversed: it was Brezhnev, not Dubcek and Czechoslovakia, who was isolated and who had to look for an honourable retreat from the situation. There can be no doubt that Dubcek and his comrades condoned the Moscow diktat, for which they can be reproached particularly in the light of the different attitude adopted by Kriegel.

But one must remember that they were in custody at the time, cut off from their country and that they took Brezhnev's threats seriously. Even if one has no illusions about the Soviet leadership, it is hard to assume reasonably that it intended to eliminate an entire people in the heart of Europe without considering the tragic and unforeseeable consequences such an action would inevitably have. The negotiating team could, indeed, have confined itself to submitting the conditions enforced by the CPSU to the Central Committee of the CPCz. The latter, without discrediting the delegation, could have rejected them by pointing out that they had been signed under "abnormal" conditions while at the same time calling on the European communist parties to send delegates to Prague to act as mediators. It is perfectly possible to assume that such an attitude would have placed the Soviet leadership in a difficult position and compelled it to agree to a solution acceptable for both sides.

On this point the Czechoslovak communists have made an irreparable mistake which for a long time will burden the prestige and future of socialism in that country. In 1938 the communists had rightly accused President Benes of accepting the Munich diktat

27

without consulting Parliament. In 1968 it was the communists — first of all the leadership of the CPCz and then the Central Committee — who accepted the diktat of a foreign country, the text of which was never submitted to Parliament and remains unpublished till this day. They did this not just in the name of the Party but equally in the name of an entire people, who trusted them. This is a heavy responsibility which must not be overlooked.

Let us just for a moment accept the hypothesis put forward by Dubcek and Smrkovsky according to which there was no other way, and the essence of the 1968 reform could be saved. The only chance of success was to rely on the support of the people, to isolate the quislings and refuse to surrender to Soviet blackmail. The leadership, fearing further Soviet intervention, was paralysed. It was also being undermined by the destructive activities of Indra, Bilak, Kapek, Jakes and other dogmatists. Instead of encouraging the activity of the working class, everything was being done to maintain calm and discipline by a constant series of appeals. Instead of standing up to Soviet pressure more concessions were made, and the demands of the ultras were being met. The weakness and hesitation shown by the leadership had encouraged them, and since October 1968 they had been on the offensive. Such a position could save nothing; on the contrary, both reforms and people were being sacrificed — in short, the entire policy of the Prague Spring was coming to nought.

At the time not many people had such a clear picture of things to come as Jaroslav Sabata, Frantisek Kriegel, Karel Bartosek, Karel Kyncl and others. The majority was in full solidarity with the leadership, though of course with certain limitations which later became embodied in the saying: "We are with you, be with us!" This was a promise and at the same time a warning to the leadership not to become isolated from the people.

In the period from September 1968 to April 1969 the supporters of the "New Course" were still in a strong position in the Central Committee as well as in the regional and district committees of the Party. But since they had abandoned active mobilisation of the masses and any chances of winning more ground they were compelled to wage a *rearguard action* against the exclusion of the progressive elements, against the return of discredited officials, against the reintroduction of censorship, the suppression of public opinion, the step by step erosion of the 1968 policy and the return to Stalinist methods. They seemed to believe that time was working for them, whereas exactly the opposite was true.

Under the circumstances it was most important to counter defeatism and resignation and to keep alive the will to struggle, possibly by different methods. This determination was demonstrated by Czech writers, intellectuals and, in particular, by the students who on 17 November 1968 declared a general strike under the leadership of the students' union and in close collaboration with the trade unions and the workers' councils. Following the example of the Prague student demonstrations in November 1939 to pay tribute to the memory of the medical student Jan Opletal and the young worker Jiri Sedlacek, shot by the SS on 28 October 1939, the workers again gave their solidarity to the student movement and to their demands. The students' strike, the position of the workers and the population in general and the support of the progressive intellectuals gave Dubcek a solid basis for going over to the offensive. The quislings, who had begun to regroup, did not yet feel sufficiently strong and secure to oppose the movement openly. But the way in which Dubcek and the progressives — under pressure from Moscow and the Indra-Bilak group — surrendered Josef Smrkovsky, the most popular champion of the "New Course", was in itself an indication of the disintegration of the collective leadership, which was by now incapable of resolute resistance. *The possibilities of putting up opposition within the Party by now appeared exhausted; thus a basis of resistance had to be found outside it.*

All the attempts mentioned earlier on emanated from the rank and file, but did not get any firm support from the leadership — and despite their positive evaluation — they were obstructed and finally banned. The spectacular self-immolation of Jan Palach in January 1969 was an expression of the despair felt by the population. His funeral became an impressive demonstration of unity at which the students and a large section of the population again showed their support for the ideals of 1968. Shortly afterwards the workers' councils held a convention and the Trade Union Congress met. That was the last attempt to ward off the seizure of power by the conservatives and total subjugation to foreign occupation. In March 1969 the people's overwhelming display of enthusiasm following the victory of the Czechoslovak ice hockey team over the Soviet Union once more affirmed the true feelings of Czechs and Slovaks towards the invaders. The demonstration was followed by a police provocation: the Aeroflot offices in Prague were devastated; this gave the Soviet leadership the pretext to oust Dubcek once and for all and to replace him by Gustav Husak who, by his intrigues, had won Brezhnev's trust.

Who Is a True Communist?

Dubcek's replacement by Husak caused further division in the progressive camp. There were some who were prepared to give in and support Husak on condition that he would prevent reprisals against the authors of the 1968 reforms. Others made a stand against the palace revolution and pleaded for the continuation of the Prague Spring experiment. Yet they had no illusions whatever about being able to prevent the return to the methods used before 1968 and to the Soviet model which had in fact been the cause of the crisis in the Party and in society. But they wanted to carry on the struggle so as to have the prestige of socialism and of the Communist Party, in the knowledge that this was important for the future precisely because of the countless violations of ideals which had taken place.

Dr Frantisek Kriegel was one of the first to translate this attitude into words. Even though he was a veteran of the Communist Party with many years of international political and human experience, the censors banned the speech he made at the Central Committee meeting of 30 May 1969 — though the text circulated the length and breadth of the country as the first Czech "samizdat". This demonstrates the aims which these Communists, who were later reduced to silence and expelled from the Party, were prepared to fight for: *national independence and sovereignty, democracy, "socialism of the people" and not of the apparatchiks, international solidarity*. While he does not speak of "opposition" he uses a new and radical tone in his speech: instead of appealing for leniency and consideration and instead of practising self-criticism — as happened in other cases — he declared that he would remain a communist even if expelled from the Party, and that he intended to act as such. After Kriegel thousands and hundreds of thousands of Communists were excluded from the Party and that is how the term "the Party of the expelled" came into being.

Kriegel's behaviour was not an isolated case, as was shown by the attitude adopted by Karel Kyncl, a communist journalist, at a plenary session of the Prague City Communist Party Committee on 2 June 1969. Kyncl asked Husak whether a comrade who could not condone a policy which was in contradiction to the wishes and interests of the people would be regarded as being in breach of Party discipline.

Just like Kriegel and Kyncl, thousands of Communists asked themselves the same question: What next? To leave the Party and thus abandon the defence of socialism? To go home, or to fight those who wanted to pervert socialist ideals and to try to salvage something for the future? They did not want to have absolved the Party of a severe historical responsibility, only to capitulate afterwards and betray national independence. The position adopted by Kriegel, Kyncl, Sabata, Bartosek, Kosik, Kalivoda and others provided one answer, namely "not to howl with the wolves" but to reject the "reality" of the occupation, its legalisation, "normalisation" and to dissociate themselves from the Husak group which had lent itself to this reactionary and anti-national step. Henceforth expulsion from the Party, even though it still called itself "Communist", ceased to be a tragedy. *They knew that the Party card was not enough to make a person a communist, and that its withdrawal did not stop you from being one. They knew that in future there would be communists and "communists".* But one thing has to be made clear: Who is a true communist? Brezhnev, who sends half a million soldiers and his tanks to mow down the freedom of a small country? Or Grigorenko and Yakimovich who in the Soviet Union declared their solidarity with Czechoslovakia? Ulbricht, who feared the contagious character of socialist democracy? Or Professor Havemann who is fighting for it in the GDR, together with Czechoslovak communists? Dubcek, Kriegel, Sabata, Hübl — or Indra, Bilak, Kapek? Where is the demarcation line? As yet it is not clearly discernible, but it is beginning to exist *and in the future it will go right across the entire international communist movement.*

Given the autonomous initiative of the workers and intellectuals and the expulsion of the progressive communists, the foundations were now laid for resistance from outside the Party. It is only logical that the first attempt to draw up a programme should have been made not by Party members but by a group of intellectuals including communists, and those without Party affiliation. The "Ten-Point Manifesto" (see Appendix, no. 1), often called the "New 2,000-Word Manifesto", is addressed to the state and Party leadership. It claims the constitutional right of citizens to petition. This absolutely lawful action makes it quite clear that the authors of the Manifesto had no intention of founding a new party or movement but much rather to work constructively and struggle politically within the framework of the existing institutions, and that they considered this possible. But this does not mean that they naïvely believed in the guarantees which ensured respect for legality. Indeed it required courage to draw up and submit such a document, as the reaction of the state security bodies against the authors was to show very soon. Three of them — Jan Tesar, Rudolf Battek and Ludek Pachman — were arrested in September 1969 and remained in jail for over a year. In January 1972 they were detained again. This time political trials followed, with heavy sentences. The others were interrogated and charged but the actual court proceedings were postponed at the last moment. Yet all the authors of the Manifesto were exposed to pressure and discrimination. Party members were expelled, they were banned from public life, lost their jobs, etc.

Almost simultaneously a further collective attempt was made to draft a programme for political opposition: the declaration of the *Revolutionary Socialist Party,* founded by Professor Petr Uhl and his friends. They came from a revolutionary youth movement which had its origins in the Prague Spring. In its struggle against the Soviet occupation and the enforced bureaucratic régime this group has declared its unequivocal support for socialism.

Its members consider the Prague Spring a significant point of departure for revolutionary progress, but express reservations and criticism about the Dubcek leadership, in particular its lack of revolutionary courage, and therefore do not share the illusions of progressive Communists towards the possibility of acting within the framework of legality. That is why they prepared for *underground activity* and pleaded for the foundation of a political vanguard organisation with a clear socialist programme, though they did not exclude work within the existing legal organisations.

If one recalls the atmosphere of that time, one must assume that this programme reflected the will of a minority of young people and workers and contradicted the feelings prevailing then in the country. The majority of the people had still not overcome the shock caused by the events of 21 August 1968: the general trend was anti-Soviet and nationalistic. It needed undeniable courage to choose such a road. One cannot but wonder whether this did not restrict the impact of the group. Yet the members of this group showed much more political perspicacity than certain leading politicians with long years of experience, and their experiment will no doubt go down in the history of the Czechoslovak socialist opposition as the first painful but useful attempt.

When Husak came to power he needed a transitional period during which he secured the co-operation of Dubcek and his friends, in order to gain time, to calm down emotions and to create the conditions for their final ousting. Following the brutal suppression of popular demonstrations on the first anniversary of the Soviet invasion — there were five dead and hundreds of injured — Husak and his collaborators felt strong enough to get rid of Dubcek. At a meeting of the Central Committee in September 1969 they launched an open attack. They had the decisions adopted by the Presidium during the night of 20-21 August 1968 annulled, just as they did those adopted by the National Assembly and the Government as well as the reply of the Central Committee to the letter from the five Warsaw Pact States of 19 July 1968 — a reply which this very same Central Committee had endorsed unanimously one year earlier. These measures meant in fact a legalisation of the occupation. Dubcek was criticised and expelled from the Presidium — he was still a member of the Central Committee — and was sent as Ambassador to Turkey, a NATO member country without a legal Communist Party where there would be no fear of sympathetic demonstrations. His supporters such as Spacek, Hübl, Cerny, Mikova and others were expelled not just from the Central Committee but from the Party.

At the Central Committee session three speeches were made — by Alexander Dubcek, Josef Smrkovsky and Milan Hübl — which, despite different approaches and temperaments, nevertheless had a number of characteristic and identical points:

— a profound conviction that the 1968 policy had been correct and clearly socialist and a refusal to consider it counter-revolutionary;

— loyalty to the Communist Party and to the revolutionary movement, and a rejection of the terms "right-wing" and "anti-socialist";

— the conviction that Husak would keep his promise and that the new leadership could continue the policy of the Prague Spring, even though within strict limits;

— a feeling of helplessness in view of the turn of events and the unjust accusations levelled against them personally;

— finally, a total lack of determination to prevent a further worsening of the situation or to mobilise the rank and file of the Party and population.

Hübl, as a historian of the communist movement, saw further and warned against repression and the demoralisation which would

33

inevitably be created: "I am aware not just of the visible components of such phenomena but also their hidden mechanism. That is why I am most concerned about the methods which are being used today to criticise and expose the 'right wing'. During the past few months a mechanism has been set in motion which — unless it is stopped at the last moment — will function in the same way as the notorious 'mills' of the fifties. . . . As distinct from then, the CPCz today has behind it the tragic experience of political trials, so that none of its members — let alone its leaders — can claim at some future date that he did not know how far things could go."

When one criticises today the position adopted by Dubcek and his supporters one must remember the atmosphere in which it was born, under what pressure the leaders of the Prague Spring were compelled to make a self-criticism, to vilify themselves and their comrades, as well as the entire policy of 1968. *The fact that Dubcek always refused to recant* — then, as later — ought to secure him a place of honour in the history of Czechoslovakia and of the international communist movement. Despite his enforced "resignation" he remains the symbol of the "New Course" and of the socialist opposition as he confirmed once more in his letter to Mrs Smrkovska (see Appendix, no. 14), and especially in his letter to the Federal Assembly dated 28 October 1974.

The speeches and the resolution of the Central Committee meeting of September 1959 provide an answer to certain fundamental questions: does the Party, as hitherto, remain the only place for a political confrontation between progressives and neo-Stalinists? Are there still acceptable compromises, with a view to a further step forward?

The answer to these questions is negative. In fact, at this point a historical stage in the development of a socialist opposition within the Party was over.

The Great Purge

For a number of Czechoslovak communists this realisation meant an end to all that had made their life meaningful. This was expressed by the Czech poet Stanislav Neuman, grandson of a well-known writer who had been a founding member of the CPCz, in his farewell letter of 18 September 1970 before committing suicide:

"I have decided to die because I can now see more and more clearly that the ideals which kept me in the Party — and for which my closest friends were executed on 2 May 1945 — are not being implemented but, on the contrary, are being trampled underfoot by the current political practices. True, I could fight them, but I no longer have the strength nor the courage. I neither want nor am I able to stand up against the Party. That is why I have chosen this way out. Mayakovsky characterised it as intellectualist, but even he chose it as the only possible road."

All that was left to the others was a return to their private lives, indifference, or a resigned wait for changes from outside. Some turned against the ideals in which they had believed until then. Yet the number of those who refuse to capitulate or to sit on the fence, and who have decided to continue the struggle under new conditions, is manifestly rising.

For tens of thousands of communists and other citizens this is a time of internal strife in which they have to reappraise existing values, in which they have to call in question an entire lifetime, and in which they reassess their fundamental political positions. They have been moulded by twenty years of socialism. In 1968 they were offered a unique chance to change their life in the direction they had dreamt of. These great hopes have now been followed by great purges: the record of each Party member is scrutinised individually, and no one can slip through this net.

Everyone has to make up his own mind: either to recant publicly, remain in the party and play a double game, or to stand up for his ideas which, while meaning expulsion, saves his honour as a communist. A difficult choice in a country and a situation where there is no other possible alternative nor prospect for change.

35

Many things have to be taken into consideration: one's own career, the result of many years of hard work which can suddenly come to naught; children who want to study and who are punished together with their parents; habits, friendships, financial circumstances. But first and foremost one's own conscience. The Government reckons with a mentality formed by centuries of foreign rule in the country: the Czechs have learnt the art of survival and the habit of regarding positions of principle as a luxury, as moral exhibitionism which a small nation cannot well afford. In this respect the purges of the seventies present a model for an accurate study of this monstrous and systematic destruction of the personality, of the mechanism of "normalisation" and of the methods used to demoralise a people and to force it into worse subjugation than could have been achieved by any genuine military defeat.

Almost 500,000 communists were expelled from the Party during the purges or left of their own free will after they had repudiated its policy. They became pariahs, anti-social elements, vilified by the press, radio and television without being able to defend themselves. They have been dismissed from their jobs, placed on a blacklist which makes any attempt at reintegration into the labour process impossible. Their wives and children are isolated and slandered. All these distressing consequences are exposed by Milan Hübl in a courageous letter addressed to Gustav Husak: he mercilessly confronts him with his own bitter past, he draws parallels with the no less bitter present and ends with a quotation by Karl Marx which both of them had not so long ago considered very apt, namely that a revolution which eats its own children is, like Saturn, on the wrong path.

Here is a brief review which shows how the avalanche of purges was set in motion. When the Party leadership returned from Moscow at the end of August 1968 — where Dubcek and his colleagues had been literally kidnapped, treated like prisoners-of-war and raised to the status of "negotiators" only after the fiasco of Brezhnev's plan to enforce a "revolutionary workers and peasants' government" headed by Alois Indra — the first victim was Dr Frantisek Kriegel, at the insistence of the Soviets. He was the only member of the delegation who refused to sign the Moscow diktat. Then followed the Deputy Premier, Professor Ota Sik, Interior Minister Josef Pavel, Foreign Minister Jiri Hajek, and the directors of radio and television Zdenek Hejzlar and Jiri Pelikan. At the end of 1968 it was the turn of Josef Smrkovsky, the Speaker of Parliament, whose political death sentence had, however, not yet been pronounced. Only then was the attack launched against Dubcek. His downfall set an avalanche in motion which no one could halt any longer. The major initiator of all these measures was already Gustav Husak, who had hidden in the background and in public acted as a loyal friend of Dubcek and of the people. He allegedly tried to save all that could be saved. Did he not say in September 1968 he "stood and fell with Comrade Dubcek"? And shortly afterwards that "no one had invited the Soviet troops"? And as late as in April 1969 that "the Prague Spring was among the most glorious chapters in the history of the Party"? All these pronouncements should be recalled by those who today still rely on Husak's "promises". The article "Husak's 700 Days", which appeared in an illegal journal of the socialist opposition and reviewed the period of Husak's leadership, aptly formulated the issues as follows: "Husak is able to promise anything and to forget everything" — depending on the circumstances. He is a man who, in spite of suffering Stalinist oppression in the fifties, became a prisoner of his thirst for power and his ambition to stand at the head of the country. Had the "New Course" continued, Husak would undeniably have been among its most zealous protagonists. But after the brutal Soviet intervention it became clear to him that "socialism with a human face" had suffered a defeat, that Dubcek and his supporters had to be removed and that Brezhnev would be looking for "a man he could trust" — a Czechoslovak Kadar or Gomulka. At the time neither Indra nor Bilak nor any of the other quislings was in a position to enforce Soviet policy. They were far too unpopular, hated by the population and virtually powerless. Husak, who during the Moscow "negotiations" had already offered himself as the "alternative solution" and later in autumn 1968 had presented himself in Kiev as a "realistic politician", was the ideal man for the Soviet leadership: a pre-war communist, a Slovak, a victim of the Stalinist trials — yet even in prison an unflinching dogmatist, highly authoritarian and reserved, without any knowledge of the world around him (which he saw merely in black and white), without illusions about abiding by Marxist ideology or the role of the USSR, but unconditionally obedient when it came to the discipline of the "socialist camp". Political power is the ultimate objective of Husak's life. The Soviet leadership did not object to the fact that during the Nazi occupation Husak had accepted an invitation from the fascist Slovak Government to go to the German-occupied Ukraine, nor had it any objection to his flirtation with Dubcek's policy in 1968. On the contrary, these are things

37

which can at any time be used for intimidation and blackmail. For all these various reasons, Brezhnev first used him as a means of pressure against Dubcek, who (honourably and not without resistance) had to hand over one post after the other to Husak. And when Dubcek had served his purpose and it was assumed that he would not be prepared to make further concessions, Marshal Grechko came forward with his ultimatum in March 1969, which placed Husak at the head of the Czechoslovak Party.

Husak realised right from the start that he had seized power only with the help of the Soviets. This had a decisive influence on his entire policy and will very likely do so in the future. Illusions in this respect are dangerous. But this does not mean that in the event of the fall of Brezhnev or substantial changes in Moscow he will not try to switch camps and place himself at the head of a movement which would aim at making Czechoslovakia independent of the USSR.

Such a merciless logic of unconditional subservience is natural for leaders who do not or cannot enjoy the genuine support of the population and whose task it is to cover up a humiliating occupation and perpetuate it. Leaders who have to uphold such a régime inevitably appear in the eyes of the population even more subservient, even more stupid and retrograde than those who prevailed during the latter half of the Novotny era. Where there is no support and co-operation from the population it is only possible to rule with the help of fear, the police and foreign tanks, whose guns keep the population in check should it forget "reality" all of a sudden.

One might argue that a similar situation exists in other European countries as well, without requiring the political trials which took place in Czechoslovakia after 1969. Of course there is oppression in these countries too, but it takes different forms. It can be assumed that the occupying power and the Czechoslovak leadership thought at first that trials were not absolutely essential for a complete "normalisation". In a developed country such as Czechoslovakia political measures and material pressure are more effective than outright force. Brezhnev and Husak know perfectly well that the assassination of opposition personalities, the resettlement of the population of entire areas, deportations, mass oppression, would only arouse strong resistance and desperate actions from the people. What was possible in certain parts of the USSR, for example in the Caucasus, in the Baltic States or in Siberia, would hardly have been possible in the heart of Europe in 1972. This applies in particular to Czechs and Slovaks, who are sufficiently realistic (especially the former) not to engage in a battle that is lost right from the start. They are accustomed to wait until the balance of forces is more favourable for them and then get completely involved, but they always act with tolerance and common sense in the struggle as well as in victory. Fear and terror, on the other hand, might inadvertently arouse their boldness and determination. In order to avoid reaching such a point, it is advisable to apply the pressure in small doses. Then people get accustomed more easily (as in the rest of the world), but the effect is all the more crushing and depressing. Oppression arouses fear in the weak, it destroys solidarity, disintegrates society, compels people to make small concessions every day which gradually turn into mass resignation. If the occupation régime can boast of any success then it is undeniably that it has applied this "normalisation technique" in masterly fashion: to divide a people that was united, to terrify people who one year earlier were prepared to give their lives for freedom, to make the people accomplices of the régime against their will. In such a way that they even fear possible changes in the future which might expose their weaknesses.

But the development of oppression depends above all on its effectiveness. If the majority of the population could be forced into obedience and loyalty, if all overt resistance could be broken and if a general passivity could be established, then Husak and his associates, in collaboration with the Soviet leadership, could keep the repression within certain limits, that is to say, they could avoid arrests and political trials. One thing is clear today: no one stages such trials or demands harsh punishment simply for his own pleasure or bloodlust. This is true especially of Husak who would no doubt have preferred not to do this. Yet merciless logic is stronger than subjective intentions: resistance against oppression followed by a policy of force inevitably gives rise to a second wave of repression, arrests and political trials.

The Party of the Expelled

From this situation, however, there emerged a new political force, "the Party of the Expelled", as it became known to the population. After many years of membership hundreds of thousands were deprived of their Party card. New ties had grown between them in the struggle waged since 1968, in which they were linked by a common ideal. They were joined by the young people who had had their first significant political experience during the Prague Spring and had achieved a political maturity normally acquired after long years in a political party. It was this maturity that laid the essential foundations for the opposition movement. Finally we must mention those people without party affiliations who in 1968 once again entered political life, when they were given the chance to participate in their own right.

One must realise that an entirely new situation has now emerged in Czechoslovakia, with the following main features:

— The 1968 movement for the renewal of socialism was not defeated completely, but merely stifled by the military intervention of foreign States, which created a close link between the struggle for genuine socialism and for national independence. This link guarantees the movement a broad basis among the population. In addition there are the 500,000 members expelled from the Party, who in most cases are experienced Party officials.

— The opposition movement, which was spontaneous at first, found spokesmen who by their public pronouncements have won the confidence and respect of the population and who constitute an alternative to the present rulers, imposed by the occupying power.

— Even though the resistance movement is extremely varied and includes the most diverse tendencies its nucleus, made up of reliable and militant progressives, pursues a clearly progressive socialist and democratic line.

— As distinct from the opposition within the Party before 1967, this movement has a programme based on the political documents of 1968, above all on the Action Programme of the Communist Party of Czechoslovakia and the resolutions and documents adopted by the Fourteenth Congress.

The "expelled" react to this entirely new situation in three different ways.

Some stress that in a socialist system, and given Czechoslovakia's particular geographic and international position, the Party remains in spite of everything the forum from which the struggle for a renewal of socialism must be waged. They reject the idea of an organised opposition movement and maintain that the majority of Party members should return to the road mapped out in 1968. Everything would have to start from the beginning again, and the communists expelled from the Party should miss no opportunity to translate this into reality.

The opponents of this position, on the other hand, claim that following the purges Husak's Party is no longer the same as in 1967 and offers no possibility of any kind of internal opposition. They do not question the good faith of the first group, but accuse it of passivity and of sitting on the fence. Even though they admit that the time when it was possible to have an opposition within the Party is over they do not think that the situation is ripe for an organised opposition, since this would give the Government its desired pretext to liquidate all its adversaries. That is why they recommend caution: waiting for a favourable situation in Moscow and on the international scene, and then taking advantage of it. The opponents of this argument point to the opportunist and spontaneous character of this trend, saying that it would lead to the disintegration of the progressive forces and to helplessness in the event of repression; they also argue that every nation must contribute by fighting to weaken the world centre of bureaucratic rule and thus help bring about transformations in the USSR and in other socialist states.

A third group subscribes to the argument that the situation created by the Soviet occupation and the purges offers no possibility whatever for a political struggle inside the Party, at least not at the moment. As a result, action has to be concentrated outside. Its supporters agree with some of the views put forward by the first two tendencies but consider that an organised opposition is absolutely essential in order to apply pressure on the Party leadership, to accentuate its internal contradictions and to create the conditions for a real alternative.

The advocates of an organised opposition have the choice of two alternatives. The first alternative is *a new Communist Party,* based on the resolutions of the Fourteenth Congress in 1968 and capable of continuing its policy without confining itself simply

41

to defending it. In view of the new situation, this policy would have to be expanded and the mistakes of the former "New Course" criticised. Such a solution would be of great significance for the future, since it would prevent the population from identifying the Communist Party and the socialist ideal with the occupation policy. In this case, the historic process of splitting the CPCz into two different parties would become evident. This split would have a theoretical content, a programme and a form of organisation. The opposition could thereby integrate itself in the international communist movement and contribute to its development in a spirit of "unity in diversity".

Members of the socialist opposition seriously considered and discussed such a possibility without, however, overlooking its negative aspects. The Communist Party had greatly discredited itself by accepting the occupation and "normalisation" after 20 August 1968. This was yet another shadow, in addition to all those dating back to the misdeeds of the Stalin era and to the present policy of Husak, which have discredited the very word "communism" in the eyes of the population. In addition, the new Party would have to be headed by leading well-known personalities who had belonged to the progressive wing, but this would only make the action of the police easier and accelerate the liquidation of the Party. Finally, in the present international situation such a new organisation was most unlikely to be recognised by other communist parties. On the contrary, it would encourage disastrous divergences, in particular in those parties which refuse to recognise the leading role of the Soviet Union but are not yet in a position to show outright resistance.

These considerations, which are tied up with a particular situation, might lose their validity later on. Precisely because of this, discussion continues about the emergence of a new party, regardless of whether such an organisation with a socialist programme calls itself communist or otherwise. But under present conditions, the opposition has arrived at the conclusion that the new situation inevitably requires new solutions. That is why the second alternative was accepted.

The second alternative was to found a *socialist movement*. As the term "movement" implies, this would not be a thoroughly structured party with its own top hierarchy, its centralised bodies, its discipline, but rather a *political trend* based on the 1968 programme and on a *socialist base in the people*. It would, however, possess an intellectual centre which would determine the general political line of the movement and take practical initiatives, *while giving groups which could be freely formed in factories and localities complete autonomy in applying the common programme.* The Centre must thus be in a position to disseminate the programme and to issue overall directives by means of leaflets, "samizdat" newspapers and a liaison and information network. After that, each group and even each individual who declares his or her acceptance of the programme can act in accordance with local conditions and choose appropriate methods of applying it.

The socialist opposition chose this structure because they reckoned with the existence of several progressive opposition trends and with the fact that it would have been extremely difficult to integrate them into one and the same organisation. Consequently, it was more expedient to give each group and trend complete ideological and organisational freedom so that each should make its own contribution to the common objective

One might oppose this conception with classical arguments based on the communist doctrine: a spontaneous movement cannot be victorious if there is no firm organisation. Such an objection is undeniably correct under certain circumstances but can hardly be automatically applied in the East European countries. An attempt to do this would be doomed to failure for the reasons mentioned earlier on.

The Czechoslovak opposition rejected the foundation of a vanguard communist party and decided in favour of different forms of organisation, not out of fundamental hostility to the vanguard conception but for the sake of ensuring practical efficiency. The "Short Action Programme" (Appendix, no. 3) explains the attitude which the authors have towards such a plan when it states that practical experience and the development of action alone will demonstrate whether it is possible to switch over from informal links to permanent and firm ones. They believe it perfectly feasible that, in the course of struggle, certain groups will develop into parties or organisations with such structures or join other groups to form a socialist movement which will become a co-ordinating centre. They leave the final option open, but consider it premature to launch discussions on the subject or to try to apply "from above" organisational forms based on a theoretical pattern.

On the road towards joint action in the broadest possible sense, the formation of the Socialist Movement of Czechoslovak Citizens and the drafting of the 28 October Manifesto by a conference of delegates from various local groups from Bohemia and Moravia

was of considerable significance for the history of the socialist opposition not just in Czechoslovakia but in the whole of Eastern Europe.

The Programme of the Socialist Opposition

The Manifesto of 28 October 1970 (Appendix, no. 2) — the anniversary of the restoration of the independence of the Czechs and Slovaks in 1918 — *represents the programmatic foundation of the socialist opposition.* It was submitted for discussion to the entire population and to the various resistance groups in the form of leaflets and in the first underground newspapers. In the course of animated debates the other groups clarified their positions, while the Socialist Movement of Czechoslovak Citizens was able to specify its programme. This preparatory phase was concluded with the drawing up of a further document of major significance, the Short Action Programme (Appendix, no. 3).

The joint thinking process developed during discussions in 1969 and 1970 and equally through joint action, such as the demonstrations on the second anniversary of the occupation. The purges and political repression which were increasing at the time made this work particularly difficult. One should not forget this when reading these and subsequent documents.

The Manifesto makes it quite clear that the movement is fighting for a socialist, democratic and free Czechoslovakia and that the aim is not just any type of socialism or one of those vague notions which are so current nowadays. It summarises its idea of socialism in the following terms: "Freedom and democracy, going beyond both the bourgeois and the Stalinist conceptions of these terms . . . We repudiate the socialism of bureaucratic machineries just as we repudiate goulash socialism" (a term used since the Khrushchev era to describe a type of socialist society which offers its citizens greater material benefits without, however, affecting the bureaucratic structures).

The movement intends to carry on along the road mapped out during the Prague Spring and to revive the principal ideas of that period, enriched by the lessons drawn from the invasion and the disintegration of the Party. The following points, which are a synthesis of the socialist alternative programme, emerge from the Manifesto and from many other contributions to the discussion:
— the transformation of the nationalised means of production into

45

genuinely collective property, to be administered by the people through democratically and directly elected bodies, notably workers' councils in the factories;

— the establishment of a *pluralist socialist political system* based on collective ownership of the means of production, in which all parties and organisations shall be equal partners, exercising their influence through legitimate political channels and free discussion, without the monopoly of one party or group;

— respect for the following rights: *free expression of opinions*, freedom of organisation and assembly, freedom of the arts, science and research, as well as freedom of information for all citizens;

— guaranteed *independence of the judiciary, and control over the police*;

— restoration of the *independence of the trade unions* and thus of their role of representing and defending the interests of the workers and all wage-earners;

— *economic reform* guaranteeing the autonomy of enterprises administered by the workers, while at the same time protecting the interests of society as a whole by scientific planning; a contribution would thus be made to the development of all material and intellectual resources;

— relations of equality between the *two nationalities* making up the Republic, thereby excluding all forms of centralism and chauvinism;

— strengthening the *sovereignty of the Republic* by promoting relations with all socialist countries, including China, on the basis of equality, solidarity and non-interference in each other's internal affairs. The Warsaw Pact is to be given back its original character of a defence alliance. Every possibility of military intervention without the explicit request of the respective constitutional Governments must be excluded.

These points make it amply clear how absurd it is to describe the movement as "hostile to socialism", as the propaganda repeats ad nauseam and as the courts of Prague and Brno state in the sentences pronounced against supporters of the movement in July-August 1972. On the contrary, it proves beyond a shadow of doubt that the movement represents opposition not to socialism but merely to the bureaucratic, authoritarian forms which distort it. *It is not a rejection of socialism but its rehabilitation.*

And this brings us to the crux of the matter. *Is there really any room for another variant of socialist society, different from the Soviet model and other existing forms of "socialism"?* Is there

46

room, in other words, for the type of democratic socialism whose initial symptoms appeared in the Prague Spring and which the movement continues to advocate? The enemies of socialism claim that such a possibility is illusory, a naïve dream — indeed, a "trap" set by communists and Marxists. And the representatives of the establishment in the East European countries claim that "democratic socialism is not even a variant of socialist ideology, it cannot even be classed as something standing between socialism and capitalism but is an integral part of the policy and ideology of imperialism" (*Rude Pravo*, 12 August 1972): except that in this case, it is apparently the imperialists who have set the "trap"! It is interesting to note how the established antagonists of East and West unite in their repudiation of an alternative socialism. But this is not surprising. If we take a closer look at the documents emanating from the Prague Spring and the Programme of the Socialist Opposition Movement we find that *this renewal of socialism is equally dangerous for the representatives of the establishment in both East and West.*

The authors of the Manifesto deny that the only alternatives are either capitalism or bureaucratic socialism. Instead, they declare that other models of socialism are possible. Sceptics, however, argue that while this may be possible in theory it is not possible in practice, and they quote the defeat of the Czechoslovak experiment in 1968 as an example. True, at this juncture we possess no experience tested in practice which would demonstrate the feasibility of such a road: but this is not sufficient to rule it out. On balance, the Czechoslovak experiment speaks in favour of such a possibility. For the first time it has been proved that a socialist society retains the achievements of such a system — complete collectivisation of the means of production, the leading role of the working class — and that it enriches them by expanding democratic liberties and a pluralist system. It is well known that this policy enjoyed the backing of the overwhelming majority of the population, which earlier on had been difficult to imagine. Such a system could be neither overthrown nor even endangered by its opponents, in spite of the fact that they were absolutely free to state their position. That is why foreign states had to intervene to stifle the Prague Spring.

Sceptics again argue that the Soviet intervention was merely in the inherent logic of things, that the same had happened in 1953 in the GDR and in 1956 in Hungary and will be repeated wherever and whenever it is deemed necessary. We have shown — and several documents and articles of the socialist opposition confirm it — *that the defeat in August 1968 was not inevitable*, that there could have been another way out. An analysis of the errors committed should not arouse any acrimony, instead one should draw a lesson from them for the future, not just in Czechoslovakia but in all East European countries. Undoubtedly, this brings us into the sphere of hypotheses. But socialism as a social system in power is a relatively recent phenomenon. It has not yet come out of its initial stages, and it has to pay a heavy price for the fact that its first victory was won in the economically and politically most backward country in Europe. This has been the cause of many of its deformations.

These considerations, naturally, do not apply to the justifiable doubts felt by those who in capitalist societies are fighting for socialist transformation and are concerned about the model which "existing socialism" offers them.

The advocates of the Soviet model like to assert that there is only one form of socialism, which is inevitably revolutionary and democratic: any other adjective added to the term "socialism" is consequently superfluous, damaging and demagogical. *They are obliged to identify the present Soviet system with socialism* at any cost. To criticise it and to have a different idea of socialism means to be exposed as an enemy of socialism, it means to advocate anti-communism and anti-Sovietism. To their way of thinking there can be no socialist opposition, only an opposition to socialism. To reject the Soviet model means to want to overthrow socialism and restore capitalism. In the East European countries this pretext is used to justify repression of the opposition. In the Western countries the same method serves to discredit socialism.

The Manifesto of 28 October 1970, as well as the other documents issued by the socialist opposition, do not just underline the socialist character of the movement, but furthermore reject every form of anti-Sovietism even though this is a stance which has spread widely among the population since the invasion. They express the hope that the socialist opposition will manage to overcome this position and be able to establish good-neighbour relations with the Soviet Union once the Soviet troops have been withdrawn. Such a possibility naturally depends on the present or future Soviet leadership: it will have to acknowledge that 20 August and its consequences have caused far-reaching political damage and that therefore some sort of compensation is required. Is such a hope realistic? At the moment certainly not. But who would have predicted at one time that Khrushchev would go to Belgrade to apologise for Yugoslavia's excommunication from the international communist movement and for her having been presented as a "base of imperialism governed by fascist murderers"? Alexander Dubcek's letter dated 18 January 1974, and his letter to the Federal Assembly dated 28 October 1974, as well as Josef Smrkovsky's letter to Leonid Brezhnev of 25 July 1973 and the book by Zdenek Mlynar written in the Spring of 1975, make it quite clear that they do not rule out such a possibility in the case of Czechoslovakia.

The struggle of the socialist opposition is a political and a constructive struggle. It excludes terrorist methods and actions, sabotage and extremist slogans. Its objective is to work for political transformation, to be brought about by political methods. This does not mean in the least that it must confine itself to debates or the distribution of leaflets. One of the crucial points of the Manifesto is the "Appeal for Action", a warning against a policy of wait-and-see, against indifference, cynicism, escape into some kind of ivory tower. There can be no doubt that the future of Czechoslovakia cannot be divorced from the development of the international situation and that the Czechoslovak people cannot change the existing power situation by themselves. Hence a "new internationalism" is a necessary condition for the success of the struggle. The future depends chiefly on struggles which will be waged by the people themselves, and on how "another opportunity", which may be closer than one thinks, will be used.

Hardly two months had passed since the publication of the Manifesto when the revolt of the Polish workers broke out in December 1970: this confirmed the optimism voiced in the Manifesto, as well as the fact that the *struggle against the centralised bureaucratic system and for genuine socialism has a truly international character.* The February 1971 issue of the monthly of the Czechoslovak socialist opposition movement features an article assuring the Polish people of the solidarity of the Czechoslovak socialist opposition and outlining the following link between the two movements: "The movement, defeated in one country, has erupted in another. . . . It is possible to keep the revolt of a people down in one single country . . . but it is impossible to resist the international alliance of all the forces which have learnt to carry on their struggle".

This is the significant lesson which the Czechoslovak workers have drawn from their experiences in 1968 and which is reflected in all the documents as well as the Programme of the Socialist Opposition. Consequently, the Socialist Movement of Czechoslovak Citizens hailed the uprising of the Polish workers in the Baltic ports while vehemently opposing a possible military intervention by the armies of the Warsaw Pact in which the Czechoslovak army would have been involved. It likewise declared its solidarity with the Soviet opposition in connection with the sentence passed on Vladimir Bukovsky.* In return, the Soviet opposition and the East German communist Robert Havemann protested against the political trials in Czechoslovakia in the summer of 1972. These are signs of a new internationalism in struggle and of new friendly and fraternal relations which could emerge between the people of the socialist countries once Soviet domination and the bureaucratic system are eliminated.

The publication of the Manifesto of 28 October in November 1970 and the foundation of the Socialist Movement of Czechoslovak Citizens, which coincided with the events in Poland, marked the beginning of an outright and dynamic phase in the activities of the socialist opposition: debates about the Manifesto and the Programme, an underground publication *Politicky mesicnik* ("Political Monthly") which has been appearing regularly every month since January 1971 in a relatively large edition and circulated through its own distribution system, a further journal *Pokrok* ("Progress"), published by communist workers at the Prague CKD plant, and the distribution of many leaflets and statements. The paper of the socialist opposition abroad, *Listy,* appears regularly, the first books circulate in the country in the form of "samizdat" publications, and finally publishing houses are being founded abroad: all this in addition to the support organised for the families of imprisoned persons and for all those in financial straits.

At the same time theoretical work is in progress to prepare a platform of pressing demands and a long-term programme mapping out the tactics and strategy of the socialist opposition. A working group has submitted a document for discussion, the "Short Action Programme of the Socialist Opposition" (Appendix, no. 3). Despite its temporary character, which is open to modification on the basis of debate, this is one of the most important documents of the socialist opposition. Many of the arguments and conclusions it contains are equally valid for all the socialist countries. Among

---

*Bukovsky, V.: *Opposition: a New Mental Sickness in the Soviet Union.*

the major issues elaborated the most noteworthy is an analysis of the process in which the bureaucratic structures tried to change into democratic ones in 1968, under pressure from below. An alliance between the progressive forces "at the top" working in leading party positions, and those fighting for a renewal of socialism among the rank and file, strove for this objective. This alliance crumbled at the time of the invasion when the forces "at the top" were isolated from the mass movement, which carried on the struggle alone and without spokesmen capable of expressing its initiatives. *It thus appears to be impossible to reform a Stalinist-type system by means of a liberal policy pursued by a leading group of the Party which, while granting more freedom to the people, is the sole body to lay down the limits within which it may be exercised.* Such a position is unquestionably a step forward compared to the Stalinist system, but it cannot solve the fundamental contradiction between a model of democratic socialism in which the people genuinely begin to participate in the running of the country, and a bureaucratic model in which they are the object and not the subject of the policy. This would merely be a *liberalisation* of the Stalinist system, not its *democratisation*. Such transformations have a favourable impact on the population and must consequently be supported and welcomed; yet they can neither eliminate existing tensions nor bring about a lasting solution. On the contrary, they are unstable, are in constant danger from Stalinist forces at home and abroad, and can at any moment degenerate into the bureaucratic dictatorship of a clique or of one single man (as demonstrated by the development of the Gomulka leadership between 1956 and 1960).

The alliance between progressive forces "at the top" and "at the base" could only be established in Czechoslovakia in 1968 because the origin and development of the Communist Party, together with certain favourable circumstances, permitted this: democratic traditions, the political maturity of the working class, the economic crisis, the nationalities problem, the after-effects of the political trials, and so forth. But such a pattern is by no means confined to Czechoslovakia, since the same conditions may arise in other socialist countries.

If, however, such a movement for the renewal of socialism exists merely at the base — which is in fact the case in all the socialist countries, albeit potentially — and has no representatives "at the top" in the Party leadership, then there arises the danger of spontaneous outbursts which can undoubtedly shake the Stalinist system and eliminate a number of its discredited leading personalities but which can in no way change its essence. An example of a country where such a situation existed is provided by Poland in December 1970 and January 1971.

This in no way means that the grass-roots movement is impotent and has to wait until a favourable situation arises at the top. Such a situation could very well be created under pressure from the masses because of their discontent and their desire for change. This brings us to the conclusion — and this is one of the major points in the documents of the Czechoslovak Socialist Opposition — that *action at the base is always decisive,* all the more so when it is taken by workers in large industrial centres.

The "Short Action Programme" rightly stresses that such a movement cannot emerge from the will of a "centre", that it cannot be created from above but that it is much rather the reflection of a serious political, economic and moral crisis in society: a crisis which is felt as such by the population, and not just by theoreticians who see signs of a crisis everywhere.

When the objective conditions for an opposition movement arise, the conditions for its success have still to be created. And this is where the "centre" intervenes, issuing correct instructions to give the discontent of the masses an orientation and to guide their energy into the right channels. This is the task of an organised opposition movement which must have a clear programme and prove capable of mobilising all the democratic and socialist forces for a transformation of the bureaucratic Stalinist system into a socialist and democratic one. The numerical strength of the opposition is irrelevant, as we can see nowadays. What is of far more substantial importance is that it expresses the aspirations, ideas and requirements of the majority of workers and of the population as a whole. At the appropriate moment it can fulfil its vanguard role and then withdraw once the population is in a position to choose a new socialist representation, elected democratically.

Another extremely important point broached in the "Short Action Programme" and in other documents is the question of relations between communists and non-communists and their respective organisations within the socialist opposition. Even though the political core of the socialist opposition undeniably consists of veteran communists expelled from the Party, this does not mean that the communists are the only nor even the major opposition force in Czechoslovakia. Neither does it mean that this automatically gives them the right to play a leading role. Czechoslovak reform

52

communists have behind them twenty years' experience of a single party régime. They realise full well that it was the *theory of the "leading role of the Party", which in fact is tantamount to a monopoly, that caused all the deformations of socialism* (in as much as the Stalinist régime can still be presented as a mere deformation). The Party stands above the people and a small group of apparatchiks rules under its protection, while all other forces, organisations and citizens are no more than transmission belts or simply objects of this policy. One of the aims of the Prague Spring was to put an end to this state of affairs. Henceforth, the leading role of the Communist Party was to be questioned all the time, it would have to examine continually whether its policy was correct, it would have to abandon authoritarian methods and cease to want to regiment all other spheres of society. Communists were to accept the fact that an opposition could develop and speak up within the socialist system; they were to accept the will of the people as reflected in democratic elections.

The socialist opposition intends to respect these principles even under the difficult conditions created by the occupation. In all its publications it insists on *the principle of co-operation among all opposition forces but likewise on the exclusion of groups with totalitarian, chauvinistic and fascist-like tendencies which have nothing in common with socialism or democracy.*

One must never forget that any socialist opposition working in a country with a bureaucratic system can under certain circumstances be confronted with the problem of a spontaneous outburst of discontent accumulated over long years of injustice and oppression. Such an outburst may be brought about by the policy of the communist party in power. Consequently, that communist party becomes the actual symbol of injustice in the eyes of the population. (In all the East European countries there exists a latent anti-communist and anti-Soviet opposition which, although not organised, is deeply rooted in the people, notably among workers, peasants and a section of the youth. But this opposition does not question the fact of nationalisation and collectivisation.) Such an outburst can result either in an alliance between Stalinists and centrists terrified by the radical temper of the masses, or else in a return to a reactionary or a military régime waving the banner of nationalism. In Czechoslovakia this danger was never as great as in other East European countries, because before 20 August 1968 anti-communism and anti-Sovietism did not have a broad basis among the people. But the Soviet intervention and the situation brought about

53

by the new leadership have given a fresh impetus to such tendencies. Today they are very strong and are manifested at the slightest opportunity. Brezhnev, Husak and all those who are defending the present state of affairs under the pretext that a change would "help the enemy" bear an extremely heavy responsibility. Precisely the opposite has come true; those who cover up and promote such a situation discredit socialism more than any reactionary propaganda.

The First Public Confrontation

As the opposition closes its ranks the occupation régime speeds up the "normalisation process". The Communist Party has been decimated by the 1969-70 purges and turned into a "party of fifty-year-olds".*

Its core nowadays consists of its own bureaucrats, its zealous officials and "old age pensioners" but not of workers or young people or any other progressive element. Tens of thousands of citizens have lost their jobs and are compelled to look for other work. Their children are denied access to universities, their families are subject to every conceivable kind of discrimination. The trade unions and other mass organisations have been purged, associations of intellectuals and artists have either been disbanded or turned into obedient tools in the hands of a clique of quislings. Likewise all traces of workers' self-management have been eliminated, with disastrous effects on the morale of the workers and thus on economic life as a whole. The first symptoms of disintegration of the economy, as before, affect the working class above all. There is a true "Biafra of the intellect" in those spheres which until now have been the pride of socialism: culture and science. The régime is aware of its weakness and its isolation to such an extent that it does not even make an attempt at convincing its citizens, but merely issues threats and asserts its authority by police methods.

Husak knows that he can only rule with the help of fear. His régime controls the entire power machinery — police, army, judiciary, Party and state apparatus. Besides this he can rely on the Soviet soldiers stationed throughout the country, who are prepared to intervene at any given moment. Husak regarded this situation as favourable for an attempt to "legalise" a government forced on the people by Soviet intervention. In May 1971 he decided to convene the so-called Fourteenth Congress of the CPCz whose delegates were chosen well in advance by the Party machinery, and he decided to hold mock elections in November.

---

*According to statistics drawn up by the CPCz in May 1972, the average age of Party members has risen to fifty.

A confrontation was inevitable. The opposition was not prepared to cede an inch of ground. The growing change of opinion as regards Husak's role has already been mentioned: first there were illusions, then a period of doubts, then came unmistakable disappointment, to be followed by rejection and finally active opposition. It must be said unequivocally that Husak has proved to be the ideal tool of Soviet policy, but his actions must not be seen merely as the result of pressure applied by the Soviet leaders and by the extremists at home. To a large extent he pursues his own line. For this he had to look for allies partly in the ranks of his one-time persecutors, as his former friend and fighting comrade Milan Hübl recalled in a poignant letter. Seen against this background he no longer represents the "lesser evil" which would justify the opposition's support against the extremists. On the contrary, his removal might even pave the way for positive changes. Any alternative team would have to reckon with public opinion, albeit to a slight extent. Prior to the Party Congress of May 1971, a significant group, consisting of members of the Central Committee co-opted at the Fourteenth Vysocany Congress in 1968 and of Party members, approached public opinion and communist parties throughout the world with an extensive analysis entitled "We can no longer remain silent". This document is not just a sad review of "normalisation" — including the first wave of repression — but places the Czechoslovak problem in an "international context" better than had ever been done before. The four years since the Soviet intervention only confirmed that 21 August 1968 had become a symbol: a symbol of the ways and means by which differences of opinion are settled between socialist countries. The international communist movement is divided into two groups depending on the position adopted towards this kind of solution. Consequently there are two ideas of internationalism, and there is a split which will come to the fore time and again when tragic acts like the invasion of Czechoslovakia, which very probably will not be an isolated case, are committed.

After analysing the results of the May 1971 Party Congress in a memorandum to the people, the opposition put the question which was also being frequently repeated abroad: could the "stabilisation" declared by Husak and Brezhnev open the way to a policy of "Kadarisation" of Czechoslovakia? Certain signs might give the impression that such a possibility cannot be entirely ruled out. Yet we regard such expectations as unjustified, and events have confirmed our view. One of the conditions of Kadarisation as a form of liberalising the bureaucratic system is at least *some measure of co-operation from the population* and especially from members of the Communist Party. Kadar was able to count on this because he came to power after a long period of dictatorship under Rakosi and after a brief uprising which was so violent that it took a large portion of communists by surprise and filled them with fear of vengeance by the people. The Soviet army intervened to put an end to the uprising. It had in fact been in the country since 1944 and had not obtained the slightest sympathy from the Hungarians.

Husak on the other hand came to power after the Dubcek era, whose reforms in those eight months had proved that it was possible to live in freedom under a socialist régime, free from oppression by the police, without censorship, without violence and in an atmosphere of national reconciliation. Husak had to show his gratitude to the invaders, whose action was regarded by the population as a humiliation. The armies of the Soviet Union had not been stationed in the country but had to cross frontiers. Finally, the Czechs and Slovaks, who had regarded the Soviets as their friends, felt betrayed. In politics, too, there was only one step from love to hatred.

For all these reasons Husak — even had he wanted to — could not play the role of a Czechoslovak Kadar. Under his régime oppression will continue to dominate, for he cannot rule without it.

That was the atmosphere in which Husak prepared the elections in November 1971. As an intelligent person he could have been satisfied had the candidates on his single list received sixty to seventy per cent of the votes. This would have been a simple job provided it was accomplished with a little intelligence. He would have been regarded as a realistic, conciliatory man who must reckon with an opposition that is inevitable but can be kept in check. Yet he is the prisoner of a certain logic: to convince Brezhnev that he was fully master of the situation he had to get ninety-nine per cent of the votes — as the Soviets are used to getting at home — and lower results would have been regarded as a defeat. Since, in addition, he had accepted a return to the pre-1968 bureaucratic system he could not afford worse results than those which Novotny had achieved during his term of office. He is the victim of his own propaganda, which repeats constantly on radio, television and at meetings that with the exception of a handful of "exhibitionists" everyone stands behind his policy. How could he then explain that there were thirty to forty per cent "exhibitionists" among the population?

So the régime set its entire propaganda machinery in motion

and resorted to oppression and terror. The Party machinery nominated the single list of National Front candidates and launched a campaign under the slogan: "Anyone not voting for them is against socialism". Alois Indra declared that the elections were a referendum for or against socialism and "fraternal help". Those who allowed themselves to be persuaded were promised leniency, others who stuck to their "errors" were threatened with reprisals. The citizens were called upon to vote in public to make the elections a demonstration for the government. Police informers went from house to house to fetch the population to the ballot boxes, polling stations were swarming with police and members of the Party machinery who made a note of anyone who failed to vote or who amended the lists. *Now that the régime had forced the people to take this first step to surrender it wanted to brand them as its accomplices.*

But it underestimated the population's capacity for resistance. When the campaign reached its climax, Josef Smrkovsky, one of the most respected leaders of the Prague Spring, gave an interview to the Italian Communist journal *Giorni-Vie Nuove.* Its publication had a strong impact on international public opinion as well as in Czechoslovakia. The régime was forced to react. Smrkovsky was accused of serving "the enemies of socialism" but they did not have the courage to arrest him — further proof that overt opposition pays and that anyone who dares to speak out in the long run risks less than he who keeps silent.

The historic significance of this interview lies above all in the fact that by his public pronouncement Smrkovsky had the courage to foil the régime's attempt to isolate him and that he, a veteran communist, asked the following crucial question: *"Do the people really participate, when their fate is decided above their heads?"* An outrageous question, coming from a communist living in a socialist country. But at the same time it was a question being asked by countless communists in the East European countries, and a question which communists, socialists and the entire Left in the Western countries fighting for a socialist alternative to the capitalist system would have to ask themselves. As long as there is no satisfactory answer all the prospects outlined by socialism here and in the rest of the world will remain dim, remote aspirations.

Smrkovsky took up an idea that he had expounded at the Central Committee session in September 1969: after twenty years, socialism in Czechoslovakia must at long last assert itself by some means other than repression. And this applies all the more to the

Soviet Union, where the revolution dates back more than 50 years!
It is high time socialism actually implemented the rights which it
promised the workers.

Without in any way exaggerating the significance of the elections, the opposition saw them as an *opportunity for a public confrontation* and for overt action in front of the eyes of the population. The appeal issued by the Socialist Movement of Czechoslovak
Citizens on 14 September and later endorsed by other opposition
groups* (Appendix, no. 4) was disseminated throughout the country
in leaflets. Husak himself spoke of a hundred thousand copies at the
December 1971 Central Committee session. The text is perfectly
clear. It explains to the citizens what their rights are and calls on
them either to abstain from voting or to cross out the names on the
list of discredited candidates forced on them by the Government.
Incidentally this possibility is sanctioned by the electoral law submitted by the régime, but is virtually denied by the authorities.

The text underlines the moral significance of such a procedure
whenever the citizen is called upon to express and defend his point
of view. It stresses that only he who fights is entitled to solidarity
from the others and wins comrades in the struggle. Those were no
empty words: the number of those arrested while distributing these
leaflets is ample proof of this. About one hundred supporters of the
opposition were arrested in Prague and other cities, above all in
Brno.

One may wonder whether an action of such magnitude, which
could not remain concealed and which to some extent made it
easier for the police to destroy the resistance network, was really
necessary. Some have their doubts and argue that this could not
have changed the political situation. This is true. But was it possible to wait? And what for? And until when? That is the constant
question which every underground movement asks itself when it
is fighting against oppression and terror by foreign occupation.

I remember that this question was asked when I was arrested by
the Gestapo in 1940, when as a member of the illegal CPCz organisation I had distributed leaflets and underground newspapers at
Olomouc attacking the German occupation. Later in prison, several
comrades wondered whether such activity directed against a mas-
sively armed enemy had any sense when the decisive battles were

---

*The Movement for Democratic Socialism; the Movement of Civic
Resistance — Czech and Slovak sections; the Opposition Communists;
the Revolutionary "Jan Palach" Movement.

being fought on the military front. An old communist answered: "The main thing is to participate in the battle, even from a distance. Otherwise we shall win neither the right to independence nor to the confidence of the people". When we met again after the war some of our comrades were missing; they had not come back from the concentration camps. And again the question was asked: "Was our illegal work and our imprisonment necessary?" Was not the outcome of the war decided at Stalingrad and on the other battlefields?" I thought about this problem all the more intensely when my mother was arrested as a hostage on my account and was later murdered by the Nazis. But finally I arrived at the conclusion that without these struggles, which at times appear hopeless, the life and the ideals which I believed in would have lost their meaning. Maybe it was someone who was just about to be arrested who wrote in *Politicky mesicnik* in October 1971: "That is why the active and passive forms of resistance are by no means quixotic but are of great significance, in the long run, and that is what must be remembered today."

Political Trials After All!

Foreign observers have wondered why this new wave of repression broke out after the Fourteenth CPCz Congress, after the election which with its "ninety-nine per cent" seemed to crown the policy of "normalisation" and "stabilisation". What people expected instead was an act of mercy for the Dubcek supporters: an amnesty, the release of political prisoners, an appeal to émigrés to return without fear of reprisal, and finally a number of political concessions. The greatest optimists (or, if you like, the most naïve) claimed that Brezhnev would "make a gesture" and order the withdrawal of his troops. Do not the Moscow diktat of October 1968 and the agreement on the "temporary stationing of Soviet troops on Czechoslovak territory" state that the Soviet army will remain in place until "a normal situation is restored"? Had this moment not come in 1971 when Brezhnev told the Fourteenth Congress in Prague that "the victory of socialism is secure" and that the CPCz leadership under Comrade Husak was fully master of the situation?

No one ever found out where these rumours came from. Did some members of the leadership really have such intentions and were they prevented by others from translating them into reality? Or were these rumours released by the Soviet leadership in order to spread doubt and confusion? The wielders of power who know that they are unable to fulfil the hopes and aspirations of the people need such a situation: they create the impression that although they were anxious to do something they were prevented from doing so. At the same time they make the people believe that they are protecting them and that things might get even worse if they were not there. But this time the mask had to drop. The Husak government has come to realise that it is facing an opposition which, while it is undoubtedly excluded from the legal political life of the country, can rely on the rank and file of the people and represents a socialist alternative. *Anti-Soviet and anti-communist pronouncements can be tolerated, but never Marxist criticism. The socialist opposition must be silenced come what may.*

Brezhnev, too, is of this opinion. He states time and again his

61

disgust at the "contacts" which the Czechoslovak opposition maintains with foreign countries and which enable it to spread information via certain socialist or communist movements in the West which the Soviet leadership finds extremely awkward. This applies, for example, to a secret speech by Vasil Bilak at the Central Committee meeting in October 1971, in which he attacked Romania and Yugoslavia and derided a solidarity campaign with persecuted Sudanese communists. The speech was published by the socialist opposition in the Western press and the result was a series of embarrassing questions put to the Prague leadership. The Soviets themselves decided to take drastic steps against their own dissidents, against the circulation of "samizdat" and against "leaks" of information destined for abroad. They encouraged the Czechoslovak leaders to deal with their opposition, above all by breaking all its links with socialists in exile, with the international progressive movement and more particularly with opposition groups in other socialist countries. But they suggested that all this be done with prudence and that members of the opposition should be sentenced only for violating specific laws. Big "show trials" as in 1949-54 had to be avoided, since this might hinder the Soviet diplomatic offensive towards the West and put at risk the preparations for the European Security Conference, one of Moscow's major objectives.

It has to be conceded that Husak never favoured political trials, and when in 1969 he maintained that he wanted to prevent arrests and trials for views or activities dating back to 1968, he meant it. Of course, his intentions were not motivated by humanitarian considerations; his well-proven political cynicism made sure of that. But he knew that even the First Secretary of the Party often finds it difficult to halt the repression mechanism once it has been set in motion, and that this mechanism could one day turn against him. At first he believed that a certain amount of political and material pressure would suffice to break the people's resistance. Yet he soon had to abandon this hope, and so did his Soviet allies. The people not only rejected "the new reality" but were anxious to change it.

So harsher measures had to be used. The first arrests and preparations for subsequent trials took place in 1969, shortly after Husak came to power. Intellectuals such as Ludek Pachman, Jan Tesar, Rudolf Battek, all signatories of the Ten-Point Manifesto, were the first to be arrested and remained in jail for over a year. An indictment was drawn up against all the signatories, most of whom were then still free, and the date of the trial was fixed for Autumn 1970. Yet it was postponed at the last moment and the three intellectuals were released from jail. They had no idea whether the charges had been dropped or whether they had been set free only temporarily. The first wave of political trials began in 1971. Among the first defendants were the writer Vladimir Skutina and General Vaclav Prchlik; then followed nineteen members of the Revolutionary Socialist Party headed by Petr Uhl and Sibylle Plogstedt; after that came Bohumir Kuba and many others.

When reading the charges contained in the indictment, one realises the hypocrisy of a man like Husak who in February 1972 assured Leroy, a representative of the French Communist Party, that no one had been or would be condemned on the grounds of his political activities in 1968-69, although he knew perfectly well that the sole accusation against which General Vaclav Prchlik, a member of the Central Committee and a member of Parliament, had to defend himself referred to his statement at a press conference in July 1968. He knew likewise that the journalist Jiri Lederer was arrested and sentenced because of two articles he had written and published in the 1968 Prague Spring period, in which he had criticised Gomulka's repressive policy during the events of March 1968 (and in far milder tones than Gierek was to do later on). It might seem surprising that public opinion did not react more strongly. One of the reasons is that the population initially expected to see proceedings against Dubcek, Smrkovsky, Kriegel and other leading politicians. That is precisely how all the trials in the Stalinist era had begun. This time different tactics were used. They were aptly characterised by Vasil Bilak, who committed a deliberate indiscretion when introducing the new Director-General of Radio to his office: "We are not so foolish as to sentence Dubcek and the others and thus give them a chance to attack us. It is quite sufficient to isolate them. But we shall punish, above all, the intermediate cadres, the journalists and intellectuals. No one will stand up for them: even the West is fed up with them."

In Czechoslovakia and abroad the public had accurate information about the arrests of Skutina, Prchlik, Uhl, Lederer and several others, but no one had the slightest idea how many political prisoners there were in Czechoslovakia in 1971 and in 1972. The last published figures refer to the first half of 1970 and are confined to Bohemia and Moravia. They state that 507 persons have been sentenced for "crimes perpetrated against the Republic", in other words for political motives. This means that the number of those arrested and sentenced throughout Czechoslovakia during that period must be over 3,000.

The Husak régime resorted to new methods. In order not to increase the number of political trials, members of the opposition were detained and sentenced for "economic offences". For example Hlavsa, the expert on trade matters at the Czechoslovak Embassy in Moscow, was arrested and sentenced for alleged embezzlements which are said to have occurred while he was Director of the aviation industry. But in actual fact he had protested against the invasion of 21 August 1968 and expressed his indignation in the presence of Soviet diplomats. Karel Bocek, Director of the Czechoslovak uranium industry, was arrested in 1970 and accused of sabotageing Czechoslovakia's economy. The true reason, however, was that on 21 August 1968 the workers in the uranium industry went on strike and refused to deliver uranium to the aggressor. Only Bocek's dramatic escape from prison in July 1971 saved him from a heavy sentence. There are countless similar cases which did not receive the same publicity. One forgets only too often that Husak is a lawyer by profession and knows his job. Time and again some of his promises have been quoted, such as: "No one is going to be sentenced for his political views of 1968", or: "There will be no prejudged trials". Yet those quoting have always omitted the last part of his statements, in which he never failed to declare: "but we shall not permit anyone to violate our laws", or "socialist laws shall be applied at all times and without exception". If one accuses him today of not having kept his promises he replies with cynicism that the accused had infringed socialist legality and were not sentenced for their views but for their crimes. Official propaganda takes up this argument and repeats constantly that in every country "the law is the law and must be observed". The Spanish anti-fascists have been and are still sentenced under the "laws" of Franco and the same goes for Chile, Iran, Brazil, Turkey, the Republic of South Africa, Paraguay etc. One may therefore wonder, *"What kind of laws are those which permit people in Czechoslovakia to be sentenced for holding views different from those held by the people who wield power, and for stating them in public?"* Are these laws not in flagrant violation of the Constitution of the Czechoslovak Republic, which guarantees the right to free expression of thoughts?

It is perfectly understandable that the rulers of the country and even some decent people in the West are indignant when one draws a parallel between Husak's judiciary and that of the former Greek junta, the Spanish régime or even the old Habsburg monarchy. Their reply is always: "Ours is a class judiciary." But what kind of a class judiciary is it when communists, socialists and patriots who without exception earn their living by hard work are sentenced and when this group of people does not include a single capitalist or fascist?

The indictments and various documents published in *Politicky mesicnik* show how the conditions for police repression and political trials were systematically created as far back as 1969 and 1970. First of all the judiciary had to be purged of all those judges and prosecutors who were not prepared to mete out "class justice" as dictated by the Party machinery. Reading these documents gives an idea of the verdicts pronounced under Husak. There was, for example, the incredible decision taken at a meeting of the Supreme Court on 9 December 1969, by which "exaggerated criticism of certain social aspects may be regarded as incitement to subversion" and punished as such. Or the juridical interpretations of Dr V. Handl, a member of the Supreme Court, according to which infringement of any one of the three fundamental maxims of the Czechoslovak social system — "the leading role of the Party", "the Marxist-Leninist spirit" and "the alliance with the USSR" — can be punished as a crime against the "socialist system". It is not hard to imagine that any criticism directed against the present régime can be transformed into one of these crimes and thus any Czechoslovak citizen can be charged accordingly.

All this demonstrates that at the end of 1971 all the conditions were there for a fresh wave of oppression.

The first series of arrests in November 1971 was followed by interrogations and further gathering of evidence against the socialist opposition. Repression broke out once more in January 1972. In Prague over 150 people were arrested and many of them released after interrogation. The police reported that it had discovered a huge conspiracy against the security of the state, and a big political trial seemed to be in the offing.

What happened afterwards is not quite clear. But it is certain that Husak and his leadership had given the green light for the arrests following reports by the secret police. Later, however, members of Husak's Secretariat claimed he had been shocked by their number, and by a certain degree of clumsiness shown by police, who arrested people such as the philosophers Karel Kosik and Lubomir Sochor, as well as Rudolf Slansky Jr and Jan Sling, the sons of leading communists executed in the Slansky trial.

Strangely enough the responsibility for the state security service, which normally falls to the First Secretary, was given at the time to Vasil Bilak, Secretary of the Central Committee and generally entrusted with ideological and international matters. Bilak was very close to the Moscow rulers and maintained particularly good relations with one of the members of the CPSU Presidium, Shelest, then First Secretary of the Ukrainian Central Committee. This transfer of responsibility was only temporary and it seemed that Husak was not keen on taking the initiative in these matters, which might place his international reputation and his future at risk. On the other hand among those arrested was Milan Hübl, an old friend of Husak's, who under the rule of Novotny and with Husak's approval had maintained contact with a number of communist parties in the West, notably with the Italian Communist Party.

All Husak could do was to insist that tangible evidence for the activities of the suspects should be presented. This was not difficult. The arrests had been prepared long in advance and leaflets, underground journals, photographs of meetings, tapes of tapped telephone conversations and of private discussions — in brief, the result of two years' intensive work — were in the possession of the police. Far from denying the views of which they were accused, the defendants took full responsibility for them.

The police were not content merely with punishing the Czechoslovak opposition; they wanted to prove its links with foreign countries, not just with the socialist opposition in exile but also with "reactionary circles". There was a plan which originated in higher quarters, possibly even in influential groups in Moscow, to use this opportunity to discredit the designated General Secretary of the Italian Communist Party, Enrico Berlinguer, whose protest against the Soviet interventions, like his sympathies for the Prague Spring, were well known. As the Congress of the Italian Communist Party was due to met in Milan in February 1972, there were some who maintained that if the complicity of Berlinguer and of the Iatlian Party could be proved his election could be prevented, other candidates could be put forward and this troublesome party could be weakened.

This is why the police arrested the Italian journalist Valerio Ochetto and accused him of having been a "courier" between the opposition and its supporters abroad. The police, who mistook him for a communist (a leading member of the Italian Communist Party bears the same name), found out to its great dismay that he was a progressive Catholic who had been deeply involved in the struggle against fascism in Greece and in Spain, as well as against the war in Vietnam. So in order to attain their objective they subsequently arrested the Italian communist journalist Ferdi Zidar, Secretary of the International Organisation of Journalists in Prague. Since he could not be forced to confess anything he had to be released and expelled, like Valerio Ochetto. A further attempt involving another journalist, the Italian Radio correspondent Dimitri Volcic, was also unsuccessful and the police had to drop its plan for an Italian "conspiracy". It confined itself to insinuations concerning my own presence in Rome, while the plot against the Italian Communist Party and Berlinguer proved a fiasco.

These arrests were usually announced in a brief communiqué without mentioning any names. This enabled official propaganda to present the suspects as "reactionaries", "offenders" or "adventurers" who hated socialism and were working for its destruction in order to restore capitalism and integrate Czechoslovakia into the Western world. Such propaganda would have been utterly ludicrous had the names been mentioned. Most of the arrested persons were well-known active communists who had fought for socialist ideals all their life.

A big international solidarity campaign was launched. "Left" groups, socialists and democrats were not the only ones who strongly deplored the latest developments in Czechoslovakia; several communist parties did the same. These waves of repression placed them in a difficult position, notably in those countries where the communists are working for a common front with socialists and other democratic forces and where they are striving to encourage a "different model" of a socialist society.

The interest shown by the world public and the movement of solidarity with the victims compelled the leadership of the CPCz and the police to yield. First of all they released all those against whom no sufficient hard evidence could be produced. Then they abandoned the idea of a political show trial in which detained members of the socialist opposition, Czechoslovak communists in exile and a few foreign nationals — especially communists but also a number of reactionaries — were to stand trial together so as to expose the united front of "revisionists, traitors and agents of imperialism". In March 1972 the police concluded its interrogations and presented the Party leadership with a dossier entitled "The case of Jiri Pelikan and his comrades" which clearly reveals the original plan, even though many of its objectives had to be abandoned, particularly as a result of the stand taken by the detainees.

Under pressure from international public opinion and following Moscow's sound advice, the Husak leadership decided against big political trials, which would inevitably have given rise to world-wide protest. It decided to have the defendants tried and sentenced in small groups and *in camera*, during the summer holidays. This was to make international solidarity campaigns more difficult. The judges and state prosecutors had instructions to adhere to specific charges of violation of the law and to stop all political arguments by the defendants. "These trials are not to become political!" was the new motto.

In the ten trials, the first of which began on 19 July 1972, this instruction was observed; but they were not a hundred per cent successful. The defendants did not deny their share in distributing leaflets and underground newspapers or their rejection of the occupation régime. *But they resolutely defended themselves against the accusation of "hostility to socialism" and referred not just to their own communist past but also made a Marxist criticism of the current régime and of the occupation of the country. They made it clear that it was causing severe damage to the cause of socialism and expounded their own programme of a socialist alternative, the only solution to the present crisis.*

The philosopher Ladislav Hejdanek, a member of the Evangelical Church, told a court in Prague in July 1972 that for religious motives he was no Marxist, but that he was for socialism based on humanism. In November 1971 he had participated in the leaflet campaign because he considered it perfectly normal to be politically involved, particularly at election time. The allegation by *Rude Pravo* and official propaganda that Jan Tesar and Jiri Müller had told the court they were "enemies of communism" are untrue. Both of them, just like all the others, insisted in their replies and in their final statement that they were socialists and that they had acted with the objective of establishing a genuine socialist society — free from bureaucratic and police deformations which discredit socialism in its present form. Jaroslav Sabata explained this unequivocally at his trial in Brno: "We are humanists, we are communists in opposition, but you who judge us, you are no communists!" And Milan Hübl said at the beginning of his trial: "Since eighty per cent of the indictment is political my defence must also be political." To enable the trials to fulfil their intimidatory objective the government did not publish the names of the defendants until six months later. This revealed the hypocrisy of a régime which at first tried to spread the version that the defendants were reactionaries and enemies of socialism. In actual fact the public know the names of Hübl, Sabata, Litera, Cerny, Kyncl, Hochman, Tesar, Müller, Bartosek and others too well to be taken in by such tricks.

A Return to Stalinism?

A return to 1949-54 and to the great Stalinist purges has often been mentioned in connection with these political trials. Many people are concerned over what they believe to be merely a beginning, and fear that the worst is yet to come. But if we make an objective analysis of Stalinist oppression such as it existed at the time of the Slansky trial and compare it with the oppression today we note quite considerable differences, suggesting that *the same process cannot be repeated.*

It is true that *the origins and motives of oppression are the same today as they were then*: the aim is still to crush the Communist Party, to deprive it of its popular leaders and of popular support in order to turn it into a mere tool of Soviet policy and to force the Soviet model of socialism upon it. Stalin wanted nothing else in the 1950s in Czechoslovakia or in the other countries, nor did he encounter any difficulties — except in Yugoslavia. From August 1968 onwards Brezhnev and the Soviet leadership have been aiming to prevent Czechoslovakia from taking its own road to socialism and to foist the Soviet model on it. The main obstacle has always consisted in the Communist Party itself, endowed with great authority, deeply rooted in the country and with its strength based on its traditions, its cadres and the support of the people. That is why it had to be crushed and reduced to a small group ruling by administrative methods, entirely dependent upon the Soviet Union and acting under the Soviet Army's protection.

The aim of the political trials and of repression in 1949-54 and 1969-72 is the same: to prevent the Czechoslovak Communist Party and the people from going their own way in building socialism. In order to achieve this, Husak had to adopt the Soviet thesis according to which the movement for a renewal of socialism was merely a form of "counter-revolution", which had to be suppressed first by a request to Moscow for "fraternal assistance" and subsequently by the Communist Party's own efforts.

The pattern of repression in such a system is well-known; for 1949-54 it can be summed up as follows:
1. The leading group defines the types of "deviation" which are

to be described as anti-Party and suppressed: revisionism, Zionism, nationalism, the social democratic deviation, Trotskyism, Titoism (and nowadays Maoism).

2. A campaign against these "deviations" is launched on every front and their representatives or spokesmen are hunted down while being attacked by the press, radio and television, etc., without having the slightest chance to defend themselves.

3. They are required to make a "self-criticism", whereafter they are removed from their posts, expelled from the Party and frequently deprived of any possibility of finding employment.

4. On the basis of their "self-criticism" or "disclosures" they are accused of intending to harm the whole of society, play into the hands of the enemy, overthrow socialism and restore capitalism.

5. Once severed from the political and ideological context the whole affair becomes a simple police and court case; neither of these two institutions can tolerate "crimes against the security of the State" and "conspiracies with foreign countries".

6. The spokesmen of "deviationism" are arrested and "admit" their "crimes"; they regret them and/or ask for stern sentences.

7. The police prepare the "script" of the trial, which is designed to contribute to the political education of cadres and of the population; the Party leadership approves this and determines the parts to be played by the individual defendants as well as the sentence for each of them.

8. Meanwhile everything is done to create a mass hysteria aimed at convincing the public of the "guilt" of the defendants; whereupon the "grass roots" demand the severest punishment.

9. The court refers to the "wrath of the people" and passes sentence on the defendants; the latter accept the verdict and declare it "just and well-deserved".

The same procedure is followed today but only up to point 4. This is where points of difference begin. Slansky, Clementis, Geminder and the other defendants of 1951 were not real but merely potential "opposition leaders". The defendants in the Summer 1972 trials are members of the socialist opposition and have never concealed their dissenting views about the policy of the present leadership of Party and country. This is why *the arrested do not play the régime's game and do not "confess" to crimes which they have not committed, they do not exert self-criticism but defend themselves in court.* But when there are no actors available it is impossible to draw up a "script" in advance or to stage a show based on it. Nor is there a public available that

71

is willing to believe in the police horror stories and in the "guilt" of the defendants. No "show trials" can be staged — on the contrary, the proceedings have to be held behind closed doors. Nobody, with very rare exceptions, demands "exemplary punishment"; the sentences are severe but they do not go beyond a certain limit.

What accounts for the difference? Is it final or only temporary? Let it be said straight away that this relative "liberalisation" of persecution is not motivated by any particular philanthropy of the present régime but rather by a *fundamentally changed domestic and international situation*. The "cold war" is over and no longer provides a pretext to justify death sentences and the most brutal kinds of repression. Of the three hotbeds of war characteristic of the 1949-54 period only the Middle East remains. Confrontation with the United States and with Yugoslavia no longer plays a part in international relations. It is true that a new tension has arisen, in relation to China: but although this increases the nervousness of the Soviet rulers it cannot — at least for the moment — be used as a substantial motive for persecution or lead to the discovery of "agents of Maoism" on a major scale. The situation has also changed *within the international communist movement; one no longer finds the same readiness to support and justify repression in the socialist countries*. We have shown that the critical stand of some communist parties can even mitigate this repression to a certain extent.

Furthermore, the role of the Soviet ruling group is limited to deciding about military intervention, ensuring political control over the socialist countries as a whole and manipulating the leading cadres in these countries. But the Soviet advisers no longer sit in at the interrogations and do not take a direct part in the repression.

The political police (the STB), the Government's mainstay and effective instrument, no longer applies the methods of the 1950s. It uses every possible means of pressure and falsification, but no longer resorts to torture or physical violence. The officials have not forgotten that in 1968 the files of the Stalinist trials were put together and made available to the public. They are no longer certain that the situation cannot change once more and that they will not be brought to book for their actions. The same applies to judges and prosecutors, who feel compelled to observe the laws more closely and do not show any excess of zeal. There are even judges who refuse to preside over political trials; they are then replaced by others who, already "branded" by their past, no longer have anything to lose.

72

There can therefore be no question of an automatic repetition of the Stalinist trials of the 1950s, although such a view can be heard from time to time. Nor, however, must one forget that the present situation is no more than an intermediate stage, which is determined by the domestic and international situation and is subject to further development.

We have repeatedly noted that the Husak régime — with him or without him — does not wish to intensify repression at all costs. It would find it ideal to perpetuate the present policy. This, however, does not depend on its wishes but on the effectiveness of the persecution. *If it proves insufficient to smother the opposition's voice and activities completely it will have to be continued and intensified.* China's increasing role in world affairs — especially in Eastern Europe, where it poses as the champion of national independence of the small and medium-sized nations — may cause an aggravation of repression. On the other hand, however paradoxical this may appear, the reduction of tension and the incipient dialogue between the socialist and the capitalist countries as well as economic, scientific and cultural co-operation between East and West make the present régimes more vulnerable and, consequently, "harder". The conservative and neo-Stalinist elements link the development of détente with increased ideological control and with the necessity of suppressing firmly any manifestation of discontent, any new ideas and any political opposition. It may be noted that the political trials in Czechoslovakia coincided precisely with the preparations for the European security conference and the conclusion of the treaty between Czechoslovakia and the Federal Republic of Germany.

Oppression is, therefore, directed above all against members of the various opposition groups and currents. *This does not mean that Dubcek, Kriegel and other leaders of the Prague Spring are permanently free from any danger.* I am convinced that Husak is intelligent enough to avoid putting them on trial, for two reasons: first, he realises that such a gesture would completely discredit him in the eyes of the world and secondly that he would be creating martyrs with an even greater halo in the eyes of the people. But there is no doubt that the pressure from the "ultras" will not diminish, and that it will increase as the internal situation remains tense and as the economic and political crisis requires a safety valve in the shape of troublemakers and scapegoats. The régime will try to shift the entire load of responsibility on to the leaders of the "new course", and one cannot tell when the step from general accusations to judicial indictments will be taken. In any event, the files on the leading figures of the Prague Spring have been prepared by the police and can be used at any time.

The opposition, too, is bound to cause a certain amount of pressure: it claims descent from the Prague Spring and its leaders, even though these latter have no share in its activities. The "ultras" might, then, one day no longer confine themselves to punishing the "apprentices" but also hit out at their "advisers" and "teachers". It may be that Husak would prefer to have them "merely" eliminated from political life, isolated and forgotten as speedily as possible, but it cannot be proved that his technical astuteness will carry the day.

In fact the great "show trial" has already begun: the entire Czechoslovak people is in the dock. Their crime is to hope that a genuine, just and free socialist society can be built. And to condemn them is to strike not only that people but the very future of socialism.

The Germs of Opposition Spread to the USSR

The historic struggle of the Czechoslovak socialist opposition is designed to prevent this hope from being eventually condemned to death. It must be waged by the opposition and by the Czechoslovak people but should not leave indifferent or idle all those people in the world who believe that socialism can offer a workable, more just and democratic alternative to capitalist society.

The above analysis enables us to assert with certainty *that the Czechoslovak people and the socialist opposition will continue their hard struggle.* This is shown by the statement of the Socialist Movement of Czechoslovak Citizens of 21 August 1972 (Appendix, no. 7) which dates from after the big political trials, as well as by all the other documents which have become known up to the present. The Husak régime — just like, strangely enough, that part of the Western press which only registers the surface of Czechoslovak reality — is convinced that it has dealt the most important leaders of the socialist opposition a decisive blow and that the harsh sentences will suffice to discourage other dissenters from carrying on the political struggle and also to prevent the people from resisting. Those responsible for the occupation régime are aware that they cannot gain the consent of the population, nor are they in the least concerned about it. They speculate on one section of the people keeping silent for a long time and the rest being exhausted, demoralised or driven to indifference and eventually accepting a limited degree of co-operation, as a result of a general feeling of defeat and disappointment. Without wishing to underrate the effects of persecution on the psychological condition of the population or the depressing consequences of the ensuing atmosphere of fear, I believe that this is a miscalculation. If the majority retreats into a temporising and withdrawn position and dares not declare its rejection of the régime overtly, this means neither that it has given up its opinions nor that its withdrawal is bound to be of long duration or final.

The socialist opposition has too broad a base and its roots strike too deep to be annihilated by a police operation. In addition the

75

dissemination of further documents of the Socialist Movement of Czechoslovak Citizens in the form of leaflets and statements after the wave of arrests shows that the police has neither eliminated it nor discovered its main leaders. What is more, other resistance groups have sprung up since the mass arrests and new periodicals have been founded. No doubt the arrest of such important figures as Litera, Hübl, Sabata, Tesar, Müller, etc. has hit hard at the Czechoslovak opposition and at Marxist, progressive thought in general. *The struggle for their release requires, therefore, equally as great energy and profound dedication as the campaigns for the release of Chilean and Spanish anti-fascists and all victims of oppression, which is almost worldwide.*

We have already attempted to answer the question of whether the losses and risks of such a political struggle are not too high in relation to its direct effect. We have mentioned the moral significance of such an opposition, the urgent necessity of its presence, which makes it possible to advocate the right ideas and the true aspirations of the people. Of course any struggle has its risks, its setbacks, losses and lost battles.

The risks are all the greater in Czechoslovakia, since the ranks of the socialist opposition include figures who are well known for their political commitment prior to and during 1968 and who have never concealed their views, not even since the beginning of "normalisation". Some of these communist veterans felt the urgent need to come out against the occupation régime overtly, in order to salvage the reputation of socialism and of the Communist Party, to show that there was a difference between communists and communists and thus to engage in a kind of public self-criticism by deeds and not by mere words. The Czechoslovak CP had not prepared for underground activity after 20 August 1968. Everything had to be improvised in the course of the struggle. The initiative had to be taken by the communists, who enjoyed great authority and were generally known, and this made the work of the police easier. But in the course of the struggle new people emerged, especially young people who did not yet have the kind of files that members of the political opposition had. On the other hand it is true that the struggle has become more difficult in that the opposition is this time not up against a foreign police force — that of the occupation power — but a domestic and, what is more, a communist police, which has a thorough knowledge of the methods previously employed in underground struggle. Nevertheless all these risks must be taken and shouldered, since the destiny of the coun-

76

try and the future of socialism are at stake in this historic choice.

Either the neo-Stalinist occupation régime will succeed in annihilating the socialist opposition and its representatives as an
organised movement: it will never succeed in annihilating its ideology, which is too deeply rooted within the people. In this case a
period of despair will set in and *a political vacuum will arise, so
that a crisis can only result in a spontaneous and uncontrollable
outburst*, the consequences of which may be extremely grave, not
excluding even the possibility of the elimination of socialism and
the replacement of one oppression by another.

Or the socialist opposition will withstand the consequences of
persecution and continue to prepare its alternative socialist programme; it will build up its cadres, encourage the people in the
hope of change and by its work and its pressure weaken the bureaucratic dictatorship right up to the moment of crisis, *so as to be able
to replace it by a truly democratic and popular socialist government.*

These are, naturally, the two *extreme possibilities*. There are
many intermediate possibilities. Politicians must possess enough
realism, but also enough imagination and courage, to understand
that the situation of a country like Czechoslovakia — as of the
other socialist states — is so rich in contradictions, in objective and
subjective influences, that no scientific analysis can predict every
possible variant or even a limited number of spectacular turn-
abouts. Who among the Kremlinologists or other Marxist or non-
Marxist experts foresaw the Prague Spring in a country which
they defined, as one of the "most Stalinist" even as late as 1967?
Who foresaw the overthrow of Gomulka, whose position had been
considered stable and even strengthened after his meeting with
Brandt a few weeks earlier? These examples remind us *how
extremely difficult it is to analyse the prospects of these countries,
in which the entire political struggle takes place behind closed
doors*, within the narrow orbit of the leading group, and in which
the divergences between the various cliques of the bureaucracy are
settled according to the rules of a palace revolution, without the
citizens having the slightest chance to see what is going on or to
intervene.

The fact is that *there exists in all socialist countries* — with differences of degree and according to specific conditions — *a situation of permanent political crisis* resulting from the discrepancy
between the socialist ideal and the reality of its practical application, between the interests of the overwhelming majority of the

77

population and the privileged group holding power, between the great possibilities of economic expansion and the low standard of living of the working people, between the population's desire for independence and fraternal solidarity and the domination of the great power, the USSR.

This political crisis, which developed in Czechoslovakia and was aggravated by Soviet intervention, can only be resolved by a radical transformation of the socialist structures. Such a radical transformation would not be a revolution of the classical type in which the social system is changed and the domination of one class is replaced by that of another. It must rather proceed from the real achievements of the socialist revolution — such as the socialisation of the means of production — and give them a socialist content. *The means of production, which the state and its bureaucracy have appropriated, must be handed back to the workers and technicians; the state institutions must be freed from the domination of a privileged group of bureaucrats and technocrats and be handed back to the citizens so that they may actively exercise all power and participate in the political and economic leadership of the country.*

This political revolution may be violent or non-violent, it may be carried out by means of *thorough reforms* or by *popular uprisings*. These two methods — reform or revolt — are often set in contrast to each other as if they represented the difference between "reformism" and "revolution" as used in classical Marxist terminology. *This is an absolutely artificial contrast in the socialist countries, where it is a question of political revolution.* It cannot therefore be ruled out that the socialist opposition will, with the help of the masses, exert such pressure on the leading group that the latter will be forced to compromise and will gradually disintegrate into its various tendencies, eventually isolating the conservative and reactionary tendencies and leading the liberal wing into a form of alliance with the socialist opposition. Such a situation may well create a movement comparable with the Prague Spring.

What applies to Czechoslovakia may well be valid for other East European countries as well, although on one condition only: that these countries, too, have *a form of organised socialist opposition* capable of formulating an alternative programme, expressing the wishes of the people and supplying cadres.

This brings us back to the original question: Is the "Czechoslovak phenomenon" relevant to what happens or may happen elsewhere in Eastern Europe, and what are the role and prospects of a socialist opposition in the socialist countries?

Even though the above analysis leads us to a positive answer to the first question, the peculiarities and differences between the Czechoslovak situation and that of the other countries should not be overlooked, especially those between the countries with limited sovereignty on the one hand and the dominating power — the USSR — on the other. The basic elements of political crisis are the same and conditions for a socialist opposition exist as well. But the state of consciousness of the crisis and of the need to create an organised force differ from country to country. The formation and consolidation of these groups and tendencies of socialist opposition will largely determine the future of socialism in that part of the world.

Political developments are never repeated in the same form. The variant of the Prague Spring, brought about by the collusion between a crisis at the top of the Party and an irresistible pressure from the grass roots, cannot be re-enacted after the 1968 military intervention and the ensuing purges in Czechoslovakia, at least within the foreseeable future. Yet it remains possible in other East European countries, especially in Poland and Hungary, where the masses are capable of exerting comparable pressure and where part of the leading group appears capable of entering into some form of alliance with the population in a favourable situation and of becoming the spokesman of the population's demands.

The signs of a gradual disintegration of the monolithic structure of the "socialist camp" — China's refusal to submit to the leading role of the USSR and the relatively autonomous foreign policy of Yugoslavia and Romania — are, if viewed from this angle, significant factors, although they appeal rather to the desire for independence and to patriotic feelings than to a struggle for a new model of socialist society. In this respect the Chinese influence can increase only to the extent to which China presents a different, doubtless poorer but more popular and more open image of socialism and to which it refrains from engaging in great-power politics and chooses to show solidarity with peoples struggling for their independence and to support the forces combating the bureaucratic system in the socialist countries. Its constantly growing presence in the world arena represents a highly positive factor for the East European countries and for the socialist opposition, even though one does not wish to replace one model by another. Yugoslavia, too, exerts a decisive influence on the progressive forces in the socialist countries. This influence has, however, been weakened in the recent period: first, Yugoslavia is too isolated from the others and consequently has not been able to demonstrate all the advantages inherent in its self-management system; and secondly, it is impossible to rule out some form of return to bureaucratic and centralist methods and to discrimination against dissidents, since the monopoly of the Party has never been questioned. The conflict between the progressive and the Stalinist forces is becoming increasingly acute and may break out at any moment: the result will determine whether Yugoslavia can play its part as an "alternative" or not.

The situation in the Soviet Union itself remains the decisive factor of change in Eastern Europe: all the other countries are subject to its control, and the Soviet Union has so far been the principal, insurmountable obstacle to every attempt at a renovation of socialism. This has led the overwhelming majority of the population — and many members of the opposition — to believe that nothing can be done until there is a change inside the USSR and its leadership, since otherwise any opposition movement in Eastern Europe, any aspiration to independence will be crushed by military intervention. We have already shown the dangers of such an attitude, which lie not only in the moral sphere but equally in the sphere of practice: Soviet intervention in Czechoslovakia could have been prevented by a different reaction from the Czechoslovak leadership. There are situations in which the Soviet Union will have neither the courage nor the ability to undertake such an action, especially if there is a simultaneous movement in several socialist countries, pressure by China, internal divergences within the USSR etc. For the first time since the 1930s one can note with satisfaction that there are signs of *an internal opposition in the Soviet Union:* dissident publications circulating as "samizdat", opposition communists, democrats, Christians, Russian and other nationalists, the movement of Soviet Jews, Sakharov's human rights committee, discontent among scientists, in the cultural sphere, among young people etc. This is undoubtedly the result of the crisis of the present régime, and clearly a sign of progress. But there is as yet no organised socialist or communist opposition movement capable of working within the Party and among the masses and of formulating a realistic alternative to the present system. Moreover, although these opposition trends undoubtedly express the latent dissatisfaction of the people and their longing for greater freedom and a better life, they appear to be confined to the intellectual "élite" of the country. This does not diminish their significance in any way: the intelligentsia has always played a great intellectual and political role in Russia, and socialist ideas were for a long time the attribute of a minority, even at the moment of victory of the October revolution. But does this mean that the influence of these groups and opposition trends is so small that they cannot directly influence political life? What are the real possibilities and prospects open for the Soviet opposition to change the political structures and replace the present leading group and its policy? To find the correct answer to this question it is necessary to review at least briefly the development and formation of this system in the USSR and in Eastern Europe.

It is often forgotten that the Soviet system was in its initial stages nothing like as monolithic as it is now, that after the October revolution and even during the civil war, foreign intervention, blockade and famine — i.e. while Lenin was alive — a lively ideological and political activity pervaded the Bolshevik Party and existed outside it, and that various groups and trends vied with one another. However much Lenin may have enjoyed unchallenged authority as the leader of the revolution there existed beside him a number of outstanding and original personalities, who voiced their opinions at meetings and in the press and frequently engaged in polemics with Lenin. In Lenin's own speeches and writings from various periods one finds both formulations liable to be interpreted in the sense that dictatorship of the proletariat is identical with the rule of one party, and the frequently stressed idea that the dissolution of the other parties and the rule of one alone are merely a transitory step, a consequence of the concrete historical situation, i.e. of the threat to the revolution by civil war and foreign intervention. A number of his speeches suggest that *his list of conditions for the construction of a socialist society did not rule out the system of a plurality of parties*. Stalin, however, raised the temporary measure of single-party rule to a dogma, allegedly valid not only in the conditions of the USSR but also, after the second world war, in the other countries in which the conditions of a socialist system then existed. The same fate was reserved for Lenin's thesis about the temporary dissolution of factions and trends within the party, which after Lenin's death led to the total suppression of all political life inside the party and throughout the country. This temporary measure, too, was transformed by Stalin into an iron law which is presented as an integral part of Lenin's doctrine on the party to this day.

These theories were to have their practical consequences: first, the suppression of any political opposition or partnership outside and later also inside the Bolshevik Party, and the ensuing and in-

81

creasing stifling of any political discussion and criticism of the increasingly narrow circle of leaders, which eventually boiled down to the rule of Stalin and the Party machinery. Any disapproval of the official policy of this ruling group or of the "leader" is then branded as the expression of an "anti-Party policy". And since the Party as a monopoly force has become the only legal political platform, and since it is also identified with the Soviet State, *criticism or opposition is now no longer merely "anti-Party" but also "anti-State": thus it comes under the penal code and is punished accordingly as a crime.* This triggered off the political trials against all Stalin's opponents in the USSR, in which political opponents, mostly Bolsheviks of long standing, were gradually to be branded as "subversives", "saboteurs", and eventually as "Gestapo agents" and "agents of imperialism". *Political opposition was thus finally relegated from the ranks of the party and from all legal positions into the underground,* and this inevitably marked its ways of thinking and its forms of struggle. And this in turn made it easier for Stalin to apply the most brutal methods for its elimination "in the interests of the defence of the USSR".

After victory over Hitler, when the authority of the USSR in the whole world had been raised in an unprecedented way, when the Soviet Union was not threatened by any immediate peril and when, on the contrary, a number of states in Eastern Europe had come under its influence, many people found it logical that there should be a certain liberalisation of the system. However, a campaign against "individual roads to socialism" started in connection with the expulsion of Yugoslavia from the Cominform, and the Soviet model of socialism was forced upon all the countries of Eastern and Central Europe as the only valid obligatory one. The change in Soviet policy towards Israel was accompanied by a campaign against so-called "cosmopolitanism", which opened the way to anti-semitism and to the suppression of every divergent, unorthodox view. As this pressure awakened resistance among the non-communist parties in the Eastern European countries, these parties were either suppressed or tied to the "transmission belts" of the Communist Party and became mere objects of strategic expediency. As, however, doubts appeared within the communist parties too, political trials were staged (Rajk in Hungary, Slansky in Czechoslovakia, Kostov in Bulgaria, Gomulka in Poland etc.) whose aim was to nip any sign of a potential opposition in the bud, to deprive the communist parties of a national basis of their own and of their natural leaders, and thus to make these parties obedient instruments of the "centre". This drove the opposition in these countries underground and exposed them to political repression, or it led to spontaneous mass outbursts once Soviet control or the national state machinery showed signs of vulnerability (Berlin 1953, Poland and Hungary 1956, the workers' uprising in the Polish Baltic ports 1970-71, etc.).

These crises and convulsions in Eastern Europe were to find their indirect echo in the USSR, where the first signs of a political awakening appeared after the Twentieth Congress of the CPSU. It is true that Khrushchev exposed and condemned the methods of political repression used by Stalin and that he obtained the rehabilitation of hundreds of thousands of executed or arrested citizens, but he did not dare rehabilitate the representatives of the "left" or "right" opposition sentenced at public trials or revise their sentences. Nor did he tolerate any form of political opposition in the Party, but eliminated his opponents — unlike Stalin — politically rather than physically. One has, of course, to consider that the "liberalisation" of any totalitarian régime is always very risky, since accumulated dissatisfaction threatens to explode. That is why it is difficult to judge whether Krushchev could have applied any milder methods against the strong position of the conservative forces in the Party machinery, in the secret police and in the Army, without running the risk of being eliminated himself.

But the fact remains that even Khrushchev did not trust the popular masses too much and that he never tried to muster the initiative of the intellectuals and workers against the pressure of the dogmatists and restore political life in the Party so as to provide for an open confrontation amongst various tendencies. This made it possible for him to be overthrown eventually by a classic type of palace revolution. Consequently this conspiracy of the Party machinery did not encounter any resistance among the people or lead to the formation of a distinct opposition movement.

The takeover by the Brezhnev leadership, and the fears of a part of the Party *aktiv* and of politically active groups of the population (including many rehabilitated victims of Stalinist terror and numerous intellectuals) that the changes at the top might bring about a revision of the results of the Twentieth Congress of the CPSU and eventually even the rehabilitation of Stalin, gave the impulse to a great number of political activities: open letters, articles, book manuscripts which were smuggled abroad for publication or circulated in the country as "samizdat".

These include first and foremost the writings of Roy and Zhores

Medvedev, Grigorenko, Amalrik, Sinyavsky and Daniel, Litvinov and Marchenko, Yakimovich, Bukovsky and many, many others, who exposed the crimes of the Stalin era and thereby helped to prevent a return to these methods; then there were the works of writers like Solzhenitsyn, especially his *Gulag Archipelago*, Maksimov, Galich, Nekrasov and others, Grigorenko's protest on behalf of the Crimean Tatars, the protest of Yakimovich, Litvinov, Larissa Bogoraz and others against Soviet intervention in Czechoslovakia, the defence of political prisoners, the publication of the "Chronicle of Current Events", and lastly the foundation of the "Committee for the Defence of Human Rights" by Academician Sakharov. This list also includes the advocacy of a greater measure of freedom in art, science and research by many Soviet artists and scientists as well as the works of writers, painters, film directors and theatrical producers, even though they may not always take on the form of an outright political protest. An altogether new phenomenon is the formation of various groups, whether they may call themselves communist or socialist or democratic, the activation of religious life, wide efforts in favour of greater autonomy or independence for the various nationalities in the USSR, especially in the Ukraine, the Baltic Republics, Georgia, Armenia and Central Asia, and the very active movement of the Jewish population for civic equality and for unhampered emigration to Israel.

Although the above is merely a sum total of isolated, uncoordinated and frequently ephemeral trends lacking a political concept and suffering from a certain naïveté, it marks nevertheless a *qualitative change in the political life of the USSR*: for the first time after thirty or forty years of absolute rule of the Communist Party and its machinery, Soviet citizens dare to voice opinions of their own which differ from official policy, they dare to criticise the ruling group, to put forward political and economic alternatives, to demand the observance of the Constitution and laws of the USSR, to defend persons unjustly persecuted, to address world opinion and ask for solidarity. This amounts to an undeniable breach in the monolithic wall of silence and isolation with which the ruling bureaucratic group has enclosed Soviet citizens. It is the manifestation of *a new degree of political consciousness, the new commitment of a section, however small, of Soviet citizens*. It is at the same time a manifestation of the continuous process of change which the Soviet system has been undergoing since Stalin's death: though the same intolerance applies to diverging opinions, the extent of repression is shrinking and its forms are changing. The post-Stalin régime is no longer capable of eliminating every divergent opinion by executions and deportations, for it no longer possesses the same authority and self-assurance which marked Stalin's power. That is why it feels compelled to tolerate many manifestations of dissent; in other cases it strives to silence the dissenters by sanctions affecting their jobs, their livelihood, and only resorts to police and judicial repression — which no longer bears the brutal features of the Stalinist era — where it feels directly threatened and where other means fail. An additional factor is that the USSR has in the meantime become a world power with manifold diplomatic and economic contacts with other governments and is therefore much more dependent on international relations than it was under Stalin; however much it may assert the contrary this makes it more sensitive towards manifestations of public opinion.

Whatever our assessment of the significance of these signs of opposition and of the dissident movement, we must give a sober assessment of their political impact and their practical ability to influence political developments in the country. We must not forget that *these manifestations of opposition do not originate in the centres of political decision-making but on the periphery of power.* This may be another factor which explains the degree of tolerance and the lack of zeal in suppressing them. After all, opposition *outside* the institutions of the régime is not as dangerous as *inside*.

A great weakness of the opposition groups as well as of individual dissidents lies in their isolation from the broad strata of the population, especially from the working class but also from the peasantry. The majority of those in opposition come from the ranks of the intelligentsia, which is understandable in view of the greater possibilities open to this group in Soviet society by virtue of its erudition, its living contact with the outside world and the respect which the intelligentsia enjoys in Russia, especially scientists and artists. Information about the living conditions of industrial workers rarely appears in the documents of the opposition, and there is hardly ever an attempt to formulate a programme containing the immediate or long-term demands of workers, farmers or young people. As far as any such demands for the improvement of working conditions and catering facilities or for the removal of inefficient management are put forward, they are mostly spontaneous and lead to wildcat strikes or elemental outbursts (e.g. in Dnepropetrovsk and Dneprodzerzhinsk in 1972) which are eventually put down by the police and army.

85

Apart from several tendencies which may be described as "left" (such as Grigorenko, Yakimovich, Marchenko, Kosterin) because they advocate the replacement of the present bureaucratic structure by new forms of people's self-management or demand a return to the system of elected "worker and peasant councils" of the period immediately following the October revolution, the most important component of the opposition current is composed of those whom Roy Medvedev calls the "Party democrats". The main demand of this current, supported by the younger and better educated Party officials, is for "thorough democratisation of the Communist Party and of Soviet society as a whole". This democratisation is to be achieved by a "return to the Leninist norms of party and state life and their increasing expansion", i.e. first and foremost by the gradual implementation of freedom of the press, speech and assembly as well as freedom for art, science and research. They do not propose the introduction of a pluralistic political system as was the case for example in Czechoslovakia in 1968, nor do they question the dominant role of the Communist Party, but they are in favour of creating possibilities for discussion within the party and for formulating opposing views, and for restoring the autonomous function of the state and its institutions. They want to submit the Party and state machinery to the control of elected bodies; these elections are not intended to be a contest between several parties but an opportunity for the citizens to decide between several candidates according to qualitative criteria, not according to the choice made by the party machinery.

In the economic sphere the "party democrats" are out to effect a reform which would permit a flexible combination of centralisation and decentralisation, of planned and market economy, of labour discipline and individual initiative of the working people. At the same time they want to cautiously test elements of workers' self-management or rather to expand elements of control, the role of the trade unions, the autonomy of enterprises and collective farms. We can summarise this attitude by saying that it is based on the preservation of the Soviet system in its essence whilst striving for its gradual democratisation, liberalisation and modernisation — a gradual process designed to avoid the crises and convulsions which in their opinion would result from a sudden liberalisation of the existing structures. As opposed to the "left" groups, this current wants all the changes to be carried out at the initiative of the ruling Party, i.e. "from above" and counts on the support of the population rather than on the population's own initiative. It is, therefore, only natural that the "Party democrats" adopt a very reserved attitude both towards the Yugoslav self-management system and towards the Prague Spring, of which Medvedev says that "reforms which are too radical may lead to dangerous situations". Interestingly the attitude of the representatives of this group towards the People's Republic of China is, like that of the other opposition groups, in most cases just as negative as that of the Soviet rulers. They have the same fear of the "anti-Russian tendencies" of the national movements in the various Republics, and fail to see that these are the expression of resistance against the central bureaucracy rather than of hostility towards the Russian people or to socialism.

Because of these weaknesses in the opposition we may expect state socialism and its political structures in the Soviet Union to remain in power for quite some time. But even though — on the basis of the rigidity of its structures, the lack of tolerance, the complete absence of popular participation in power, great-power foreign policy, ideological stagnation, etc. — we may speak about neo-Stalinism, a return to the excesses of Stalin's régime — mass murder of innocent people and of entire populations, the monopoly of decision-making and unlimited dictatorship vested in one man — is hardly probable. There is, rather, a growing *alliance between the Party machinery, the upper sections of the technocracy and the managers of the economy,* with the support of the Army, which is constantly increasing in importance as the only well-organised and unified force. It requires modern, highly effective weapons, whose production means that they play a crucial role in industry and science; this in turn requires efficient administration and a political leadership which does not take too risky decisions (and does not leave it to the Army to atone for the consequences of its blunders: Cuba, the Middle East etc.). The present leadership, furthermore, knows that it cannot keep power by repression alone — though this remains an integral part of the system — but that it must provide for sufficient economic development in order to raise the living standards of the population, who are no longer ready to make unnecessary sacrifices.

To achieve these aims, economic co-operation with the highly developed capitalist countries is imperative, especially with the USA, the Federal Republic of Germany and Japan, whilst the political status quo in the world is preserved — in particular, respect for the Soviet sphere of influence in Central and Eastern Europe and the geographical and military encirclement of the

People's Republic of China. Even if this co-operation remains confined to contacts between the governments it is certain to have a gradual influence on the country's internal situation. It may well lead to a "technocratic" variant which will limit the power monopoly of the party machinery in favour of "liberal" technocrats and managers, who aim consists of making the Soviet Union — or rather Russia — a modern state with a sound and efficient economy capable of satisfying the needs of the population. The presence and capabilities of the socialist opposition currents will decide whether or not this transformation of the Soviet Union into a modern State will take place within a socialist framework.

Yet this development will be equally influenced by pressure from the socialist countries and the international communist and socialist movement. The latter will have to choose between the role of passive witnesses who accept everything and are always ready to pay for the mistakes of the "socialist world centre", and an autonomous stand, not merely in order to take their "own road" but also to exert influence upon the USSR.

The Responsibility of the Left in the West

Let us establish a daring hypothesis — one, however, which cannot be withheld from this kind of analysis of the prospects for a socialist alternative: the hypothesis of a *situation in which an alliance of communist and socialist parties, together with other forces of the Left, would in the long term accede to power in certain Western countries like, for example, France or Italy.* We fully realise that this will be extremely difficult in the present circumstances, and we do not wish to reiterate all the arguments which seem to point in the opposite direction. But such a possibility cannot be ruled out entirely in a new climate of international détente which would lead to the American commitment in Europe being phased out and to the gradual dissolution of the present military and political blocs. *This, in fact, offers socialists a hope*: the hope of socialist changes in society in the economically and politically most developed capitalist countries — in keeping with Marx's and Engels's forecasts, though with a delay of over fifty years. *Since the unexpected birth of a socialist society in Europe's most retrograde country brought the fatal disease of Stalinist deformations upon socialism, is one not entitled to hope that the new socialist reality in the developed countries would contribute to radical changes in the system as they exist in the East European countries, facilitating and accelerating the transition to democratic and humane socialist structures there?* Such hopes are encouraged by the efforts of those communist parties in the West European countries which advocate a pluralistic political system guaranteeing the preservation and development of personal and democratic freedoms (cf. especially the programmes of the Italian, French and Spanish CPs). If such socialist systems based on political plurality existed would it then be possible for communists like Milan Hübl, Sabata, Tesar, Litera, and others to be held in jail simply because they had advocated the same system in another socialist country?

If this prospect gives rise to hopes within the socialist opposition, can it be promoted and supported by the Soviet leading group, whose interest lies in exactly the opposite direction? Two completely different possibilities arise here:

1. In the midst of the process of socialist transformation these countries may have to face up to such a serious situation — pressure from the reaction at home, economic mismanagement and shortcomings, but also pressure from America or elsewhere or an economic blockade — that they will be compelled to ask the USSR and the Soviet bloc for material assistance as they have always done so far. Experience shows that their development will then probably proceed in an identical manner as in the other Eastern European countries, especially Czechoslovakia: at the international level, from a voluntary and enthusiastic alliance to increasingly stifling dependence; at the internal level, from the elimination of "reactionary agents" and political opponents of socialism (on the pretext that they weaken the state in a period of crisis) to the consolidation of "class unity" and discipline by uniting communists and socialists within a "united Party of the working class"; and later from the leading role of this Party in the country's political life to purges of "revisionist", "anti-socialist", "trotskyite", "liberal", "zionist", "individualist" elements etc. — with the same result as in the East European countries: the establishment of the "Soviet model" (united Party and authoritarian structures) and integration into the "worldwide socialist camp" (limited sovereignty, "guaranteed" by the USSR).

Such a development is not inevitable: one can reckon with the existence of traditions and socialist forces in these countries which would recognise the peril in time and oppose such a policy with greater success than has been the case in other countries. In this hypothesis a new "Yugoslav" or "Czechoslovak" affair (this time a French or Italian one) could usher in a conflict between the "centre" and the "periphery" whose outcome would depend on one factor alone: whether the will of the country was expressed by a personality of the rank of Tito, who refused to bow to Stalin's pressure in the 1950s, or by a new Dubcek, who, with a broken heart, allowed the Soviet Army to march into his country as a guarantor of the future of socialism.

2. The other alternative is that the communist parties of these countries, and with them the socialists and their progressive allies, will wish to keep their promises and build a *socialist society of another type*. The alliance between communists, socialists and other political forces is based on co-operation between equal partners, the rights of political opposition are safeguarded, democratic freedoms, especially of speech and assembly, are protected, the workers participate in the management of the economy; an idea of

national sovereignty is fostered which is not in contradiction with international solidarity but does not contain any trace of interference and domination by the "world centre". It is, in brief, a socialism which is supported by the majority of citizens and does not need to resort to repression.

This alternative would offer the peoples of Eastern Europe a new "centre of attraction"; it would be all the more vital and dynamic since it would be based on one or several concrete examples of democratic socialism, on a different concrete model of the socialist society. This would usher in a new stage of development of the international communist and socialist movement, which would be characterised by radical transformations within the communist, socialist, social democratic parties and the various left-wing trends, both in the "socialist camp" and in the capitalist societies. In this context *the socialist opposition in the East European countries would appear to be the natural ally of this new trend.*

Many communists and democrats in Eastern Europe have set their hopes on this kind of development and consider it the only way to reshape the systems existing in their countries. I can remember what a leading figure of the Prague Spring said on returning from a "pressure trip" to Moscow: "From now on socialism can only be saved by the communists of Western Europe, who have no Soviet tanks standing outside their windows." An interesting reflection, even though it shows a lack of deep knowledge of the complex logic inherent in the international communist movement.

Many members of the socialist opposition, while voicing the wish to see such a tempting prospect come true, are concerned with the following question: what will happen if democratic socialism comes to power in some Western countries in the present situation while "existing socialism" in the USSR and Eastern Europe still holds fast to its bureaucratic structures and is considerably stronger, above all in the military sphere? Is it not more likely, in this case, that it will first be influenced by authoritarian socialism, then eroded and finally dominated by it? This question ought to worry not only the members of the socialist opposition in Eastern Europe, who are anxious not to forfeit their great hope, but equally their Western comrades, who would face the same danger of seeing the very meaning of their struggle go to pieces.

Jacques Julliard wrote in *Le Nouvel Observateur* on 28 August 1972: "Historically speaking, democracy in the socialist countries has so far always been smothered under the impact of three factors: civil war, foreign intervention, and the existence of an all-powerful Party organised on the Leninist pattern." For the West, an addition should be made: "Total lack of knowledge of the Soviet model." True, the attitude of communists and other members of the Left in Western Europe towards the Soviet Union and the régimes in Eastern Europe is less euphoric and more critical today than it used to be. But this is still a long way from a thorough analysis; there is a tendency to criticise details rather than the principles of the matter, especially where the Soviet Union is concerned. Any radical criticism is met with the accusation of anti-Sovietism and "playing the enemy's game". Yet this is precisely the pattern on which repression in the Socialist countries works.

Such phenomena are in no way confined to the countries in which the communist party is in power. They already exist within the revolutionary movement even at the stage of preparing for a struggle for power. *They must be analysed and fought here and now if one is to prevent a return to the same "deformations"*, the same mistakes, which can no longer in fact be described as "deformations", because they have been the rule and not the exception, and have apparently so far been an integral part of the process of building socialism.

They must therefore be reckoned with; they must be examined and analysed well before accession to power. One must assess to what extent they are inevitable in the process of building a new society and seek the means not of avoiding them completely, which is impossible, but of overcoming them. This does not offer a foolproof guarantee against a repetition of such phenomena, but it does make it more probable that the "new course" will not suffer the same disaster.

This task cannot be mastered by the members of the socialist opposition in the East European countries alone. There must be an awareness of these problems among communists, socialists and Marxists in Western Europe. *They must support these efforts and consider them a decisive element of their common struggle. This is a crucial problem for the future of socialism: either it will be proved by practice and force of example that there can really exist a model of socialism other than the Soviet — authoritarian and bureaucratic — one; or the entire theory and practice of socialism must be subjected to a new analysis, a new assessment. and consequences must be drawn from these.*

92

A New Alternative

When we look at the programmes and demands of the various groups of the Soviet opposition and of the opposition forces in the other Eastern European countries, notably Czechoslovakia, Hungary, Poland and Yugoslavia, we notice, despite many differences stemming from conditions in the countries concerned and notwithstanding different formulations and tactics, a number of fundamental demands and objectives which together make up a political opposition platform. But we must not forget that apart from the socialist opposition in the USSR and in the East European countries there exist opposition groups and individuals who reject socialism as a system and show a preference for a Western type of parliamentary democracy, or who advocate a state system based on Christianity, or authoritarian régimes with an anti-communist nationalist character. These groups may enjoy some measure of support among sections of the population who have been disappointed by the existing system which professes to be socialist. But if we take into account their development so far and the division of the world into Soviet and US spheres of influence, these tendencies have no chance of influencing future events.

What then are the major objectives of the socialist opposition in Eastern Europe?

1. To maintain the nationalisation of the means of production but to transfer them from the present state ownership to popular ownership, with a broadening of the range of various forms: from State ownership which is suitable for large industry, to group ownership which is advantageous for medium-sized and smaller establishments, to co-operative ownership which is suitable for services and various crafts as well as for agriculture and trade. Some groups have come forward with the demand for "workers' " or "factory councils" as a form of self-management through which manual and white-collar workers are to decide production plans, technical equipment of factories, the distribution of surplus value and the appointment of managers and leading officials. However, this demand is raised only seldom by the Soviet opposition, where the tradition of workers' struggles is much too remote, while the socialist opposition in

Czechoslovakia, Hungary, Yugoslavia and Poland gives it top priority. In a number of East European countries the opposition envisages the existence of a private sector in the service sphere, though with strict limitations and supervision laid down by law so as to prevent any exploitation of workers or accumulation of private capital. The Soviet opposition places greater emphasis on the need to raise the efficiency of production and management in the economy and not so much on self-management and workers' control.

But all the groups in the USSR and in the East European countries have one thing in common: they want to retain the collective ownership of the means of production, and they reject a return to private ownership of these means of production by capitalists, though official propaganda deliberately imputes this idea to them.

2. On the basis of collective ownership of the means of production, they demand the creation of a socialist political system which would genuinely guarantee the broad participation of the working people in the political and economic running of the country, as well as equal rights for all citizens. Here the main obstacle is the monopoly position of the Party and its identification with the state. That is why virtually all opposition programmes in the USSR and in the other East European countries underline the need for a *democratisation of the Party,* and the forging of new kinds of relation with people who have no party affiliation. In the USSR, as distinct from Czechoslovakia, no demand is made for political pluralism. One of the reasons is certainly that during the past fifty years they have had no tradition of party political confrontation. They demand discussion within the Party and debates on differences of opinion; that decision-making party institutions should consider alternative proposals and lastly, that the Communist Party must win the people's confidence and the right to a leading role by the correctness of its policy, which should be put to the population for judgement.

In the other socialist countries it is the need for a system of *political pluralism* which is stressed, the need for other political parties, representing the various interests of other groups in socialist society, to participate in political life and in decision-making. The relations between these parties and the Communist Party should be based on partnership and co-operation instead of that of a "transmission belt" acting on instructions from the Communist Party.

The various opposition groups are identical in defining socialist democracy as a system which grants its citizens more rights, more freedom and influence than bourgeois parliamentary democracy — and obviously also far more than a Stalinist bureaucracy does. It should be a combination of *representative democracy* in which the citizens choose their representatives by direct and secret elections at various levels and with a wide range of programmes and candidates, *and direct democracy*, which means direct participation of the citizens in the administration and supervision of power by workers' councils, by the self-administration of local government and by other forms of self-management.

3. Practically all opposition programmes "discover" the role of the trade unions to be that of representatives of the workers' interests in relation to the state body. It is recognised that under socialism, too, the interests of working people may well run counter to those of the state administration and that consequently *the working people must have their own autonomous organisations* such as trade unions, youth organisations, farmers' associations, women's organisations, co-operatives, associations of artists, scientists, etc. In addition to defending the interests of their memberships these mass organisations should be able to participate in decision-making, first of all by expressing their views on government proposals in their own independent press, and secondly by sending their delegates to Parliament and other bodies of workers' power.

4. All the documents of the opposition in the USSR and in the other socialist countries without exception place special emphasis on the absolutely guaranteed *freedom of opinion, assembly, criticism and information for all citizens.* The Left in the West frequently underrates this demand or views it as the expression of an intellectual élite which remains of no consequence for workers and peasants. But it is this demand, which the socialist movement has put forward right from the start, that is *the prerequisite of each and every democratisation process and of the mobilisation of the working people.* If the working people are kept ignorant of the actual economic situation in their own factory and in the state as a whole, of domestic and foreign policy, of the conflicts in governing bodies, of the various opinion trends etc., they will never be in a position to state their views on fundamental issues and formulate their own position; it will make them dependent on bureaucratic groups who speak for them and in their name. *Without these freedoms, even if they are only carried out gradually and partially, there can be no renewal of political life just as there can be*

95

no fundamental transformation in the USSR and in the East European countries.

Certain opposition groups, however, make the mistake of expecting pressure by Western governments to bring these liberties for them instead of waging their own struggle and exerting their own pressure on their ruling groups. In the USSR, moreover, the demand for tolerance within the country and the right to emigration, especially — though not exclusively — for the Jewish population plays a particularly important role; it is, of course, valid elsewhere too.

The intellectual opposition groups attach major importance to the demand for *freedom of the arts, science and research.* This may appear as an élitist demand confined merely to those whom it may concern or to the cream of the intelligentsia. But it is of major significance for the development of society as a whole, especially for the increasing elimination of the distinction between manual and intellectual work.

Under the conditions which exist in the USSR and in the East European countries the opposition can do no more than protest against violations of the law and deformation of socialist ideals, expose the worst injustices committed by the system, fight in defence of this or that member of the opposition, or at best try to bring about a partial improvement. It cannot, however, elaborate complex conceptions and programmes, discuss them with the working people, work out an organisational structure and so forth. It has the role of a beacon lighting the road in the dark, or of a fuse exploding in an untenable situation and releasing revolutionary forces, rather than that of a conscious "alternative" or a real political force. This applies in particular to the USSR, but also to countries with a political tradition such as Czechoslovakia.

Marxist theoreticians and politicians rightly criticised the Dubcek leadership and all those who held leading positions during the Prague Spring in 1968 for failing to give the entire process a clear conception, a political programme and correct tactics. Yet they forget that one needs time to work out a conception and tactics and that conditions for a political life must be created which is impossible under the rule of the Stalinist bureaucracy. That is why every movement for the renewal of socialism in the USSR and in every East European country will first of all take the form of a spontaneous outbreak with contradictory views and hazy conceptions. Differences will be cleared up, a programme worked out and tactics outlined in the course of development. This is precisely why opposition movements, groups and individuals such as Sakharov and Medvedev are of great importance for the future because at least in the initial stages they make possible a differentiation or a presentation of problems, thereby laying the foundations for future development.

Many of the objectives of the opposition in the USSR and in the other countries come under the same influence. And on this hinges the second important question: *how are these objectives to be implemented and translated into reality?*

After the Twentieth CPSU Congress it seemed possible to discuss and carry out some of these objectives within the Party, and within Soviet institutions. That is why most of the proposals were addressed to leading bodies of the Party, while a number of later "dissidents" participated in the work of various commissions and working groups which drew up alternative proposals for the leading Party and state bodies. Even after the fall of Khrushchev Sakharov addressed his well-known memorandum to the CPSU leadership, Yakir defended his ideas in the Institute of History of the Academy of Sciences, and Roy Medvedev offered his study on Stalinism to the Party Publishing House.

When it became clear that the conservative forces in the leadership were not prepared to discuss these proposals but, on the contrary, to suppress them as expressions of a policy hostile to the Party, several groups and individuals made an effort to maintain their activities on a legal basis and decided not to embark on any kind of illegal activity. The initiative of Sakharov and of his friends in forming the Committee for the defence of Human Rights falls into this pattern. The Committee set itself the aim of campaigning for the rights enshrined in the Soviet constitution, and of protesting wherever valid laws were being violated. The first opposition groups in Czechoslovakia after the Soviet occupation likewise stressed their legal character (see the Ten-Point Manifesto of August 1969). In the same way, the criticism of the bureaucratic system of sociologists of the "Budapest school" was done in public and by official institutions.

As intolerance and repression were stepped up a number of opposition groups and individuals wondered what organisational forms to choose which would make it possible to attain the set objectives. This discussion went further in Czechoslovakia than anywhere else, as this study and the published documents show.

It became clear that possibilities for opposition activities within the Party were extremely limited after August 1968, and especially after the Husak régime came to power. Consequently, the main task had to be to build up a socialist opposition movement outside the Party.

On the other hand the "Party democrats" in the USSR saw the only serious opposition current to be exclusively within the party and within official institutions. They considered this the only possibility of becoming active and of pressing for their objectives. But it is not clear to what extent this current has been successful in forming itself within the Party, and whether its sole objective is to back up the moderate wing in the leading bodies of the CPSU.

The socialist opposition in Czechoslovakia never ruled out the need and the possibility of acting within the Party and within legal institutions, in short whenever an opportunity should arise. Yet it opposed the erroneous view that there was no possibility for a political struggle outside the Party and the existing institutions. Instead, they arrived at the conclusion that in the given historical situation the crucial point of the opposition's struggle lay precisely outside the Party and that this was an independent political struggle. There were, however, different opinions as to who should be the mainstay and organiser of the struggle. Some leaned towards the view that a new illegal communist party had to be formed which would draw on the results of the Fourteenth CPCz Congress, thereby continuing the line of the Prague Spring. Others maintained that the Communist Party was far too discredited and that the existence of two communist parties would make the masses feel that this was a struggle within the Party among communists, which would in turn isolate the opposition from the people.

The socialist opposition in Czechoslovakia is the first example of a political opposition in a socialist country. Its existence will unquestionably meet with a response in the other countries, including the USSR. At the moment it is too soon to conclude whether this form has proved itself in Czechoslovakia and whether — naturally in different variants — it can be applied also in other East European countries. The repression which the occupation régime set in motion against it in 1971-72 and which reached its climax in the series of political trials in summer 1972 only goes to prove that the ruling bureaucratic group was fully aware of the political weight of a socialist opposition and that it was determined to crush this opposition in Czechoslovakia before its example could find followers in the other socialist countries.

At the same time the Soviet leadership struck at the opposition in the USSR, in particular its most interesting journal, the *Chronicle of Current Events,* which has become an important source of information on the activities of the Soviet opposition for the world public. At the same time it acted as a potential centre around which the various opposition groups and individuals could rally. The trials of Yakir and Krasin, the sentencing of Amalrik and Bukovsky, the detention of Grigorenko in a psychiatric clinic where he was to be completely silenced, and the campaign against Sakharov and Solzhenitsyn, were aimed at destroying and demoralising the Soviet opposition even before it had had time to become organised and to establish contacts with similar groups in other countries in Eastern Europe as well as with the Left and the democratic movement in the West.

The form of open political struggle in which Sakharov, Solzhenitsyn and their friends stood up to this campaign of vilification deserves our admiration and solidarity. Yet some of their statements reveal the weaknesses and limitations of the Soviet opposition, particularly when they talk about the Western world and call on Western governments to force the Soviet leadership to agree to a democratisation in return for economic and other forms of cooperation. It would appear that these representatives of the Soviet opposition failed to recognise the true situation which has arisen out of the mutual interests of the Soviet and American establishments and their Western allies and which results in *the common interest of both partners to maintain the political status quo in the world.* This kind of notion also demonstrates a certain despair among the opposition or at least in some of its sections at the political indifference of the Soviet population, and a certain indecision on the question of how to obtain their objectives by a political struggle within the system and by the forces of the people. This demand to the West obviously gives official Soviet propaganda the pretext with which to brand not only Sakharov and Solzhenitsyn but the entire opposition as "enemies of détente and co-operation", which is of course untrue because it was precisely they who were among the first to press for such co-operation in which they saw a possible improvement in the situation. Yet they were disappointed; they had harboured unjustified illusions. This strengthened the hand of the communist parties which support the Soviet policy of peaceful coexistence and which can now accuse the Soviet opposition of joining forces with the champions of the cold war (see Moreau in *L'Humanité*). But the main reason for such a confusion of ideas lies in the fact that the Soviet opposition and similar movements in the East European countries — with certain exceptions — re-

99

ceive no help from communist and socialist parties and from the West European Left as a whole. That is why out of despair and because of their lack of understanding of the situation a section turned to those quarters where this support or at least publicity is forthcoming. This paradoxical situation was explained by the Italian Marxist Rossana Rossanda, expelled from the Italian Communist Party, in an article in *Il Manifesto.* She speaks of *"the considerable blame and responsibility which the European Left has to bear".*

The tragedy of the Soviet opposition lies in the fact that it is being condemned by communist parties for maximalism and impatience while the rest of the Left reproaches it for "liberalism" and lack of "class consciousness" as well as "reformism". Here we come back once again to another instance of the fetishism which burdens the international communist movement and the Left: the unbridgeable gap between "reformism" and "revolution". In countries like the USSR, where there is a certain basis for a socialist society, even though it is thoroughly imperfect, this point of dispute is absolutely irrelevant. As we have already demonstrated through the example of Czechoslovakia in 1968, *under certain circumstances, and given the activity of the masses, reforms can create the conditions for qualitative transformations of the system towards a more extensive socialist democracy so that the masses can in fact play a revolutionary role.*

Against this background it becomes clear that a truly revolutionary activity in the USSR and in the East European countries would today mean speeding up those reforms of the given system as would provide for a greater participation of the working people in decision-making and in leadership, even though such measures may prove to be entirely insufficient and would only gradually approach the ultimate objective — a democratisation of the Soviet system.

In the leadership of the CPSU a struggle is beginning to brew very quietly between the moderate wing, which considers certain reforms indispensable, and the representatives of the old dogmatic policy who fear reforms and change, which they consider an overture for upheaval and a threat to their privileges. The moderate wing concentrates for the time being on better relations with the USA, the Federal Republic of Germany and other capitalist countries so as to take advantage of new opportunities in the economy and in internal reforms. On certain questions the standpoint of the opposition coincides with that of the moderate wing, and the possibility cannot be ruled out that the hysterical campaign against Sakharov, Solzhenitsyn and other representatives of the opposition by exponents of the harsh line is being waged as an indirect struggle against the moderate wing with the aim of creating difficulties for the latter in foreign policy. One must not forget that a large section of the Soviet military and its allies in the armaments industry and in the ideological sphere constitute a numerically strong and influential group in society which is directly dependent on the foreign policy of the day, and which at any given time is ready to defend its own interests against all who threaten them (remember the Army's resistance to Khrushchev). Today this group does not want Brezhnev's policy of rapprochement with the West to make too much headway and it would even not object if this policy were to result in a fiasco. It is perfectly possible that it is using the current campaign against the opposition for these objectives. An indication of this is the inconsistent reaction of the Soviet leadership which on the one hand presents Sakharov, Solzhenitsyn and others as "completely isolated individuals" while on the other hand conducting a vast public campaign against them. Apart from the fact that, via Sakharov, the conservative forces are aiming at the supporters of reform in the leadership, they realise that while he and the others are undeniably in a minority they voice the views and aspirations of broad sections of Soviet society. It is hard to tell to what extent these views are backed, as there is no possibility of open dialogue.

That is precisely why the reform programme, most clearly formulated in Sakharov's Memorandum and in the 1972 postcript, and the programme of the "Party democrats" as expounded by Roy Medvedev, are for the time being the only real concepts for change in the Soviet system. The experience accumulated in the USSR and more particularly in Poland, Hungary and Czechoslovakia demonstrates that far-reaching *political transformations are only possible when they are advocated by forces within the ruling Communist Party, even though the initiative may emanate from the population. Only a combination of pressure from the masses with the activities of the political core of the Party and the institutions can create the conditions for political and economic reforms of fundamental importance and for a genuine democratisation of the system.* This is borne out above all by the example of the Prague Spring in 1968.

On the other hand, wherever there is only a movement or discontent among the rank and file which has no support from an opposition inside the Party, there may be outbreaks which shake the régime and may topple some of the most despotic and discredited leaders but which cannot bring about fundamental changes of the system, as demonstrated by the outcome of the Polish workers' uprising at the Baltic ports in 1970-71.

In both cases, the existence of a socialist political opposition proves to be decisive: even though it may be numerically weak it nevertheless expresses the requirements of society and the mood of the majority of the population. It can, furthermore, formulate a programme for change and turn it into a demand of the masses as well as of the reform section of the Party leadership. The socialist opposition is the main guarantee that the upheavals and eruptions which inevitably accompany every political transformation in the socialist countries will not turn merely into spontaneous outbreaks, nationalist outbursts and even counter-revolution. The opposition offers the only *socialist* alternative to the present régimes.

In this connection we may be accused of limiting the possible alternatives for development in the East European countries to the framework of a socialist society, and to exclude every other course, in particular the establishment of a Western-style parliamentary democracy. We are not unaware that such endeavours exist among a section of the population, particularly in reaction to the authoritarian model of socialism, to the monopoly of the Communist Party, to repression and to errors in the economy. But we do not rule out this possibility simply because we are socialists. Indeed, it rules itself out because of the reality which has come about in these countries since the second world war. It is true that the foundations for a socialist system were not always laid by the will of the majority of the population but enforced at times by a minority supported from outside. Yet the transformations which have taken place in the meantime are so profound and concern such broad sectors that *a return of the means of production, factories, mines, banks, and collectivised land to capitalist private ownership is out of the question.* Neither does the majority want this. It has become accustomed to collective ownership, to a certain social equality, to a significant advance in the education and health services and to a greater democratisation of culture, even though a high price has to be paid for this, even though new kinds of discrimination arise, and even though the privileges of the leading group cannot be reconciled with all this. Neither are the capitalist countries nowadays interested in "exporting" the capitalist system to the East European countries. For them it is far more advantageous to expand trade with these countries and to make this a lucrative business by

102

exporting the products of capitalist industry and importing the required raw materials.

Such an attempt to return to a capitalist system would only be possible in the event of an outright conflict between the USA and the USSR. But the consequences would be catastrophic and would presumably have nothing in common with democracy or with freedom, nor with the aspirations of the East European peoples. There would rather be the danger of a civil war which would end either in a chauvinistic military dictatorship or in a seizure of power by the most reactionary forces of the Party machinery, who would then present themselves as the guardians of order.

For all these reasons, democratic socialism is the only acceptable prospect both for the USSR and for the other socialist countries in Eastern Europe. It takes account of the reality in these countries and at the same time of the profound aspirations of their peoples for freedom, for a share in the affairs of the state, for national independence, equality and brotherhood in relations with other nations.

The Opposition and International Détente

The question remains whether international détente and broad East-West co-operation are beneficial to the activities of the opposition or whether they hinder them. The events of 1973-74, especially the increased repression in the USSR, Czechoslovakia and the other countries, would indicate that the conservative forces are on the offensive there and that they consider the elimination of the opposition to be one condition for any kind of détente and co-operation. Roy Medvedev was certainly right when he wrote in November 1973 that "the process of détente, more extensive trade and other forms of economic co-operation will not automatically change the political climate in the USSR, nor will they lead to greater democratic freedom and respect for the political and civil rights of the citizen" — as some commentators in the West assume. But Medvedev does believe that "international détente — though not in itself — represents the prerequisite for a democratisation of Soviet society".

For the socialist opposition the alternative is not: either détente, co-operation and co-existence between states with different social systems, or cold war, boycott and isolationism.

The true alternative is contained in the question *what kind* of détente is being sought: détente based on the ossification of the political status quo, on the division of spheres of influence between the two super-powers and on "contact" limited to the official representatives of the two establishments, or détente which not merely eliminates military conflict but also loosens the military and economic blocs, limits the monopoly position of the two super-powers whilst strengthening the role and capacities of medium sized and small states, which bans military intervention against other countries and creates opportunities for human contacts between citizens of all states, for the unhindered exchange of information and opinions and for political and cultural dialogue (including polemics), and which makes possible a political development independent of spheres of influence, without jeopardising the security of this or that great power.

The policy of the 1968 Prague Spring proceeded precisely from this latter conception of détente and international co-operation — with the awareness that the Czechoslovak experiment in democratic socialism was possible only in such circumstances.

Today, as in 1968, the political forces which have remained loyal to the Prague Spring and which are gathered around the socialist opposition — both in Czechoslovakia and in exile — support the policy of détente and, far from wishing to hinder it, strive to extend it so that all nations, large and small, and the ordinary citizens may benefit by it. At the same time they criticise the conception of peaceful co-existence which leads merely to the ossification of the existing situation and to the consolidation of the hegemony of the two super-powers. They also criticise the great-power policy of the present leadership of the USSR, their deformations of socialism and their repression of the political opposition. They reject the Soviet thesis according to which anyone criticising the negative aspects of Soviet policy automatically becomes an opponent of détente and a champion of the cold war.

When supporting the policy of détente and co-operation we proceed, moreover, from the historical experience of the past twenty-five years in Czechoslovakia and Eastern Europe, which proves that *the cold war and the state of international tension not only failed to weaken the Stalinist régime but, on the contrary, strengthened its most reactionary dogmatic elements and enabled them to justify the policy of repression, of dogmatic rigidity and of isolationism.* In contrast each subsequent easing of tension has brought about a relaxation of oppression and of censorship and created scope for better information, for new ideas and the resurgence of new political forces. The preparation and realisation of the Prague Spring would have been impossible without such an atmosphere.

It could be argued that the Stalinist and conservative forces have drawn the lessons of the 1968 events and will permit détente only to the extent that it is strictly controlled by themselves. There is undoubtedly an element of truth in this assertion, and one cannot fail to note that the suppression of the Prague Spring by Soviet intervention has exerted and will continue to exert a long-term influence on developments in Eastern Europe. From this also results the apparent contradiction of present-day Soviet policy: on the one hand there are attempts to widen co-operation with the West (for economic and strategic reasons, the latter with regard to China) but, on the other hand, there is a fear of facing the consequences of this policy and an ensuing tendency to intensify repression and ideological control.

This is the reason why the so-called peace offensive of the Soviet Union is coupled with a new wave of repression, administrative sanctions and ideological militancy, not only in Czechoslovakia, which is today the most vulnerable spot in the Eastern bloc, but also in the other countries and in the USSR itself. But this does not mean that one should reject the policy of détente in these circumstances. This policy acts in a long-term way. Even co-operation limited in the above-mentioned manner can produce positive results after a certain period of time: it does away with the "bogey" of the external enemy; it alleviates fear in people and activates opposition; it permits wider contacts with the outside world, even though within certain limits; it influences the intelligent part of the Party and state machinery; alongside trade, technical and scientific co-operation it inevitably leads to exchanges of documentation, literature and specialists; it accelerates the differentiation within the ruling groups. All this does not, however, mean automatic liberalisation or any other fundamental changes in Eastern Europe, as many naïve minds would have it. This is the kernel of the dispute between the two groupings of the Soviet opposition as personified by Academician Sakharov and by the historian Roy Medvedev: *should "liberalisation" be a precondition of détente and co-operation, or should it be a characteristic or — more precisely — a consequence of the development of relations?* I rather agree with Medvedev that the main problem of Soviet society is its democratisation, and that this will essentially result from the pressure and struggle of internal forces, for which external relations can merely create favourable conditions. Western governments cannot put forward ultimatums or preliminary conditions regarding their relations with the USSR and Eastern Europe, because this would not correspond to their general conception of those relations. Besides, any monopolistic authoritarian system possesses sufficient resources to withstand even an isolation of this kind. External pressure produces counter-pressure by the conservative, dogmatic forces which have a strong hold over the machineries, especially the police and army.

On the other hand, relations in various spheres will bring about a certain mutual dependence, and not merely in economic matters. These relations also give the other countries of Eastern Europe a certain room for manoeuvre with regard to the Soviet Union. Overt repression is made more difficult where public opinion plays a more important role, and in individual cases a partner can intervene more effectively than an opponent. In this sense we are in favour of the expansion of all forms of contacts and co-operation, including at government level, provided, of course, that this is not taken as settling the whole problem of détente and peaceful co-existence. It must include criticism of all negative phenomena, in particular of the suppression of civil rights, of disregard for international agreements such as the UN Charter of Human Rights, and of every form of repression, which are contrary to the true spirit of détente and co-existence. Particularly dangerous is the assumption, very frequent in the West, that political and trade relations preclude open discussion and criticism and demand a certain form of self-censorship. This would amount to applying the rules of diplomacy to the spheres of politics, ideology, human rights and freedom, and this is extremely dangerous. The East European partners must become accustomed to seeing the above principles and demands as an integral part of European co-operation; they do not represent an "ideological diversion" but aim at better mutual relationships and a genuine dialogue without discrimination.

Western public opinion ought to defend the right of the political opposition in Eastern Europe to express dissenting views, to formulate alternative solutions and proposals, to participate in the political life of its respective countries, to raise protests in the event of persecution and to manifest its solidarity with the persecuted. *The demand made by the socialist and democratic opposition in Eastern Europe that it be permitted to act within the legality of the constitution is equally in the interest of European co-operation and détente*, for it is the best guarantee that accumulated problems will not one day lead to spontaneous outbursts whose catastrophic consequences could exert a negative influence on future political developments throughout Europe and the world.

The result of the opposition struggle — which is sure to be very protracted, difficult and full of setbacks — is important not only for the future of the peoples of the USSR and Eastern Europe but for socialism in general as well as for the further development of Europe and the world. That is precisely why the struggle of this political opposition deserves not only a better understanding from public opinion in the West but also effective solidarity and political support. This in no way contradicts the justifiable desire for the development of good relations between East and West and for true détente, for progress and world peace.

The socialist opposition may be shaken by repression, it may suffer temporary losses and defeats, but it cannot be destroyed: being deeply rooted in the people, it is the herald of the future.

A Common Road

At a time when the English edition of this book is coming out and when the public events of August 1968 appear to be increasingly remote, we are witnessing a whole series of public pronouncements by leading figures of the Prague Spring whose voices have penetrated the wall of official censorship in Prague and Bratislava. First, there is the authentic testimony of Josef Smrkovsky on the events of 1968, then Alexander Dubcek's letter to the Federal Assembly on the harassment of expelled communists and the discredit brought to socialism by the ruling clique; a letter from the eminent Marxist philosopher Karel Kosik to Jean-Paul Sartre on the persecution of all unofficial thinking; a letter from playwright Vaclav Havel to Husak on the mechanism of fear; another from the communist scientist and world-famous biologist Ivan Malek on the liquidation of scientists, from the writer Ludvik Vaculik to the Secretary-General of the United Nations and from another writer, Pavel Kohout, to Heinrich Böll and Arthur Miller on his hopes and doubts in connection with the Helsinki summit; and finally a new book by Zdenek Mlynar, a former member of the Dubcek leadership, on the essence of the 1968 reform and on a possible way out of the present crisis. In addition there is a whole series of further letters, documents, petitions, protests and extremely valuable works of literature and the social sciences circulating in Czechoslovakia in samizdat form. Their publication in foreign languages would certainly greatly enrich socialist thinking and European culture as a whole.

All this prompts the question: why is it that after so many years of the country's occupation by Soviet troops and a régime of "normalisation" it has not been possible to silence and uproot the spirit of the Prague Spring? What is the message that these voices of the socialist opposition bring to the Left in the West? Why does Czechoslovakia remain an open wound — and will remain one until such time as a political solution is found or another attempt is made to combine socialism and freedom for all those who regard socialism as a better alternative to present society?

There is one common answer to all these questions: the entire

108

political and intellectual movement which is nowadays summed up under the term Prague Spring was the logical climax of a crisis of socialism into which Stalinism had plunged it, and at the same time an attempt to find an answer to a question which hundreds of millions of progressive people throughout the world today ask themselves, namely whether a socialism different from the Soviet system and its dogma is possible.

What was at stake in Czechoslovakia in 1968 was this cardinal question, which until then had been but a theoretical problem. And that is precisely why the high-ups of the ruling bureaucracy in Moscow, Berlin and Warsaw had to strangle the Prague Spring on 20 August 1968: they were afraid of the bacillus of a "different socialism" which might infect the people in Eastern Europe as well as in the West. The present ruling group in Moscow is not in fact at all keen on genuine socialist transformations in Western Europe because it is afraid of their possible reflection on its "empire". We can well imagine what would happen if a government of the Left in France really wanted to apply the principles of "a programme of liberty" as the Communist Party of France recently proposed. What would happen if the communists and other citizens in Czechoslovakia, Poland, Hungary or even the USSR were to insist on their application in the countries of "existing socialism"?

And that is precisely why a "Kadarisation" was not possible in Czechoslovakia after 1968 to preserve at least some of the 1968 reforms. Instead, Czechoslovakia had to be mercilessly thrown back years so that the others should not be inclined to follow its example. All that has happened since 1968-69, that is to say since the Husak régime came to power, has been described in many articles and books; and yet the extent of the damage and the destruction of the intellectual potential of the country are beyond the imagination of most foreign observers.

First of all, the Communist Party has been destroyed, the party which despite all the errors and crimes at its door remained up to 1968 a living organism linked with reality, capable of discerning the depth of the crisis and finding within its ranks sufficient strength for the renewal of socialism in 1968. That is why it had to be punished, demoralised and reduced to an organisation which cannot exist without the presence of the Soviet Army and the supervision of the secret police: half a million of its most active members were expelled, with the harshest consequences for their livelihood and that of their families. New members are being admitted predominantly from among the ranks of careerists and cynics who adhere to the principle of "no changes while we're alive" and "anyone against us misses the bus".

The workers' councils — the foundation of self-management and socialist democracy — have been eradicated without a trace and declared to be "an instrument of counter-revolution". The trade unions, which after a long time had turned back into autonomous organisations of the working class in 1968, have been turned into a "transmission belt" of the Communist Party or rather of its apparatus, and their main task is once again to force the workers to fulfil the norms laid down by the central bureaucracy. Strikes are again illegal and punished as sabotage. Likewise, autonomous organisations of youth, students, peasants and intellectuals in the sphere of science and art have been eliminated. The intelligentsia is punished with particular severity for the progressive role it played on the side of the people in the preparation and carrying out of the Prague Spring.

The repression which affects people's livelihoods has no parallel in the history of Czechoslovakia: anyone who is not obedient or holds views different from the present leadership and refuses to "recant" is sacked and does not find another job in his own profession. It is easy to imagine where this leads, since everyone is an employee of the state and has something to lose, including the worker who may be transferred to a worse-paid job. Worst off are the children, who have to suffer for their parents by not being admitted to universities or higher secondary schools irrespective of their excellent results. How many young talents will have been lost and how many young people will thus have become "enemies of socialism", as a result of an injustice which they will bear throughout their lives.

There is hardly any need for me to write about the "blacklists" of writers, scientists, painters, film directors and actors. The public in the West is informed, at least partly, about this, in view of the popularity of many of these Czechoslovak artists. But who will write down the hundreds of thousands of acts of discrimination and personal tragedies of ordinary officials and citizens, who for their support of the "new course" in 1968 find themselves in the "ghetto", deprived of all civic rights and of the possibility of defending themselves?

Those who, in spite of all this, have not been broken by the mechanism of pressure and fear and job deprivation have experienced harsh police and judicial repression. True, it is not as brutal as in the fifties, but it is no less effective, merciless and

110

depressing: hundreds of thousands of citizens, the majority of them communists, young people and workers, have been sentenced on political grounds often camouflaged as "criminal offences". As I write this, Milan Hübl and Jaroslav Sabata, former member of the CPCz Central Committee, and the student leader Jiri Müller, have been in jail for four years simply because they advocated a different conception of socialism from that propounded by the leading group. All that is Left-wing and progressive in the West is counter-revolution and reactionary in today's Czechoslovakia. It is not difficult to imagine that the authors of the common programme of the Left in France, the ideologists of the Italian and Spanish Communist Parties and enthusiastic members of Left-wing groups in the West, would be declared "agents of imperialism" in Czechoslovakia today, arrested and sentenced.

Is this an "internal affair" of Czechoslovakia as some want to assert, in order to excuse their silence? Does it not rather discredit socialism throughout the world? Is it possible to advocate in Paris a programme of political plurality and respect for civil liberties, while at the same time keeping silent or even justifying the state of affairs in Prague? Does this silence not weaken the credibility of socialism in France, Italy, Britain and throughout the world? Who plays more into the hands of the Right wing and the reaction: he who talks about the deformations and crimes in Eastern Europe or he who commits them?

All these facts demonstrate that the present occupation régime in Czechoslovakia has the narrowest social foundation any leadership has ever had since 1945, or even since the restoration of the Czechoslovak State in 1918. Its representatives are fully aware of this and do not even try to convince the population. They do not want support but obedience. That is why they rule openly by means of fear, with the help of the state police and the Soviet army in the country.

But in one thing they are willing to make concessions to the people — in the economic sphere. Between the lines of their speeches one can read: "What else do you want? We guarantee your wages so that you can feed and clothe yourselves properly. You can even buy a car or a cottage. Yet we know very well that you are shirking at work and some of you are stealing state property. We tolerate all this provided you do not meddle in politics." People are not badly off, they are indifferent to the régime and that is why they seek refuge in their privacy, where they can grumble as much as they like. Even though the régime has thus — and with the help of repression — neutralised a considerable section of the population, the voices of Dubcek, Smrkovsky, Kosik, Kohout, Malek, Hajek, Vaculik, Havel and the others are not calling in the wilderness. They represent various trends of the socialist opposition which, although not organised, express the feelings and aspirations of the majority of the people, and therefore exercise political influence. This is the only way to explain the hysterical reaction of Husak and Co. to these pronouncements by the opposition, recurring purges, searches and interrogations, dismissals and various types of discrimination.

If everything depended on the internal balance of forces there would be absolutely no doubt about the outcome of a confrontation between the occupation régime and the socialist opposition.

But the European summit in Helsinki has to some extent "sanctioned" Soviet hegemony in Eastern Europe in return for hopes by Western statesmen that the USSR will not interfere in developments in the West. This only confirms that the "Czechoslovak problem" has become a problem for the whole of Eastern Europe as well as an international issue. The conditions for its solution are, first of all, changes in the Soviet Union, and secondly, a new balance of power between bureaucratic and genuinely democratic socialism throughout the world, especially in Europe.

But the external conditions are not enough, and they will not appear of their own accord. They must be complemented by a systematic and persevering struggle of the socialist opposition in the country. The above-mentioned statements by the representatives of the Prague Spring, and also a number of further facts about the resistance of young people, workers and other sections of the population, testify that this strength and determination do in fact exist. For the time being it is not very likely, but one cannot rule out that even within the "normalised" communist party forces will gradually appear which will realise the need for a change of the present entirely negative and hopeless policy, which is leading to stagnation and may possibly give rise to a spontaneous outburst of discontent, the effect of which can today hardly be imagined. A certain link between the pressure of the opposition and the forces within the "establishment" will permit the emergence of a new movement which will exert such pressure that the ruling bureaucracy will no longer be in a position to resist it. We can well expect that the present régime is becoming such a burden for the Soviet policy of dialogue with the West, and that the Moscow leadership will sooner or later try to throw off this millstone.

It is in this spirit that we must understand Dubcek's letter, as well as the writings of Zdenek Mlynar and earlier on of Josef Smrkovsky. They proceed from the assumption — which need not come true, of course — that in the end the Soviet leadership will understand that it is better to have a group in power in Czechoslovakia supported by the majority of the people than to have *gauleiters* who rely solely on the presence of Soviet troops in the country. Neither can the CPSU completely ignore the fact that some of the foremost communist parties, for example in Italy and Spain, and also in Britain, have already publicly opposed the methods of ruling Czechoslovakia whereby the rights of communists such as Dubcek or Kosik to state a different opinion are suppressed. Moscow is also fully aware of the views held by a number of socialist parties with whom it wants to co-operate for various reasons.

The socialist opposition in Czechoslovakia understands its struggle as part of the international struggle of the Left for socialist transformations in Western Europe, too. But from our own experience we know that this fight for a socialism different from the Soviet type will encounter the same opposition from dogmatic forces in the West and from the strong bureaucracy in the USSR as did Czechoslovakia in 1968. The Left in the West must realise that its endeavour for a "different socialism" can be crowned with success only in the event of a democratisation of the USSR and of the East European countries. The militarily and economically strong bureaucracy in Moscow cannot tolerate authentic socialism in Paris or Rome just as it could not tolerate it in Prague, Budapest or Warsaw.

It is this realisation, at which we have arrived on the basis of our experience and which must become the point of departure for a new strategy of world socialist forces, that is the basis for the necessary mutual solidarity between the Left in the West and the socialist opposition in Czechoslovakia and in Eastern Europe, as well as the community of their struggle for a genuine, that is to say a democratic and self-managed socialism. Unless this is grasped in time, a great historic opportunity for socialism will be lost.

DOCUMENTARY APPENDIX

1 The Ten Point Manifesto

[This manifesto by a group of authors is the first document in which the opposition spoke out against the occupation. Resistance to Moscow and the neo-Stalinists had previously been voiced, for the most part, in individual statements. The opposition inside the Party had found neither a common political platform nor a means for countering the offensive launched by Husak and the "ultras". Dubcek was still a member of the Party's Presidium and Chairman of the National Assembly, while a considerable section of his supporters persisted in the belief that the battle could and must be waged inside the Central Committee and in the Party itself.

It was in the tradition of the Prague Spring that a group of Communists and politically unaffiliated people should take the initiative in drafting a document which contained what might be termed a minimum programme for resistance to "normalisation", in order to keep as many of the fruits of 1968 as possible. To understand the document correctly we need to recall that the massive purges had not yet started and that the spirit of the "new course" was still alive both within the Party and in the public mind. Taken out of its political context, the document might well sound very naïve today. Yet the authors are fully aware of the deep-seated conflict between the supporters of socialism and democracy and "those who have for twenty years been deforming socialism and are now shielded by the foreign occupation". They are anxious, however, to take advantage of all the opportunities for legal action which they believe have not been exhausted, and they have confidence in public pressure. They refuse to assume voluntarily the illegal status which the authorities would be glad to force upon them. Nevertheless, they harbour no great illusions about the institutions of Party and state; they proclaim a form of civil resistance by refusing to recognise non-elected office holders (that is, the new leadership of Party and state). And from April 1969 until the great purges of spring 1970 people did, in fact, follow this course; then came the point when they realised its ineffectiveness.

The authors of the manifesto did not confine themselves to rejection and criticism; their intention was also to formulate a posi-

117

tive programme capable of uniting the communists who had remained true to "socialism with a human face", as well as the socialists, democrats and unaffiliated progressively-minded people. They rejected all reactionary, anti-socialist, indeed all nationalist or anti-Soviet trends. Finally, they appealed — true, hesitantly as yet — to the international solidarity "of all socialist and democratic forces" throughout the world.

The document takes the form of a petition to the organs of Party and state, in accordance with the right conferred by the constitution of the Czechoslovak Socialist Republic. Three of the signatories — Rudolf Battek, Jan Tesar and Ludek Pachman — were promptly arrested and held for over a year in prison. The rest were interrogated by the police, charges were laid against them, but their trial was continually postponed. Other signatories, Jiri Hochman and Vladimir Nepras, who were arrested in January 1972, were then charged with other "offences". Pachman and Tesar were rearrested in January 1972 and brought to trial, Pachman being sentenced to two years', Tesar to five years' imprisonment.]

TEN POINTS
addressed to the Federal Assembly of the CSSR, the Czech National Council, the Federal Government, the Government of the Czech Socialist Republic and the Central Committee of the Communist Party of Czechoslovakia.

It is now a year since several of our Czechoslovak representatives were transported to the meeting which resulted in the production of the so-called Moscow protocol. It is a protocol about the humiliation of adult and sovereign nations which bore no guilt, but had the bad luck to come between two great powers battling to dominate the world. The power which sent us the troops invoked socialism, which was allegedly threatened in our country. But the threat here was not to socialism, it was merely the position of those who had been spoiling it for twenty years that was in danger. Our reform process gave cause in 1968 for the almost universal belief that mistakes could be corrected, that the wrongs would be remedied and that it would once more be possible to work with a will. In those days the Government and the regenerating Communist Party were well on the way to demonstrating that socialism does not necessarily have to be permanently associated with compulsion, restrictions and deprivation, that it can give people all the traditional freedoms won in earlier revolutions, and then build up on them a society which is more advanced not only economically, but also morally. Our endeavour was in tune with the time-honoured ideals of the socialist movement which strove for the right of nations and mankind to freedom, rejected great power domination, secret diplomacy and politics behind closed doors. It was therefore the international duty of all who still in any way acknowledged the original socialist aims not to hinder our work, to treat us decently and to let the Czechoslovak people decide how to prevent reactionaries at home or abroad from forcing upon them some rotten old order.

So now we have been living for a year under conditions imposed upon us. Life has simply grown worse in that time. The supply of goods is bad, prices are rising, industry is disrupted and nothing has been done about the real causes. Many able, gifted and properly elected people have had to leave their employmnt or their posts. The Action Programme adopted by the Communist Party of Czechoslovakia in April 1968 is being scrapped point by point, public organisations have been paralysed by coercive measures, the public is denied a voice in shaping government policy, important issues are decided by groups of individuals in place of the democratic organs of the state. Not a single organ of power of the Czech nation has been established by the will of the people. The mandate of the joint Parliament has expired. What is more, the censorship prevents any public discussion of these matters, which suits people with petty minds and domineering natures, the old opportunists and the new careerists; they are able to say what they like, twist the facts, slander people and launch press campaigns which no one has a chance to answer. And they have the impudence to declare that now at last it is possible to speak and write the truth. In fact one has to seek the truth in ways so devious that no one can vouch for their reliability and where provocations can also occur. Many people are now facing charges, and some, it seems, may be imprisoned, for trying to substitute for the function which in a civilised state is performed by the free press.

We cannot agree with this state of affairs and we do not wish to remain silent; therefore we are addressing ourselves in this manner to the legislative bodies of the Republic, to the Federal and National Governments and to the Central Committee of the Communist Party of Czechoslovakia with a declaration in which we want to state openly, and at the risk of suffering the familiar primitive reprisals, the following standpoint:

1. We reject what happened a year ago, because it amounts to

119

the trampling of international law, defiling the name of socialism and infringing the principles of common decency. We are in favour of observing international treaties. Socialist states in particular need, however, to maintain meticulously the sovereignty of each. We demand that their governments should show the world a somewhat more mature mode of overcoming misunderstandings and conflicts. We regard the presence of Soviet troops in our country as a cause of unrest and an obstacle to the renewal of friendly relations. We demand that the supreme organs of state should start negotiations about the withdrawal of the troops.

2. We do not agree with the policy of continual retreat in face of threats and we reject, in particular, the consequences of foreign interference after April 1969 when the bureaucratic mode of government was stiffened, and a purge was made in the state, party and economic apparatus in favour of less competent but more obedient people, or of those who have lost the confidence of the public. We protest at the disbanding of voluntary organisations which have in no way contravened the law, and the attempts to split some organisations. We condemn the banning on false grounds of the Co-ordinating Committee of Cultural Unions. We reject the coercive intervention in the affairs of the university students.

3. We scorn censorship, the imposition of which has placed us among those unhappy nations which are not allowed to speak either to themselves or to the world. The censorship has put us back a hundred years. It blocks the exchange of views and information, it prevents the formation of informed public opinion, it encourages the reading of trash, it hampers the checking of power, it protects incompetent officials and, finally, it allows further political immoralities to be committed. It signifies a step towards art and learning becoming mere servants of power, tolerated as decorations on the facade of state.

4. So long as the security force is not placed under the effective and visible control of civil organs, especially the legislative bodies, we have no faith in the assurances that in future the law will be observed and there will be no repetition of the institutionalised crimes of the 1950s. On the contrary, we observe that legal sanctions against people who have broken the law are weakening or ceasing to be applied and that such people remain in their posts and cannot be criticised. We see the banning of the Society for Human Rights as a bad sign. We want the international pact on civil and political rights, and the pacts on economic, cultural and social rights to be ratified and implemented without delay.

5. We do not recognise the role of the Communist Party as an organ of power and its elevation above the other organs which are responsible to all the people. To place the category of party affiliation above the category of citizenship is an abomination. We insist that the Communist Party should earn its leading role in society solely by winning confidence through its excellent fulfilment of society's prime desires. The relations among the political parties in the National Front cannot be other than those of partnership. Non-communists, who are the majority, have no obligation to live in conditions which they cannot influence. We respect those communists who endeavoured to free the Party of distortions and who saw their job as being to serve what is referred to as socialism with a human face. We support those of them who insist on the legality of the Fourteenth Party Congress convened last year.

6. The foreign intervention in Czechoslovak affairs has had particularly unfortunate consequences in the economic field. Here free discussion has been halted, the drafting of the law aimed at legalising workers' councils has been held up and where the councils have been established their activity has been crippled. Economic stimuli have again been suppressed and we note a renewal of the vain attempts at arbitrary dictation of economic relations. The blame for the growing crisis is attributed to those who backed the economic reform, although everyone knows that the measures have not been properly implemented. The workers, too, are blamed for bad working morale and low performance. In reality, however, they are often uncertain whether to work at all since the results are not to be seen, or in part they vanish into thin air and in part they are used for purposes with which the workers cannot agree — to pay for the inflated state administration and the coercive apparatus such as the censorship, the secret police or the armed forces which never shoot at the right moment, for the economically unprofitable propaganda which is noted for its ineffectiveness, and for corrupting the hosts of officials in various organisations. Why should the workers work to keep in their posts people who just a year ago were on their way out? Should they work harder when more money is often of no use to them? We consider such attitudes to be understandable. After all, people need to know the meaning and the purpose of their work, to assure themselves daily that they are under good management, and they must have the right to voice their opinions on economic matters from the standpoint of their particular job and from the standpoint of the state as a whole. However, with every job left undone or done badly we punish each

other for something which is not of our doing and which we should be able to remedy. In our view, where employees are working under directors, scientists and officials in whom they have confidence and whom they respect, they should give every support by means of good work and discipline; but at the same time we feel that to work under incompetent bosses or those forced upon one is intolerable. Conflicts cannot, however, be solved at the expense of society, but by the departure of such people. To bring this about by legal means is the right of the trade unions. We therefore demand the prompt enactment of a law on socialist enterprises enabling expert staff to decide about production with due respect for the state plan, and allowing the workers a say in allocation and investment. We demand that the rights of trade unions deriving from the Charter of the World Federation of Trade Unions be maintained. If there is talk about the workers' class interests, then these are now their class interests, in accord with the interests of everyone.

7. We do not agree with the postponement of the elections to national committees, and especially to the legislative organs, because delay means prolonging conditions resembling a state of emergency. We want elections conducted according to an election law which will strengthen socialist democracy. The law must embody the right for citizens' nomination committees to run their own candidates, and also a method for recalling members from their posts. We reject any elections conducted on the previous lines and we shall not take part in them.

8. We are glad that out of the extensive programme of reforms contained in last year's Action Programme of the Communist Party of Czechoslovakia, the federalisation of the state has been accomplished. We wish the Slovak nation prosperity, we are for competition and for our economies to complement each other. We shall oppose any stirring up of conflicts and suspicion, and any petty squabbling over the little we possess together. For what matters is what is to come. And there we note that federalisation has stopped short at the decisive organ of power, the Central Committee of the CPCz. We are in favour of genuine federalisation, that it should not turn again into a merely formal confirmation of decisions made about our nations by a small group who require no federalisation for the exercise of their power.

9. With critical debate silenced by the censorship and gross interference in the make-up of state organs and public organisations intended to frighten people, and with unscrupulous scribblers in third-rate newspapers obviously preparing the atmosphere for

worse things to come, we say plainly that the right to disagree with the Emperor and the Government is an age-old natural right of man. Enlightened monarchies already knew how to use it as a constructive force. Therefore we ask how this question will be solved here. And until it is resolved, we reserve the right of dissent which we shall exercise by opposing by legal means anything that goes against our reason and our human conscience, and against our convictions as citizens striving for socialist democracy and humanism and which conflicts with the good traditions of our country. We have no wish to resort to illegal methods; we shall, however, employ the organs hitherto existing to defend our rights. We shall try to maintain horizontal links among sections of the public organisations. Just as we reject the use of force in international relations, we reject its use in domestic political conflicts as well; consequently, we show our opposition to officials, who under normal circumstances would have to be removed, by not seeing and not hearing them, by not meeting them and not employing their services. We express our solidarity with people who are persecuted for their political views.

10. But negation is not our programme. In the worst situations life has to go on. We believe that no oppression can entirely silence thinking or kill all work. We are in favour of every citizen doing all the good he can, above all that he should do his job well, especially jobs which serve his fellow citizens, for instance, in the distributive trades, in transport, the health services, education, crime prevention and so on. Workers in research and culture can never stop working. New work will continue to appear, professional contacts will be established. Young people will study, they will learn not only to the extent that is allowed or obligatory, but as they wish. Even when unfree politically a mature nation can defend itself by asserting its lifestyle, its philosophy of life and its character by means of practical deeds of an unpolitical nature. We can, for instance, although with difficulty, improve our homes and communities, make our living and working environments more healthy, limit economic losses, manage with what we have. We can entertain ourselves in a manner that suits us and not those whom we have no wish to entertain. We can cultivate and extend our hobbies and interests. We know we cannot change our situation on our own, because we are not the centre of the world or the main force behind its movement. There are times when one simply has to keep going and hold on to what one has. That we shall try to do, in the belief that progress cannot be halted.

In conclusion, we reject *a priori* the usual accusations and abuse which we can expect. We are not opportunists because, as always, they are the people who have known how to sail with the wind and are now among the powerful. We say nothing that is anti-state, because no set of people who may feel they have been attacked can consider that they are the state, and because we are not out to disrupt the organisations of the state; rather, we demand that they should function in accordance with the Constitution. Our ideas are not anti-Party, as free discussion in the Party would prove, nor are we anti-socialist, because we are concerned with socialism of a kind which can be successful in an advanced country and with freeing it of the repulsive features imparted by a set of feeble-minded dogmatists, power-hungry careerists and depraved bullies. We have no reason to adopt an anti-Soviet stance in so far as the affairs of the Soviet Union are concerned; we are merely against the gross interference in the sovereignty of other states. We wish success to the Soviet people. We shall support the democratic and socialist forces in the world in their efforts for international disarmament, peaceful settlement of disputes, the disbanding of military blocs.

We are communicating this standpoint to the Federal Assembly of the CSSR, the Czech National Council, the Federal and National Governments, the Central Committee of the Communist Party of Czechoslovakia, that they may take it into account.

Prague, 21 August 1969

2 The Manifesto of 28 October 1970

[28 October occupies a special place in Czech and Slovak history — with the founding of the Czechoslovak Republic on 28 October 1918, the people achieved national independence after three hundred years of subjection to the Habsburg monarchy; on 28 October 1945, the Government decreed the nationalisation of heavy industry, mining, large landholdings and the banks, thereby laying the foundation of the socialist order; on 28 October 1968, federalisation of the Republic was announced, a measure intended to give equal rights to Czechs and Slovaks.

This, then, was the date chosen by the representatives of various regions, groups and the different trends within the opposition to issue the Manifesto of the Socialist Movement of Czechoslovak Citizens; it was distributed throughout the country in leaflet form. It is a basic statement of views by the socialist opposition, later to be elaborated in other documents. That Slovakia was not represented on this occasion was due to the fact that the socialist opposition made a late start there, thanks to certain illusions about the federalisation measure and, indeed, about Husak.

In 1970 came a turning point: two years of occupation and of the Husak régime had provided ample proof that the hopes of salvaging something from the 1968 reforms, even of a move towards "Kadarisation" in Czechoslovakia, were unfounded. Opposition had become impossible inside the Party, although this in no way signifies that the million "tested" members should be equated with the supporters of the occupation régime, still less that the *apparat* and the leadership are now free of conflicts which may one day precipitate a new crisis in the Party.

Despite its narrow power base, the régime was now firmly in control of the Party and state machine, the police and the armed forces, while also relying on the Soviet army of occupation stationed throughout the country.

Public resistance to the occupation, though considerable, was unorganised; it surfaced mainly at sports and cultural events, through boycotting the press, radio and television, absenting oneself from work etc. Moreover, there was a danger that these actions could degenerate into nationalistic outbursts, giving the authorities new pretexts for strengthening their repressive measures.

In this situation the emergence of the Socialist Movement of Czechoslovak Citizens represented a new chapter — the opposition had assumed an organisational form, it had been co-ordinated and had produced a joint programme which could provide a basis for united action by the various groups and trends. While being open to a variety of trends, the framework represented a strictly socialist political platform. There is no question here of opposition to the socialist system as such, solely to its bureaucratic, centralist, police-state and Stalinist nature.]

Citizens of Czechoslovakia!

The representatives of Bohemia and Moravia met in Prague recently. They have reaffirmed the attitudes and ideas supported by the broad masses of people in 1968 and 1969 that were so unanimously manifested then and that today still live on in the minds of the people of Czechoslovakia, in altered or hidden forms perhaps, but in spite of official propaganda and notwithstanding the way people have to behave when at work.

The vast majority of our people in 1968 welcomed the fact that our society was endeavouring to give socialism its true meaning, to combine freedom with democracy, to aim at a conception surpassing bourgeois definitions of socialism and Stalinist interpretations, to develop the whole structure of civil rights, ensuring the legal rights and liberties of all citizens, creating a political and social system in which everybody would find his rightful place and be able to expand his ideals in a life based on happiness. We reject forms of socialism that are bureaucratic, goulash types of socialism that cannot free Man from the sense of alienation that is a malady of both East and the West. Those in power today in Czechoslovakia, through their own deeds and actions, have discarded the ideals set up by socialism and are using socialist terminology to camouflage a bureaucratic dictatorship.

There is no need to organise a movement of resistance against this type of régime. The movement exists and will go on existing as everyone can see. It is supported by thousands of workers, both in the towns and the villages, by the intelligentsia, members of the Czechoslovak Communist Party who were or still are in the Party, members of other political parties in the National Front, people who are not members of any party, those working in the factories, scien-

126

tific institutions, the state political apparatus, in trade unions, youth movements, in the mass media, free professions, members of the Army and State Security, and those whom the present régime has forced in tens of thousands to leave their posts.

Members of this movement are also those citizens who refused to betray the common ideal, by leaving Czechoslovakia after the August 1968 invasion and seeking temporary asylum in other countries, either for fear of persecution and possible loss of work or so that they could continue to fight for the ideals of the post-January policies elsewhere. We refuse to brand them as traitors! They have chosen a way, out of their own free will, that was paved for them by thousands of others, throughout the centuries.

The real state our country is in is evident: there is a political, economic, ideological and moral crisis that can hardly be compared to any other period in our history.

Politically we have been robbed of our rights. The servile policy of our present régime endangers the very future of our nations and state entity. In spite of statements of an opposite nature and the futile attempts of some of our functionaries, our best people are being purged in all fields of work and science. The régime is annihilating our scientific institutions. It is silencing our culture. It has put our trade unions, youth organisations, women's organisations into fetters. It has liquidated the idea of workers' councils. It is returning the whole economic structure to the old system of centralisation that in the past, more than once, has proved itself a failure. The present régime is not supported in its efforts by the much needed enthusiasm of the greater majority of the Czechoslovak people or the Czechoslovak intellectuals who in the nineteen fifties managed to compensate for the inadequacies of the state plan by correcting it, or the inefficiency of those who planned it and the authorities. The régime today talks of scientific and technical revolution at a time when it is purging its economy and scientific departments of fully qualified staff and specialists.

Into state, social, economic and administrative posts are today nominated people who have in the past been capable of little more than merely destroying existing values, people who were police informers. This potentially weak group of activists of the present régime considers itself to be the élite class which alone can provide all the solutions, can lead the country out of its present crisis. This so called élite is imposing the most primitive type of political, economic and ideological dictatorship, which is prevalent in the sphere of culture too.

127

This sort of development is not only a threat to the people of Czechoslovakia. The political line being followed by the present leadership of the Czechoslovak Communist Party and the Czechoslovak Government is seriously obstructing the continuation of a progressive development of the entire Eastern bloc. We are being forced into accepting a primitive type of dictatorship at a time when all the five states, which sent their armies to invade us, are themselves trying out methods and means of accelerating their progressive development or at least putting a brake on the development leading them to economic and political chaos. And at this moment we are not even mentioning the liberalisation struggle of the progressive groups and movements in the socialist states that are demanding structural reforms and, most of all, democratic reforms that would help them overcome the Stalinist model of socialism.

The Socialist Movement of Czechoslovak Citizens is leading a struggle for a socialist, democratic, independent and free Czechoslovakia, a fully sovereign Czechoslovakia with full control of its internal and external policies. A Czechoslovakia that would be allowed to find its own way and means of development and progress and the fulfilment of the ideals and wishes of its citizens. We have not chosen at random the date 28 October to manifest our aims. For this day symbolises the re-instatement of the Czechs and Slovaks into one state, on this day many years later the monopolies belonging to wealthy capitalists and landowners were nationalised, this day is the symbol of the establishing of a just political structure, the alliance of two nations with equal rights, the Czechs and Slovaks.

The existence of the Czechoslovak state has always in the past been seen as linked with other states. This idea has in the past been propagated in the foreign policies of the country. The existence of our nations and our state will always be dependent on the creating of better relations throughout the world between individual states and on the relaxing of international tensions, especially in Europe, on the basis of mutual co-operation and full sovereignty.

The biggest political issue in Europe at this time is the problem of the two German states. It can only be solved by recognising them as two independent, sovereign states, while their own mutual relations are decided upon by themselves. The latest political developments, especially the Soviet-West German treaty, have proved that our foreign policies in 1968 were correct. We continue to be convinced that West Germany does not cradle only revanchist forces but that through the signing of a Czechoslovak-West German agreement relations between the two countries are possible, without Czechoslovakia having to abandon any of her basic principles. An understanding of this sort and the restoring of diplomatic relations between the two countries, the frontiers of which are at the same time the frontiers of two different political blocs, would greatly contribute to the easing of tension on the European scene and be a vital step towards the establishing of real peace throughout Europe.

The problem of our relations with the Soviet Union is of vital importance. The Soviet Union is our most powerful neighbour and a world power. It will be necessary to overcome the uncomprehending, negative and at times hateful attitudes which are professed today, for obvious reasons, by the majority of our people towards the Soviet Union.

Czechoslovakia was not occupied by the Soviet people or by the nations of the Soviet Union. The present situation though was not created by us and we cannot change it by ourselves. The changes can only be effected by the present or future leadership of the USSR, if it recognises that 21 August 1968, and its consequences, must be repudiated, if it realises that only a neighbour that does not see in the Soviet Union a danger to his own sovereignty is of real value, a neighbour that sees in a relationship of this sort mutual respect and an alliance. We shall at all times continue to let the Soviet Union know that freedom and good relations with other countries cannot be enforced by military might and through the medium of people who have been compromised by their past, but only through a sovereign and truly free people who cannot and need not have other aims than the creation of such friendly relations and alliances, based on equality with other countries. Internationalism does not mean the sending of military forces of one or a group of countries into another country. Internationalism expresses the aim for equality and alliances based on equality, the uniting of modern, progressivey minded states, socialist states, the uniting of movements, political parties, of all these without any exception. If the atomisation of progressive elements in the world is not to continue then it is necessary to move forward to a new type of internationalism, towards a unity of different opinions and attitudes. Those who enforce their ideas on others through the use of force are not bearers of progress.

The political set up in Europe today is still in the grip of the post-war division of it between two world political blocs that both respect the existing status quo. This unnatural and dangerous policy of power blocs can be eliminated if the states of the Warsaw Treaty and the North Atlantic Treaty all get together and agree on a joint plan of action together with the non-aligned countries. Czechoslovakia's foreign policy should be based on this principle and should be supporting all measures leading towards this aim: bilateral and multilateral agreements on non-aggression and the renunciation of force, agreements on the creation of nuclear free zones and zones with only limited armament, zones in which the use of arms is forbidden altogether, especially in the area of frontiers between two power blocs, treaties dealing with the withdrawal of all foreign troops from the territory of another country.

While these sort of treaties are still in the making, or non-existent, Czechoslovakia can only accept the existing status quo and in this situation, which demands an active initiative of all states, Czechoslovakia's foreign policy remains practically non-existent.

All the lies and distorted information with which the present régime in Czechoslovakia is trying to prove to the people that our aims in 1968 were the overthrow of socialism and a restoration of capitalism, the linking of Czechoslovakia with the West European military bloc, only demonstrate the evil intentions of their authors and their inability to understand that the alternative to capitalism is not only a bureaucratic form of socialism but other more modern forms of socialism. None of the other Communist Parties in Western Europe accept the idea of a monolithic type of socialism. They are for a pluralistic system, a political partnership of different interest groups, acting with full autonomy and with no one's sponsorship.

The nationalisation of our industry was an important step of liberation in our history. It later became evident though that the nationalised property did not belong to the nation but to the state apparatus. It was not the property of the workers but of the state bureaucrats. It was not used to finance a government of the people but a bureaucratic régime.

Our aim is to fight for the true rights of the people, so that their property is handed back to their admiinstration, workers' councils that would be elected by the people while the state, the true representative of the people, would put into effect the interests of the whole society, through a direct price control system, investments, rates and tax policies.

The equal status of the Czechs and Slovaks was firmly anchored in the declaration of an independent Czechoslovakia on 28 October

1918. The new arrangement was greatly valued by both Czechs and Slovaks. The federal structure joining the two nations together at present is greatly endangered by the policy the CPCz is carrying out. The Stalinist model functions on the basis of one directive centre. Centralising tendencies which are once more apparent after the plenary meeting of the Central Committee of the Czechoslovak Communist Party in January 1970, are not as evident on the surface only because at the head of the Party is a man long known for his struggle for the equality of both nations. The federation however loses its meaning because Czechoslovak politics are determined neither in Prague nor Bratislava.

Our struggle is a political struggle and a positive one. Its methods are not the methods used by force or sabotage. We do not propagate the motto: "The worse, the better!" as official propagandists would have us do. Most of our work is done with enthusiasm and a sense of initiative. Our efforts are directed only by a sense of professional honour and human conscience, and it is only at the very last stage that they are affected by material interests. A deliberate slowing down process or the sabotage of the economic process will not lead us out of our present critical situation, nor any hysterically organised campaigns that are supposed to solve the economic crisis. The issue at present is not how we work but what is happening to the results of our work, why these are being wasted.

Our country has been in need of economic reforms for the last ten years. In 1968 we did not have enough time to put them into effect and since then the necessity has greatly increased.

Our aim is not the division but the unity of our fellow citizens. The unity that was so symbolic of the year 1968 beyond dispute showed that an understanding among all men in our country is possible, that there is much more that unites us all than divides us. It is not a question of revenge, it is a question of creating conditions that would enable any decent and industrious man to live happily. The people we cannot agree with form only a small group. We shall fight for every man who wishes to lead a decent and free life in this country.

There are many people who have not given up and reject all the lies told to them, among them are those who have made this gathering possible. Many others, on the surface adapt themselves to the prevailing conditions so that they and their families may at least have a chance to live. The others are tired out by the long crisis and cynicism of present day politics. They seek asylum in their own homes, work within themselves, for their families — for these

131

are the last values left to them. But they too realise that despair, apathy, cynicism, escapism into the privacy of their own homes are dangerous. By doing this they are reinforcing the lack of existence of even a small, humble aim, they are encouraging ideological and economic chaos, the false scheming of would-be intellectual speculation, prophecies based on looking at the map of the Sino-Soviet frontiers, the accumulation of gossip escaping from parliamentary lobbies etc.

If there is any moral to be learned from the modern history of our country then it is this: the more we come to depend in hard times on the fact that our problems will somehow solve themselves in conjunction with the larger scale problems of Europe and the rest of the world, the more we are turned into mere passive reflections of some newly formed structures, created by world powers. The future of Czechoslovakia is firmly linked to the future of world development and it is only we and we alone who can decide to make use of certain situations, to fulfil our aims, to take full advantage of each chance we get.

No citizen of Czechoslovakia is excluded from any sort of action. Do not let us wait for a leadership to form, or leaders to emerge, if we do not want to, once again, succumb to the subjugation of power politics. Let us be tolerant, let us help the oppressed, let us not make things worse for those we cannot save. Solidarity has always been our strongest weapon. Let us fight for every single thing, in the struggle that is going on at all levels, everywhere, in families, in our places of work, everywhere.

We are fully aware of what we want: it is a political socialist system. A system in which there will exist a partnership built on equality between political and non-political organisations, a system in which there will be self-government both in communities and institutions, where there will be an institutionally anchored control of power, all the basic freedoms and freedom of religion, all the freedoms formulated in the Declaration of Human Rights, ratified by Czechoslovakia.

Our manifesto today wishes to help in this struggle. Let us distribute it through every possible channel. Let us work on the preparation of a new complex programme of action. Our basis for this will be the Action Programme of April 1968, the documents put forward at the Fourteenth CPCz Congress, discussions throughout the mass media on the structure of a political system, economic reforms, workers' councils etc., topics about which we were once wholly united. These ideas are not to be allowed to rest, they must

132

be put forward again and again, compared with the changing face of the existing reality. They must be made to live again in private conversations and in public. The present day régime cannot abolish its party organisations, trade unions etc. It must be surrounded by a facade of assent. It is quite aware this is only a facade and though it can keep on replacing functionaries, it cannot expel all the members of the Party. The régime cannot go on waging a destructive war forever with the population. If it does not want to destroy itself it must go on to the formulation of a pseudo-constructive programme and cannot continually purge society of its best elements on a mass scale. This affords opportunities to everyone to propagate again within their own organisation ideals which are indestructible.

The present régime may propagate terror but it is a régime built on insecurity. It arrests people without any reason for it is in need of scapegoats. It has to establish their guilt and as this is difficult it holds them in prison for long periods of time. The régime has no arguments it can well use. Its only weapon is phrases that are supposed to convey truth but are totally outworn.

Because all the ties existing between the political system and the social structure crumbled in 1967, the present day régime cannot even turn to the pre-January policies for precedence. It managed to destroy the positive values and ideals of 1968 but it is forced to go on existing in their name. There is no better medicine it can prescribe for itself. The régime is incapable of determining the difference between the positive and negative values, these are determined by everyone of us, by those whose aim it is to continue to work in the name of these very ideals in our families, on a social level, in our working environments, in all the state organisations and within the state apparatus.

One of the most frequently formulated questions is whether we are optimists or pessimists about the future of our country. Gramsci wrote that optimism derives from one's will power.

If we wish to live in a socialist, democratic, independent and free state, if we want to enjoy the right of self-determination and to search in our own way and on the basis of our own conditions, for the right model of socialism and for such ways that can give the people of our country a happy life, if we want to believe that we shall see this happen still in our lifetime, then we must act at once.

That is why our voice is to be heard today. The development of international events, the development going on within the socialist camp, within the Soviet Union itself, in Europe and the whole world, offers to us another opportunity today that we must make

133

full use of at once.

Read this carefully, think about it and pass it on. In this way you too are acting.

28 October 1970

3 The Short Action Programme of the Socialist Opposition

[This is among the most interesting documents of the Czecho-slovak socialist opposition. It was drafted in January-February 1971, two or three months after the publication of the Manifesto of the Socialist Movement of Czechoslovak Citizens on 28 October 1970. It must be emphasised, however, that the draft is no more than a basis for discussion, intended for further elaboration. During the political trials of July-August 1972 the prosecution mentioned several versions of the document which were, in fact, debated among the socialist opposition groups. This in no way detracts from the importance of what was, actually, the first venture in pro-jecting the strategy and tactics for socialist opposition in the social-ist countries — related here to the particular conditions obtaining in Czechoslovakia.

We have already analysed the document as it relates to the poli-tical fight of the opposition; here we would simply wish to under-line its *socialist* character. And that must be stressed all the more strongly in view of the fact that the law courts in Prague and Brno, and Husak's propaganda, have tried to paint it as "a programme for the step-by-step liquidation of the socialist system" and for "the establishment of an openly bourgeois-type democracy" (*Rude Pravo*, 16 August 1972). This line of argument is typical of those who uphold the one and only (Soviet) model of socialism, in Czechoslovakia and elsewhere. Determined that this is the only valid and conceivable model, they automatically condemn as anti-socialist and "counter-revolutionary" any attempt to take a dif-ferent view of socialism. In their view the basic principle of socialist society is the leading role of the Communist Party; he who wishes to replace that role by a system of political pluralism is an enemy of socialism, "an agent of the class enemy". It is not hard to imagine the reaction of the French and Italian socialists, for in-stance, who are prepared to co-operate with the Communist Parties in the common fight for socialist change, were they to be con-fronted with the choice: either accept the Communist Party's "leading role" (that is, its monopoly of power), or be classed as "enemies of socialism".

The reader can judge Husak's propaganda for himself: the same article in the Party paper flatly declared that the Short Action Programme aimed "to detach Czechoslovakia from the community of the socialist countries, to impose *neutrality* on her, and to link her foreign policy *exclusively* to the western capitalist countries, this being the framework of the so-called mid-European solidarity"! The occupation régime is in a position to put over this sort of story to *Rude Pravo* readers, who are denied the right to read the document for themselves. A fine example of "socialist discussion"!

The western reader would be well advised to pay special attention to the section of the Programme dealing with the need to confront the experience of the Czechoslovak socialist opposition with socialist thinking in the rest of the world.]

We offer here to the circle of people concerned with these matters an outline of a "Short Action Programme". In referring to the circle of people concerned, we have in mind primarily those engaged, in one way or another, "professionally" with the programmatic and tactical questions of the socialist opposition. It is, in any case, a strictly controlled and therefore fairly restricted circle. Our draft is not intended for publication, even in the form of an internal ("self-service") document. It summarises discussions which the Manifesto of the Socialist Movement of Czechoslovak Citizens of 28 October 1970 (published abroad as a programmatic document reflecting one of the trends in the socialist opposition) aroused in several initiatory groups. This concerns, in particular, the section of the draft dealing with tactical questions. Programmatic principles are treated only marginally in this very incomplete outline. So the "Short Action Programme" is not a political programme in the true sense, nor even an action programme. Hence its working title: the *short* action programme.

Of course, that is not to say that the socialist opposition has no need for a thoroughly worked out and well-founded political and tactical programme. On the contrary, it is already extremely urgent. And we had it in mind when deciding to draft and present for discussion a document with a single purpose — to hasten the maturing of conditions for the formation of a guiding political force which could put forward a representative programme and, as a genuinely representative force, provide backing for that programme.

Many weeks have passed since the decision was taken to draft some kind of "memorandum" as a basis for discussion about the further concrete steps to be taken by the opposition forces. In the meantime we have experienced in rapid succession the Polish events, the December meeting of the Central Committee and the publication of the so-called "Lessons", the convening of the party congress, and further movement in the opposition camp at home and elsewhere. The resultant shift in the angle of vision has aggravated the difficulty of formulating any kind of programmatic document, however modest its nature. More detailed consideration was needed to decide the immediate steps required by the course of events.

Consequently, we regard the "Short Action Programme" primarily as serving to prepare the ground for the coming debate which can be expected to result in a further concentration of the opposition forces. With this in mind we have gone deeper than originally intended — it is no longer sufficient in January or February 1971 to record the outcome of discussions around the Manifesto of 28 October 1970, because the confused situation of autumn 1970 has now, in many respects, been clarified, the possibilities for advance by the opposition are more evident and moreover — and this is the most important thing — new possibilities have emerged.

I

The initiatory groups which have come together to consider future action by the socialist opposition grew out of radical opposition to the policy of enforced normalisation and bureaucratic consolidation. And their overall political purpose derives quite naturally from this origin, that is, they work for a socialist alternative to the prevailing socialism "of bureaucratic apparatuses" (Manifesto of the Socialist Movement of Czechoslovak Citizens). They follow on from the movement for the democratic revival of socialism initiated in January 1968, the aims of which were stated in the Action Programme issued in April of that year; it is a question of a new democratic model of socialism suited to the Czechoslovak conditions.

As an *organised* force, however, the post-January movement has disintegrated. This fact — however bitter it may be — has to be taken as the starting point for any realistic political thinking. The post-January movement no longer exists in the form it possessed in 1968-69. Yet one can say that it persists. And in a sense, it does actually persist. One can say that its ideas live on; and that, too, is undoubtedly true. Nevertheless, the peculiar ideological-political formation which rightly bears the name "post-January movement" is a thing of the past. To overlook this reality would be to stand first with one foot, then with the other, outside this world.

This fact compels us, above all, to be clear about the question: what, actually, is the basis from which the socialist opposition of today wants to carry on? A general reference to the ideas of democratic socialism cannot provide the answer. However, it is important to realise that democratic socialism is not identical with "socialist democracy" which simply requires to be deepened, developed and improved; we are concerned with a system requiring radical, revolutionary (structural) change — but this strategic goal does not in itself provide an answer to the question of what forces will accomplish the change.

The post-January movement reflected a specific alliance between the forces "at the top" (the progressive forces in the Communist Party which held power) and the forces working for a democratic revival of socialism "from below", or vice versa. This alliance was not static; both its base and its apex were constantly shifting, and it was, of course, neither straightforward nor free from conflict. Its quite fundamental positive contribution was, however, that the progressive forces "within" the given (legal) structures channelled the initiative (or pressure) from "below" or from "outside".

To a point, the mechanism was effective — the old bureaucratic structures were transformed into democratic structures. A new political representation was rapidly formed and consolidated within the Communist Party and outside it, a new vanguard political structure was emerging.

The effectiveness of that mechanism was, in fact, demonstrated by the August intervention itself.

The August intervention stimulated a dual process: on the one hand, it provided an impetus to developments from below. The progressive forces which had been constituted within the post-January movement freed themselves, and the forces inclining to a conservative solution of the crisis also strove to free themselves from the forces "below" — they tried to break free from the pressure from below. There was no halting the split in the Communist Party; its "central current" fell apart, and with it the entire post-January movement in its former clearcut guise.

The freeing of the progressive forces was hastened as step by step the post-January movement lost its positions in Party and state and in the trade unions, that is to say, the power positions on which it had previously relied. From stubborn insistence on the

138

post-January aims a new vanguard orientation was born. This orientation could not, however, link up directly with the structures of the post-January movement — these rapidly disintegrated before one's eyes. The stronger the shift by the "establishment" elements of the post-January movement to the side of the conservative order, the more resolutely the emancipated elements turned to their only possible support — to the *social* base for a democratic revival of socialism. The ancient truth that freedom and democracy have to be won by the people themselves began to assert itself as a sober reality; the battle was on against the illusion that the road to victory for socialist democracy is easy and quick, straight and short.

The break-up of the previous structures confronted the vanguard socialist forces with an urgent choice: either to fill the vacuum left by the disintegration as an organised force of the post-January movement with a *new type of organisation*, in which case they could stand on their own feet and survive, or else to capitulate and disappear. For the genuine vanguard there could be but one answer.

The events in Poland found the progressive forces at a stage when they had already, by and large, solved the question of "self-preservation". They had posed a number of new questions and put the old ones in a new light — they reaffirmed the permanent and universal nature of the crisis in which the bureaucratic systems of the socialist countries are involved; they restated the old truth about the significance of "workers' actions". Strong emphasis was placed on linking the progressive forces in different countries, on forming an international alliance of the forces fighting for the democratic revival of socialism.

The whole range of these questions has one common denominator: the need to form a new political vanguard of socialism. This somewhat abstract conclusion indicates the basic strategic orientation for all true vanguard forces in the socialist opposition. But being in the vanguard is not a matter of reiterating this abstract truth, but of the ability to move towards its actual realisation.

That is the angle from which our document has been written. It sets out to examine, as concretely as possible, the conditions which have to be taken into account and met if the "self-preservation" phase is to be definitely transformed into a new, steady advance.

II

It cannot be said at the time of writing that the opposition forces have anything in the nature of a fully developed leading structure. But there are, on the one hand, initiatory groups which are trying to achieve closer contact with each other, and on the other, a *potential leading political stratum* which represents a sufficiently firm base for the fairly rapid formation of the requisite leading structure.

This stratum consists of several tens of thousands of people who — thanks to the overall political development and to their own ideological and personal roots — represent a coherent body which can justifiably be regarded as a potential vanguard of the opposition, that is, it is a body whose separate parts (groups and individuals) are capable of developing *independent* initiatives and of building up an increasingly organised ideological and political formation.

The people belonging to this stratum enjoy a natural political authority and prestige, and they have considerable experience of political, organisational and ideological work. As a potential "leading team" they are distributed all over the country — true, not entirely evenly, but nevertheless they do represent a network with a nationwide field of action. Several years of political struggle in a situation of open crisis have established very many informal linkages within this group. The destruction of the legal structure, however, has split this coherent body into a multitude of autonomous centres of potential or actual activity, but the atomisation is being gradually overcome. Despite the drastically limited possibilities for legal communication, more and more new linkages are still forming spontaneously (and broken linkages are being re-established).

The leading political stratum ("élite") should, however, be seen as part of a broader structure embracing hundreds of thousands of those who were politically involved in the post-January movement — a kind of "membership base" for the leading team. And the entire structure is, in turn, rooted in the wider hinterland of "sympathisers", with a whole variety of ties linking it to the broadest masses of the population. The political atmosphere in the leading stratum is, of course, determined by the movement in the whole complex web of relationships among "the masses", by the *general* atmosphere, the degree of spontaneous activity among the social groupings etc.

Our purpose in sketching this very rough and abstract sociological pattern, which says very little about the actual state of the "general political atmosphere" and all the other factors of the political movement, is to underline the necessity to activise the *entire* leading (potential) political stratum. We shall not be able to speak of a genuine leading political structure until the potential coherent body becomes an actual force.

In this connection it must be noted that it would be useless and highly illusory to think of shaping this coherent body into an organisation with the traditional hierarchical structure, some kind of party of the "Leninist type", or — at worst — some version of the strictly centralised party of the Stalinist type. The procedure here must, on the contrary, be entirely "untraditional" or, better, it must draw on the best traditions of the undogmatic and non-bureaucratic mode of developing informal linkages. Whether permanent and firm linkages (possibly "formalised") plus the appropriate structures will develop, and how this will come about, remains to be seen. For the moment, whether a procedure is productive should be judged by the simplest and simultaneously the most comprehensive criterion: whether it develops the coherent body as a *coherent* body, that is, that it strengthens all the bonds of "solidarity", personal and impersonal, ideological, political, thus stimulating creative political thinking and political activity appropriate to the given conditions.

No great progress on these lines may occur for a fairly long time. But what matters is not the extent of the advances but rather that they should happen, in other words, that things should move in a certain direction. From this angle one must welcome any progress in the direction indicated, because it will create conditions for establishing the leading structures rapidly and promptly when the circumstances are more auspicious, and it will reduce the risk of a loss of tempo occurring in any future political crises.

III

In considering a potential political vanguard in terms of a structure embracing tens of thousands of people, it is obvious that we must also consider a specific leading structure as well, or a leading component of the vanguard, a "vanguard of the vanguard", so to speak. In keeping with what has already been said about the "organisation of the vanguard", it must be noted that this component cannot be seen as an authoritative centre issuing directives and allotting tasks, that is, a centre in the bureaucratic sense. But this does not mean that it should not fulfil the function of a centre in a non-bureaucratic sense, a focal point of activity concerned with co-ordinating the forces awakening spontaneously to political activity, while at the same time taking the initiative in bringing to life in a planned way all the potential sources of political activity in

141

all the most important centres — in localities and workplaces. The number of these "important centres", that is, the big enterprises, the larger localities (not merely the district towns) can be estimated as being in the order of several thousand units nationwide. The prospective strength of the envisaged leading component should match this; it should be a "centre" of considerable scope, but of a quality ensuring that its separate parts — each group and individual — are capable of framing, according to the local circumstances, the goals and tasks for the movement's vanguard components as a whole.

The initiatory groups, having already established themselves as independent sources of activity, represent quite naturally the point of departure for building up this leading component. None of them can be excluded from the overall framework of the socialist opposition (in so far, of course, as they accept a socialist, anti-capitalist programme). And to none of them can the range of their opposition activity be prescribed — it will be whatever they are able to develop. The weight which this or that group carries within the movement as a whole will depend on its political calibre and not on any *a priori* doctrinal requirements (by political calibre we mean here the ability to express the needs and interests of society's progressive advance, the ability to attain the goals deriving from this, and a constructive approach to integrating all the opposition forces, etc.). What holds for the socialist-oriented groups applies, ultimately, to groups which, while not accepting a socialist programme, remain within the framework of generally democratic criticism of bureaucratic socialism, because objective principles are involved here. The difference is, however, that the relations between the two types of political orientation are bound to evolve differently. Within the socialist opposition one is justified in assuming a tendency to co-operate as closely as possible. The relationship of the socialist (left) opposition to the right wing (stream) in the opposition will necessarily be complicated by a multiplicity of ideological and political barriers.

We are not concerned with developing this abstract schema. Without some deeper analysis of the state of the opposition, that would be quite unjustified. By posing the principle of "plurality" within the opposition we wanted to indicate no more than the starting point for resolving the real problem, namely that of solving the question of co-operation among the various communist and socialist (non-Marxist, non-communist, but not anti-communist) ideological political currents and their representatives. The problem relates not only to the relationships between communists and non-communists, but also to those among communists themselves (within the communist ranks).

The problem is basic: it concerns the *politically representative quality* of the vanguard's leading component — without all-round ideological and organisational work by this leading component it would be impossible to form an effective and viable leading political force of the opposition. We have discussed so far the "cadre composition" of the political vanguard, and we have treated it very generally, primarily in quantitative terms. But the question of forming a socialist political vanguard is not primarily one of numbers, but of the political quality, and the criteria of this quality are not abstract, they are *historical* — they are tested in the course of political development. Whatever corresponds to the needs and interests of historical social development will stand the test; whatever conflicts with these needs and interests will be superseded.

In its unique guise of 1968 and 1969 the post-January movement has been superseded, but that does not signify the superseding of those elements in it which reflect the interests of the true motive forces of society's development — the interests of the broadest working masses (which, in our society, means all sectors, all citizens in the society). If we consider the ideological-political cross-section of this movement, which expresses the society's interests through its ideological and organisational efforts, we arrive at the conclusion that the new vanguard comprises various socialist currents and that their gradual unification is necessary for the establishment of a productive vanguard force. We may describe this plurality concept as an *"alliance* of vanguard forces". When we come to consider a name for a political formation which is in some way integrated, the concepts "movement", "league", "union", or "front" come to mind (Socialist *Movement* of Czechoslovak Citizens, *Union* for Democratic Socialism, *League* of Democratic Socialism, *Front* for the Democratic Revival of Socialism, etc.).

The idea of "alliance" does, however, presuppose a tendency towards unity and integration, convergence rather than divergence. The natural basis for the process can be seen in the fact that the bonds linking genuinely vanguard socialist forces must be *internal;* they cannot rest on what the different elements in the socialist opposition do not want. Internal bonds are positive. They grow around long-term goals and not around short-term, partial and transient goals. Thus the alliance of vanguard forces is not a product of any loose and temporary ("tactical") association of *diverse* forces, it is a dynamic formation in which co-operation is deepened among relatively *uniform* forces and currents deriving from various and relatively *diverse* environments, sectors and groups.

This alliance is not a force establishing itself *alongside* its natural hinterland, above the broadest sectors of society and the various ideological and political currents; it is formed within all these components, and in the endeavour to expand the natural potential and disposition of each. Only in this manner can the new political vanguard, we are also saying that they are, to some extent, diverse. This structure; for the vanguard quality is not a privilege, nor is it the preserve of some closed group with "a monopoly of wisdom"; it is a matter of productive, constructive and positive political activity stemming from the aims of the socialist programme as a whole.

When we speak of *relatively* uniform components of the vanguard, we are also saying that they are, to some extent, diverse. This diversity and the differences it produces should not be concealed or brushed aside, because contained in them are the specific potentialities of each separate part of the socialist opposition — be it a communist part, or the various non-communist components. For the same reason it would not be right, or even possible, to aim for a uniform (homogeneous) structure which would entirely and without trace erase the ideological differences. Communists are socialists who regard socialism as the era of "transition" to communism, and the socialist state (the political organisation of society = "state-semistate") as the instrument by which to do away with any kind of "state" (political) organisation. Non-communist socialists are sceptical about these "ultimate goals", or they reject them as utopian, unrealistic and so on. All, however, agree that the era in which we live is the era of socialism, of the socialist democratic state, and that progress (whether or not we are moving "towards communism") is dependent on the measure of intellectual and political freedom (i.e. the degree of democracy) and on the all-round development of the potential offered by social ownership. This programmatic assumption and basic political goal links communists and socialists not only in the fight for democratic socialism, it also creates internal bonds between them for the entire era of "socialism", however the relationships between them may be shaped (in the formal sense). And it is certainly desirable that these relationships (of views, and in organisational terms) should develop in an optimal manner and be as close as possible. But even here we cannot give priority to abstract criteria — although it holds in general that a tendency to integrate is progressive because it is functional, effective, and it may prove ineffectual and dysfunctional if it oversteps the limits set by the current possibilities and conditions for the functioning of the individual components.

This concept of the vanguard as an *alliance* of vanguard forces is — as we see — in direct contradiction to the traditional image of a revolutionary organisation which is strictly centralised and ideologically monolithic. Yet it is not, basically, a new concept. Its general outlines can be deduced from the efforts of the progressive forces throughout the international Left, not excepting the communist parties.

Putting the plurality concept into effect is, however, a matter for the entire vanguard, for all its parts and all conceivable levels, but in the first place it is a question of productive ideological effort by its leading elements. We underline the function of ideology and the function of the leading component because without them it is impossible to develop *rational* thinking and activity at the required level; and without rational endeavour we cannot overcome the obstacles that are holding the movement back, nor can we formulate a new system of views (corresponding to present conditions), values and standards of "ideology".

IV

The most numerous and compact part of the socialist opposition consists of communists, that is to say, the force in the communist movement known in the official sectarian, dogmatic terminology as "the Right". This force represents tens of thousands of expelled office-holders and hundreds of thousands of former rank-and-file Party members, as well as a section of present CPCz members and office-holders who have passed the "checking". This part of the Left opposition draws significant moral and political support from the identity betwen its attitudes and those held by important forces in the international communist movement; in some respects (for instance, the view about the entry of troops into Czechoslovakia) these are forces constituting the *majority* in the world communist movement. The core of this group has preserved a clear awareness of the progressive goals of the post-January policy and a self-confidence stemming from their certainty about the legitimacy of their political endeavour; they carry on organically from the ideology of the post-January reform movement. The gradual crystallisation of attitudes and views in this group (plus the countervailing process at the other pole, in the so-called Marxist-Leninist Left which has assumed hegemony in the ruling party) led through a number of stages (January 1968, August 1968, April and September 1969, the Party membership screening in the spring of 1970, the "Lessons" published at the end of 1970) to the actual splitting of the pre-January CPCz into two opposed parties.

"The Party of the Expelled" (of course, the term is inaccurate in several respects) is not, however, an undifferentiated formation. More precisely, although the differentiation process has passed from its highly dynamic phase to a somewhat more static stage, it has not yet ended. Alongside the less essential differences (stemming from the aftermath of distinctions in tactics, from the social environment and national differences — Slovakia! — and possibly from local and generation differences) one elementary political factor has come to the fore: the willingness or unwillingness to continue political activity under entirely new conditions. In other words, the question *how* to proceed is prefaced by the question *whether* to engage in opposition at all. Not only personality factors enter into this, there are also those of an ideological nature (the concept of legality takes first place here).

In so far as the active wing of this group is concerned, it may be assumed that its various sections will approach each other in their views. As an illustration: the most representative statement yet published, the *Manifesto of the Socialist Movement of Czechoslovak Citizens*, met with responses from two groups — one signing itself "Communists", the other the group which issued an appeal to workers and technicians signed "Workers — legally elected functionaries of the CPCz". Both expressed disagreement, but from totally opposed standpoints. The second group categorically rejected the "Communists", on the whole from the same positions as those of the Manifesto authors. So they have come closer to the group behind the Manifesto (other circumstances point to this, too). But the group signing themselves "Communists" have also undergone rapid development (influenced particularly by the Manifesto and by the Polish events); they have made far-reaching amendments to their initial attitude, saying they were mistaken in their estimate of the potentialities of Husak's "centrist" leadership.

But it must be noted that, in its present state, the Party opposition is extremely undeveloped; its consolidation is at the embryonic stage. Much of the theoretical, programmatic and analytical work essential for defining any ideological positions remains to be done; in this connection we need to organise political discussions (as broad as possible under the circumstances). Both jobs require the co-operation of all the initiatory groups concerned and a con-

146

siderable, manifold extension of the circle of people participating (in accordance with their possibilities and their roles).

In the context of the communist component of the left opposition, a special problem is presented by the group of Party members who have passed the screening test but who inwardly disagree with the present course or have basic reservations about it, but who do not (at least for the present) come out actively, and who sometimes support the official policy directly or indirectly (alongside reasons of an opportunist and personal nature, ideological motives also play a part here — the mystique of the Party and the Soviet Union, etc.). This group (oriented "towards Husak" and against the "leftists" — that is, "centrist" in attitude) represents the transition to the most opportunistic section of the "deleted" membership — or vice versa. (One cannot equate them with those who have remained in the Party by agreement with the expelled and who are determined to work in the spirit of opposition.)

The ideology of the group (especially their illusions about "centrist" policy and the role of the "centrist" politicians) needs to be criticised just as strongly as that of the "Marxist-Leninist left". Their responsibility for the conservative course is no less than that of the extreme dogmatists and sectarians. Which does not exclude — in certain circumstances — various kinds of co-operation when the opportunity arises.

The same goes for all the other groups operating within the legal structures and assuming more or less undefined attitudes — in the non-communist parties, in the trade unions, the state apparatus, the youth organisations etc.

V

Of an entirely different order is the problem of co-operation by communists and socialists with the non-communist (non-Marxist) trends. Experience is rather lacking in this respect — in some places there is more, in some less. The inclination towards the "plurality" concept is stronger in the Czech areas than in Slovakia, in Moravia it is stronger than in Bohemia.

As with the communist sections of the opposition, the question of co-operation is primarily a matter of the actual constitution of the groups. Where they have not constituted themselves as initiatory groups, there can be no grounds for co-operation.

The basic significance of the post-January movement stemmed from the fact that bonds of far stronger trust developed between communists and non-communists. This does not exclude the pos-

147

sibility of conflicting trends operating within the various sections of the non-communist opposition — leaning, on the one hand, towards co-operation with the communists and, on the other hand, rejecting the idea. Experience so far, however, gives grounds for optimism. Indisputably right-wing (pro-capitalist and pro-imperialist) attitudes are a minority, even out on the fringe.

Nevertheless, the communists themselves exert a considerable influence on the internal development of the non-communist groups: "as you call into the forest, so the forest speaks". There are no grounds for supposing that the non-communists will believe the communists merely because they declare themselves to be "progressive" and opposed to the policies of the present Party leadership. That position, too, is — generally speaking — compatible with the "spirit of domination" and "hegemony" that characterises sectarian and authoritarian communism. Over the past twenty years many things have served to repulse people and frighten them off, and thus to prevent many of them from joining with the communists. It is all the more understandable, then, that there is a demand for the communists to display "willingness".

The prolonged split between the communists and socialists has necessarily led to the formation on the soil of socialist society of strikingly new non-communist and non-Marxist opposition currents which, while having an affinity with traditional ideological and political formations such as national or democratic (Social Democratic) socialism, or Masarykian realism, or Christian social teaching (left-wing Catholicism, an ecclesiastical council movement!), go well beyond the limits of the traditional formations in their current political function.

And alongside tendencies of traditional hue we also have some less traditional attitudes, especially among the younger age groups and the liberal and technological intelligentsia, or among the young intellectuals (students). In this category we have tendencies reflecting the influence of the West European and also the non-European Left ("The Revolutionary Socialist Party") and some following the more traditional domestic concept of "above-party" and "unpolitical" forces ("The Club of Committed Non-Party Members").

In accordance with the theses concerning the importance of a union of vanguard forces, it is necessary to regard co-operation among all these trends as an indispensable condition for the growth of a new political vanguard. Positive co-operation multiplies or at least extends the forces, it prepares the ground for a more integrated society of the future, it overcomes limited group mentality and egoism (clinging to traditions and symbols, to received values in general, to the accepted style of language etc.) against which even the noblest ideals provide no safeguard.

VI

In considering the force capable of transforming the existing structure in a democratic spirit, it goes without saying that it cannot be the vanguard "as such", it must be a mass movement headed by the socialist political vanguard. There is no need to elaborate this key point of revolutionary strategy and tactics. Its basic aspects are well-known: a mass movement cannot be wished into existence, it represents a complex, peculiar structure of the most varied "objective" and "subjective" elements, it is an expression of acute political crisis (born of crisis, the movement stimulates the growth of the crisis) etc.

At the moment one can hardly speak of an acute crisis or of spontaneous political activity by the broadest sections of the population, or even of activity among the key sections. The open political crisis has passed into its "hidden", "chronic", "quiet" phase; the popular movement for the democratic revival of socialism has been "pacified", and its disintegration is marked by the familiar symptoms of passivity, escapism, apathy and so on.

Nothing, however, could be more unreasonable than to absolutise these things. Any schematic approach to these matters is bound to backfire. And that goes for the other pole of the same problem — the questions associated with the tempo and the forms of transition to socialist democracy (to any structurally distinct stage of social and political development). We are familiar with the scholastic disputes about the relations between revolution and reform, and we have no intention of adding to them. We will confine ourselves to noting that structural changes ("revolutionary reforms") should involve sudden upheavals, an immediate transition from one set-up to another, in short, "leaps" converting an unfree society into a free one, without any intermediate stages. And vice versa — a high probability of "evolutionary" development in one direction in no way excludes the possibility of sudden change and convulsions which few could have foreseen before the event. And this holds all the more for a "consolidated" society, as ours has been.

In addition, there are the problems associated with combining the methods of struggle "from above" (and impulses "from above") with those "from below", in other words, the fight "from

149

within" and "from the outside" to which we referred in the introductory section.

The key question in this whole complex of issues is, however, that of the main "motive force" of revolutionary change. In tune with the rational (not the doctrinaire) tradition of revolutionary socialism, we find that it is the masses of industrial producers concentrated in the big urban enterprises, and primarily the mass of manual workers.

The attention of all vanguard forces should be focused on this field; it is then necessary to work out as definite a plan of procedure as possible for this sector, aiming to establish, on a realistic time-scale, footholds in all (or nearly all, that is, the biggest) major enterprises.

The plan should be guided, among other things, by several basic tactical considerations which we will merely note here in schematic terms:

(a) The problem of linking the most varied particular and specific interests of the most varied groups of working people with the general political movement (the following list is far from complete): defence of workers' rights of all kinds, protection against attacks on wages, the provision of a safe and healthy environment, criticism of arbitrarily appointed and incompetent authorities, criticism of abuses in organisation and administration altogether, exposure of the insulting treatment of people, demands to participate in management as provided for in the appropriate regulations, and attention to workers' suggestions, the fight for trade union democracy and democratic representation as a whole, the fight for economic reform in its particular and its overall aspects, the endeavour to establish democratic bodies such as workers' councils or enterprise councils etc.).

(b) The problem of utilising legal organisations — trade union and public organisations, and also the Communist Party, organisational links between enterprises, conferences, consultations, collective agreements — any gatherings and any actions offering an opportunity to assert the true interests of the working people against those of the bureaucracy.

(c) The problem of the relationships between workers and the technical intelligentsia (specifically, between the workers and the economic apparatus); in general — aiming for the closest possible bond between the workers and the technical intelligentsia (the difference between the bureaucracy and the tech-

150

nical intelligentsia), the fight against caste distinctions and hidebound sectional attitudes, against the bureaucratic tactic of "divide and rule".

VII

The foregoing section needs to be supplemented by another traditional theme, that of the allies of the working class:
(a) the peasant movement,
(b) the youth movement,
(c) professional organisations of the intellectuals.

All three "sectors" have much in common with the tactical elements of the basic (industrial) sector: specific programmes linking particular interests with the general movement for the democratic revival of socialism, the drive to develop the group's progressive awareness, the formation of autonomous links of a "horizontal" type, utilising legal structures of all kinds etc.

Some comments on the sectors:

(a) The peasant movement. The post-January movement of cooperative farmers which first established the Farmers' Union and was later switched to the less dangerous channel of the Union of Co-operative Farmers, proclaimed the programme of "equal rights" for farmers with the rest of the population, in other words, equality of agriculture and industry. This programme was buried, and the co-operative farmers' oganisation was reduced to being one of the transmission belts, its political character has been destroyed and its function limited to that of a cultural society. Moreover, in the interests of "strengthening state control", the leading elements of the self-managing agricultural organisations (the agricultural associations) have been liquidated. There is considerable resistance to this policy; not only the majority of the villages but also the overwhelming majority of co-operative officials take a progressive stance.

(b) The youth movement. Students, young workers, their cooperation and their efforts to get an alliance of all social groups among the youth; the significance of the Socialist League of Youth (youth clubs!); the relation between radical criticism of bureaucratic structures and the specific possibilities open to youth organisations; the adaptation of Hungarian experience with juvenile law; the so-called complex programme for handling the problems of the young generation as a whole (see resolution of the SSM congress); the protest movement

151

by youth, and particularly by the students (the campaign for the release of Revolutionary Socialist Party members) — its national and international dimensions (our students — Angela Davis!).

(c) The intellectuals: (i) centres of scientific work (although the disbanding of the Scientific Workers' Union has made organisational work even more difficult, the negative effect of this action should not be overestimated; it would be as well to consider co-operation among people who know each other from this sphere); (ii) the artistic unions; (iii) doctors; (iv) teachers and education workers (libraries!); (v) the legal profession (judges, prosecutors, advocates!).

The exceptional pressure by the state bureaucracy on all sections of the intelligentsia, and especially on those concerned with the humanities who are within its immediate reach (state employees!), causes a profound and damaging differentiation which cannot be underestimated: alongside the small band of active agents of government policy, there is a numerous and varied body of loyal people, embracing a highly diversified spectrum from the most active to the most passive. This section generates not only a strong pragmatic conformist tendency, but also some pronounced "centrist" (opportunist) ideological influences. The ideological counter-pressure from the vanguard groups should be linked with an extremely circumspect political approach, because this broad current of indeterminate forces includes a large number of progressive impulses and opportunities for all kinds of co-operation, and the vanguard cannot afford to ignore them.

VIII

All the foregoing remarks about the composition of the vanguard forces indicate a complex set-up presupposing co-operation among various and specialised groups. Such co-operation is conceivable only on the condition that it develops as independently as possible (according to the nature of each component or "sector") and, at the same time, as far as possible in a planned manner, i.e. that it will be deliberately geared to the goals of the overall movement for the democratic revival of socialism.

Obviously, the undertaking is ambitious, and the proposition underlying it might well seem utopian were it not for the fact that we have set ourselves and are guided by certain simple organisational principles which are based on realistic possibilities and, in a way, are already, or are about to be, realised.

Where opportunities for "normal" communication are lacking, "self-service publishing" (samizdat) is naturally of prime importance. The circulation of diverse documents providing information and enlightenment is a fairly simple technique ensuring the necessary linkages among the most varied groups. Therefore any initiative in this direction should be *generalised* to the utmost. The means required for the simple reproduction of documents are minimal and they are available to almost any circle of people. And naturally no bounds are placed on independent initiative; any group can, according to the possibilities open to it, produce translations, draft appeals, issue information and exposures, link local matters with the general matters etc.

In addition to this elementary and highly centralised activity, which will become more difficult and vulnerable the more it spreads, two other essential forms are available: the distribution of materials published abroad (a possibility not widely used as yet, but psychologically extremely important and effective), and the publication of longer documents of all kinds as "occasional" publications and "periodicals" (symposia, editions of more extensive studies, regular "notebooks", collected papers etc.).

The publication of this kind of material is more difficult to arrange, however, and the risk is incomparably greater. That must be taken into account in preparing such undertakings. Here, too, considerable decentralisation is needed, but in contrast to samizdat activity the work cannot be isolated. The content should be regularly assessed and checked to ensure that all programmatic, theoretical, analytical and polemical activity is closely linked to the needs of the movement.

IX

From the organisational standpoint one can establish as the simplest principle for immediate purposes that the *leading body* of the political vanguard and the group responsible for the *distribution* of the longer documents should *coincide*.

We have referred to the leading body of the political vanguard as a circle of people numbering thousands (whereas the political vanguard itself is in the order of tens of thousands). In this category belong the most active and committed (and, of course, the most reliable) representatives of the "Right" from all areas of political and public life. We consider it unnecessary to list all these areas: what has been said about the structure of the vanguard should suffice. The entire grouping should be seen as a highly dynamic formation which will grow in numbers in proportion to the circulation of the more substantial and important publications, and it will, in its turn, influence the level and quality (content) of the overall ideological activity. The organisational work cannot be tied to any set pattern; nevertheless, a few general principles may be mentioned.

(a) Establishing the leading collective of the vanguard requires time (which cannot be measured in weeks or months); the job calls for caution, but also for energy and determination. If this condition is to be met, *first* some kind of staff needs to be set up. For the immediate future the basis is provided by the initiatory groups which have joined together with the aim of generalising their findings to the widest possible extent. But this innermost circle needs to be extended several times over within a fairly brief period. We believe this can be achieved most readily if the "Short Action Programme" is discussed in the *circle of people concerned,* as mentioned in the very first sentence of our document. For this purpose, after discussion in the innermost circle, final editing is required. The selection of people from this circle calls for the most careful consideration. It should not be mechanical, nor should the communicating of the text itself be a mechanical, passive act confined to reading what is written; it should lead to further elaboration of the programmatic and tactical principles of the socialist vanguard and of the organisational steps. (In addition to reading the document, it would be useful to organise discussions in twos, threes and fours etc. — there are no limits to initiatives in this respect.)

(b) In selecting the people to represent the leading body of the vanguard, two complementary sets of guidelines should be observed: on the one hand, taking full advantage of all the opportunities offered by the old linkages established by the post-January structures (officials of representative bodies and people whose abilities and authority are not in doubt) and, on the other hand, paying attention to people not publicly known who have proved that they can provide a valuable reinforcement to any kind of specialised activity (political, organisation, ideological etc.); in general, the criterion of usefulness should have priority over that of *formal* representation.

(c) The organisational procedure for setting up the movement's leading body (and consequently, the entire movement) should not adhere — at least, not *strictly* — to territorial and administrative divisions; the coverage of "regions" and "districts" should be flexible. All the most important "regional" and "district" centres should be covered (that is, not merely the present regional and district towns, but other centres as well) and the connections with localities should be continually extended, with priority given to contacts in the big industrial enterprises; this does not exclude the formation in particular places of the most varied kinds of set-up according to local possibilities and depending on personal ties among members of the movement. A network of contacts of all kinds should not rule out the existence of several lines of contact to one local centre, or various overlappings (especially temporary ones) in so far as they are expedient for particular personal links — in general, the principle should be that differences of opinion or personal conflicts should be loyally overcome, not perpetuated.

Alongside these general principles of organisational work, there are problems of a specific nature ("Prague", "Moravian", "Slovak" problems etc.). Since these are peculiar to each area, we shall not comment on them. Loyal co-operation by all parties concerned is assumed here, too.

X

The most serious, but also the most difficult and demanding aspect of forming the vanguard is the international aspect. Its solution requires a sober and dispassionate approach based on a thorough examination of the prospects for a variety of alliances within the socialist countries, and elsewhere.

In principle, however, one must proceed from the fact that the movement for the democratic revival of socialism is an international movement, although its level varies in different countries and it has quite different aspects in the "Soviet" camp and in the capitalist countries.

The attitude to the emigrant population must also be resolved from this standpoint. Knowing how differentiated its composition is, we must choose the most careful approach to developing political co-operation, which should not mean mutual isolation. On the contrary, by mutual co-ordination we should arrive at the most productive procedure and the "internationalisation" of progressive efforts throughout the European Left.

The orientation to Europe should not mean ignoring any, even the most modest, potential opportunities for co-operation outside Europe; careful consideration needs to be given to the complex of Chinese and Sino-Soviet questions.

The first and basic tactical aim should be that the left opposition in Czechoslovakia should win the support ("recognition") of the West European Left; that the Party (communist) opposition in the country should win recognition from the West European communists. Here we need to achieve even the most modest successes (intervention at various levels on behalf of Czechoslovak communists, information in the communist press, open statements of solidarity). As an immediate matter, consider the international aspect of possible actions in connection with the coming congress of the Czechoslovak Communist Party, and possibly in connection with the CPSU Congress (joining in discussion prior to both congresses; linking both things).

January-February 1971

4   The Election Appeal

[This appeal was distributed in Prague, Brno and other Czechoslovak towns between 14 September and election day on 28 November 1971. Issued by the Socialist Movement of Czechoslovak
Citizens, it was later signed by other opposition groups, including
the "Jan Palach Revolutionary Group", the "Civil Resistance
Movement" (Czech and Slovak sections) and the "Communist
Workers' Movement". Its wide distribution (Husak spoke in the
Central Committee of 100,000 copies, only some of which were
seized by the police) and its effect on the public irritated the ruling
group, who proceeded to launch a witch-hunt against the authors
and distributors of the leaflet. During one of their raids the police
arrested in rapid succession the two sons and the daughter of
Jaroslav Sabata, followed by Sabata himself and some fifty students
and young workers in Brno. In Prague, the "Czechoslovak
Brethren" group (Rev. Jaroslav Dus, Dr Hejdanek, Jiranek and
others) were detained. The wave of arrests in Prague started at the
beginning of January 1972; among the victims were Milan Hübl,
Jaromir Litera, Karel Kyncl, Jiri Hochman, Karel Kaplan, the
sons of Otto Sling and Rudolf Slansky, and around one hundred
other oppositionists.

Despite the repression, the socialist opposition was successful in
its campaign, which conformed strictly to the Constitution and,
indeed, to the election law approved by the Husak régime, which
guarantees the citizen the right to abstain from casting his vote or
to withhold his support by deleting the name of a candidate — in
Prague and other major towns abstentions amounted to 10 per cent,
no-votes to 10-25 per cent (Husak himself was given a 20 per cent
anti-vote in the Prague Vysocany district, which in no way deterred
the election commission from declaring him elected by 100 per
cent of the poll!). In a speech to the Central Committee in December 1971, Husak railed against the leaders of the "Right" for not
taking part in the elections (he referred in particular to Dubcek,
Smrkovsky, Kriegel and their wives, also to Pavel, Hübl, Silhan,
Litera, Vodslon, Kosik, Vaculik, Hanzelka, Bartosek and Samalik,
who were among the people subsequently arrested in January
1972).]

Citizens of Czechoslovakia!

We are required to go to the polls at the end of November. The régime's representatives are turning the elections into a referendum in which the electorate is obliged to express its approval of the occupation and of the destruction of all hope of democracy in the future and the violation of civil rights, by voting for the official candidates. The canvassers tell us that whoever abstains or does not vote obediently for the official list is an enemy of socialism.

These are not genuine elections in which we shall be able to choose our own representatives in Parliament, in the National Council and in local government committees. The political leadership has decided not only on the candidates but also on the total percentage of the electorate declared (by the electoral commissions) to have voted and on the percentage of votes cast for the régime. The elections are a fraud, and the results have already been fixed. However, it is not a matter of indifference whether we go to the polls or not, and whether or not we cross out candidates' names. The electoral commissions will secretly report to the leadership the number of voters who boycott the elections and the number of deletions, whatever the figures announced officially. If the citizen expresses his opposition to the current situation, this has a great moral significance, and it will also have an international impact: the world will hear about us only if we stand by our principles and defend our rights. We must not forget that the world will only think about us if we ourselves remind it of our fate.

We will not be surrendered to our fate, as long as we do not surrender ourselves to it! Every one of us must each decide individually how to act, according to our personal and family circumstances. If you want to reject the current situation or criticise it, then you have the choice: either boycott the election or cross out the names.

1. Abstention is the most open form of rejecting the current policies. Voting is not a legal duty but a civic right. It is the business of the citizen himself how he exercises that right. He cannot be punished for abstaining; he can only get his cards endorsed. The canvassers are not state representatives, and they have no right to force anyone to vote. It is the business of the citizen himself whether he allows them to enter his living quarters or regards them as unwanted intruders. If you decide to go to the polls, remember that:

2. Voting is secret. The law says that there is a secret ballot; and demonstrations of so-called group voting are not provided for by law. Paragraph 34 of the election law speaks about the voting

booth ("A space for filling in the ballot paper"). Since the elections *are* (not "may be") secret, the booth must be secret too, and should therefore be situated so that voters *must* (not "may") enter it. Pay attention so that this is held to, whether you are going to cross out names or not; it is a question of respecting civil rights.

3. Negative votes are indicated by crossing out the whole name (first name and surname).

The electoral commissions, in accordance with their instructions, will count incomplete deletions as votes cast for the list. If there are indistinct marks on the ballot paper, these will likewise be counted as positive votes.

In the smaller parishes, candidates for the local government committees can be voted for and the names of candidates to higher bodies crossed out. One may replace the official list of candidates with a list of one's own, or put a slogan on a piece of paper into the voting envelope: for example, the electoral commissions will certainly understand the slogan "January, not August!"

The Socialist Movement of Czechoslovak Citizens

September 1971

5 The Workers' Proclamation

[Describing themselves as "Workers — legally elected officials of the CPCz" is a group of communists expelled from the Party during the big purges who maintain, however, their strictly Marxist view; they are active predominantly in factories and among the working class. Their main base lies in Prague's big industrial enterprises, and their underground paper *Pokrok* ("Progress") circulates in the various branches of CKD-Prague, the firm in which the Extraordinary Congress of the CPCz met on 22 August 1968.

The group's political approach is underlined by the document published here, which was distributed in Prague in January 1972 to mark the fourth anniversary of the "new course". Its interest lies in its being addressed exclusively to workers; it states the tasks and demands of the socialist opposition in industry. The Czechoslovak working class has a long tradition of struggle, especially by legal means. Under the Habsburg monarchy it won the right to vote and to strike, the right of trade-union organisation, and achieved a higher standard of living than existed in the neighbouring countries. Under the First Republic after 1918, the tradition was maintained; the two working-class organisations — the social democratic and the communist parties — were among the foremost political forces in the country, campaigning in an entirely legal manner. During the Nazi occupation, while the working class showed its hostility by go-slow tactics at work and by sabotage wherever opportunity offered, the risk of direct confrontation with the enemy was avoided.

After the liberation in 1945 the workers played an important part — with the help of the CP (which had emerged as the strongest political party, with industrial workers accounting for over fifty percent of the membership), through the unified trade unions and the factory councils in nationalised industry. In February 1948, by means of a general strike and bringing out the workers' militia, they helped the Communist Party to achieve absolute power. Subsequently, however, the Party isolated itself by posing as the sole representative of socialism and the working class, placing itself above the workers. In this manner it turned the dictatorship of

160

the proletariat into a dictatorship over the proletariat.

Twenty years of Stalinist rule witnessed a systematic depoliticising of the workers, with the ruling group imposing its concept that the workers' part in building socialism was a matter of raising labour productivity and carrying out the economic plans decided by the power centre. So the workers were robbed of their leading role, and equally of all the political rights won by the struggles of previous generations: the right to strike, the right to independent trade union organisation, to defend their economic interests etc. The situation was reflected in the steady decline in the working class membership of the party (fifty-two per cent in 1948, twenty-two per cent in 1967).

Following Dubcek's dismissal and the Husak takeover, many workers showed their revulsion against politics by leaving the party and the trade unions. There was a danger that the apathy of the past twenty years would set in once more.

The aim of the socialist opposition is to revive activity among industrial workers by providing a platform for their immediate demands and by encouraging them to join with the technicians, seeing them not as enemies but rather as a vital contingent in the common struggle.]

Comrade workers,

Four years separate us from January 1968. In that time the few months of hope, with the prospect of settling our country's political and economic problems in a genuinely socialist way, were forcibly cut short by the entry of foreign troops. With their aid, contrary to the will of the people, power was taken over by the dogmatic-bureaucratic clique which is ruthlessly suppressing all the rights and democratic freedoms of our citizens.

The majority of people in both our nations disagree with the presently ruling power and do not support it. The major part in this resistance is played by the working class. The workers not only accepted the January ideas as the correct way out of the crisis of the Novotny era, they started above all to put the Action Programme immediately into effect at their places of work.

The temporary interruption by force of the post-January course gave the workers new revolutionary experience. They soon realised that the so-called consolidation is primarily a frontal attack on themselves. It has deprived them of progressive leaders who are devoted to socialism. Thousands of worker functionaries were

161

expelled from the party. Thousands more have been driven out of their posts in the enterprises. The central trade union organisations have been converted into an obedient tool, willing to approve any anti-working class measures, as has already happened with the amendments to the Labour Code. The workers' councils, the most significant product of the post-January course, which gave workers a real share in the management and control of their own enterprises, were liquidated.

The main blame for economic failures is increasingly placed on the workers. The ruling group blame them for its inability to steer the socialist economy in a new way. It enforces a strict wages ceiling in an effort to increase output and halt the mounting inflation. But prices continue to rise and the living standard of the working people is declining. Our export surpluses in the socialist countries have been exhausted and our debt with them is growing. Our funds in western countries are used for importing goods, often of inferior quality, which are sold to the public at high prices. These measures are intended to give the impression of a well-supplied market, while at the same time the most ordinary or cheapest products of daily consumption are often unobtainable.

The ruling group proclaims itself as the spokesman of the working class and the sole interpreter of principled marxism-leninism. It labels anyone holding an opinion other than the officially approved as being a right-wing opportunist, an anti-Soviet and anti-socialist element. But there is no unity even within the group. The different factions squabble over positions of power, over well-paid posts in the party, the administration and in industry. Nothing can be more at odds with the revolutionary interests of the working class than this government of incompetent careerists which has set itself up as the representative of the workers, which forcibly suppresses all vestiges of socialist democracy and is leading our society into a profound political and economic crisis.

The fate of nations is not decided, however, by small groups of dogmatists, no matter how they may surround themselves with the biggest possible apparatus of bureaucrats and police spies. The further advance of socialism in our country will be decided by the millions of working people, headed by their revolutionary core, the workers in industrial and production enterprises. That is why we are faced today with the need to unite our forces and to concentrate them on these main tasks:

(1) At the annual general meetings of the CPCz, not to elect extreme leftists [i.e. dogmatists — *trs*] to posts in the basic organ-

isations and enterprise committees, and not to nominate them for public office. Demand that the party rules be observed and do not let office-holders be forced on us by the party apparatus.

(2) At trade union annual general meetings and conferences, insist on a secret ballot. Nominate for office comrades who are capable of resolutely defending the workers' interests.

(3) Insist that workplaces are equipped in accordance with the regulations on safety at work. Demand that prompt steps be taken to reduce noise and dust, to provide machines with covers and safeguards against accidents. Your health is the most precious thing you have.

(4) Through the workshops and enterprise trade-union bodies take a determined stand against further inroads on workers' rights, demand that at least the Labour Code be fully observed.

(5) Use collective agreements as a defence against further attacks on wages, for improving health care, catering and the working environment.

(6) Criticise concretely and openly the incompetence of the newly-appointed managers and demand that they should bear full responsibility for their work, as the worker has to bear responsibility for faulty products. Don't go along, however, with any vague and generalised criticism of technicians as a body. The great majority hold the same views as the workers. Don't forget that this method of dividing people was often employed by Novotny in order to distract attention from mistakes by the leadership. The present ruling group will also try to use it as economic difficulties increase.

(7) Don't take part in mass parades intended to demonstrate to the public abroad that the working people agree with the political set-up in our country.

Comrades, every factory, every workplace must become a fortress where the workers themselves will have the decisive voice. We are no longer alone in our fight. The same problems that we wanted to solve in January 1968 are now beginning to be understood by more and more workers in the other socialist countries, and in the USSR. Fighting alongside us are also progressive people in other countries, people who are not indifferent to the advance of socialism.

Workers, legally elected functionaries of the CPCz

Distribute this at your workplace and in other enterprises.
By doing this alone, you are fighting.

6 Declaration against Oppression

[This declaration by the Socialist Movement of Czechoslovak Citizens was distributed in February 1972 in Prague, Brno and other Czechoslovak cities. Thus the arrests of November 1971 and January 1972 had succeeded neither in unearthing the resistance network, nor in striking at the "centre" of the movement, which continued its activity despite the increasingly difficult conditions.

The document reveals the "revanchist" tendencies displayed during interrogations by the State Security officers when seeking "evidence" against the former leaders of the "new course", for instance, Dubcek, Smrkovsky and Kriegel (the Italian journalist Valerio Ochetto describes in his book how the police tried to make him confess that he visited Bratislava to meet Dubcek), and also against the new leaders, such as Husak, whom they held to be lacking in severity.]

Citizens,

The régime which declared that it wanted no political trials and that it would not penalise anyone for their political views proceeded, after the elections, to throw off all inhibitions and to launch a furious attack against those who have refused to submit. Already before the November elections such prominent politicians and scholars as, for instance, Jaroslav Sabata, Jan Tesar, Rudolf Battek, Ladislav Hejdanek, the student leader Jiri Müller and tens of others, were arrested. They are accused of distributing election leaflets. Even were that true, they would be being persecuted for wanting to remind Czechoslovak voters about the passages in the election law concerning elector's rights which the press had deliberately suppressed. When should citizens voice their political views, if not at election time? Arrested at the beginning of January were former members of the CP Central Committee Milan Hübl, Rector of the Political University, and Alfred Cerny, Secretary of the Party Regional Committee in Brno, and then journalist Karel Kyncl and Jan Sling, son of a member of the CP leadership who was executed in the 1950s.

During the first week of February the persecution not only intensified, it also assumed new forms. The targets of police raids were not the usual thieves and prostitutes, but Marxist intellectuals. In Prague alone some hundred people were involved in arrests, interrogations or house searches. Held for several days in solitary confinement in Ruzyn Prison were Rudolf Slansky junior, son of the former Party General Secretary who was executed in 1952, the wife of the already imprisoned Jan Sling (her mother, a pre-war party functionary, was detained in Bratislava), prominent Czechoslovak scholars, professors, assistant professors, Karel Kosik, Jaroslav Klofac, Karel Kaplan, Robert Kalivoda, Lubos Sochor, Frantisek Samalik, historians Karel Bartosek, Josef Belda, journalists Jiri Hochman, Jiri Dienstbier, Cestmir Suchy, Vladimir Nepras, political workers, formerly of the Prague City Committee of the CP Jaroslav Litera, Adolf Dorn, the former head of information compiling at the Central Committee, Jan Kaspar, two staff from the Political University, the painter Jindrich Heger and others. The raids were so unsuccessful that the majority of those detained had to be released, but they are still threatened with re-arrest, or further interrogation without detention. Among those kept in custody were Karel Kaplan, Karel Bartosek, Jaroslav Litera and Jiri Hochman. Karel Kaplan is particularly in danger; as a historian and CP official, he was in charge of the work of the so-called Piller Commission which reviewed, summarised and assessed the documents concerning the crimes of the 1950s, and the security officers whose crimes he knows about are filled with pathological hatred for him. Also in considerable danger is Jiri Hochman who suffers from chronic pneumonia and has recently had a recurrence of active tuberculosis. People are still being taken daily from their workplaces for interrogations lasting many hours, or all day.

The security force pretends it is exposing some kind of "criminal activity". But interrogations involving hundreds of people have demonstrated that they are really looking for something different — for an opportunity to take their revenge for 1968. Some of the interrogators have made no secret of the intention to arrest Josef Smrkovsky, nor of their hatred for Alexander Dubcek, and even for Gustav Husak. The security raids were accompanied, in a number of places, by demands from the most reactionary elements for new purges and "check-ups".

This course has a logic which is familiar to all of us and which someone once described as "the action of the mill". The net is cast not only around those who openly voice their disagreement with the régime. It can close on anyone, at random and without discrimination, including those now in power, or those who share with them the slender hope of preserving a quiet life, at least for themselves and their families. We know that open resistance is futile in this situation and would only lead to further losses. But to look on passively would be to assume guilt, so that one day someone would again be able to declare that we all bear our share of it. Each of us can do something to counter the persecution of our friends, acquaintances, fellow workers and neighbours. Let us express our solidarity with the persecuted, help their families, insist that the law be respected, let us not give the police more power than it actually possesses, and let us not allow the victims to be dismissed from their jobs. Their are other ways of helping, too — don't talk unnecessarily about matters that interest the security, don't keep leaflets and journals, pass them on safely and at once! When we are interrogated, we know nothing, we remember nothing, we can recall nothing even if we should feel that they know all, or if they really know something. In any case, confession will not help us, and by talking we simply provide them unnecessarily with further testimony against ourselves or against others.

We wish also to bring the dangerous course of events in our country to the attention of the international communist movement, of communists, socialists, democrats and friends of Czechoslovakia, and their organisations. The present régime is destroying the last vestiges of civil rights and freedoms, and by posing as socialist it is also destroying the socialist ideals of our people. With the voice of the Czechoslovak people silenced, your voice can contribute to alleviating the persecution and to preventing the fate of Czechoslovakia and her people being forgotten at the coming meetings on European security.

Socialist Movement of Czechoslovak Citizens

Prague, February 1972

7 The Socialist Movement of Czechoslovak Citizens on the Political Trials

[This document confirms that the police oppression and the trials have not destroyed the socialist opposition and that the movement is determined to carry on the fight. It underlines that the defendants and the convicted are all convinced socialists or communists, that they are all fighting for a socialist order and that they behaved steadfastly and with courage before the court. Moreover, it emphasises that the currently valid laws under which the defendants were tried are in contravention of the Constitution and the principles of socialist society; consequently, citizens are entitled, and are in duty bound, to reject these laws and to press for them to be repealed.

The reader will note once more how the opposition values international solidarity, especially from the Left. The régime endeavours to suppress the expressions of solidarity, but people learn about them nevertheless — they stiffen morale and represent a considerable obstacle for the régime.

Having reiterated the principles of the socialist alternative — a society offering more freedom than the capitalist system allows, with direct participation by citizens in the political and economic management of affairs etc. — the statement calls for action to change the present situation in Czechoslovakia by means adapted to the concrete political conditions. The debate on questions of European security appears as an advantage in this fight for democratic socialism — providing that the occasion is not confined to concluding a treaty between governments, and that it offers the opportunity for an open discussion, an extensive exchange of ideas, experience and information. Genuine socialism is not afraid of informed citizens — on the contrary, it needs them. Those convicted in Prague, Brno and Bratislava fought for this kind of socialism, and their comrades are determined to carry on the fight.]

Citizens,

The series of political trials held in Prague, Brno and Bratislava has marked a further stage in the crisis into which the Czechoslovak people were cast four years ago — on 21 August 1968. Party and government officials, and Gustav Husak in particular, have repeatedly proclaimed that no one would be placed on trial for their opinions, that there would be no political trials. These promises, as many others, have not been kept — trials have been going on for a long time now. It suffices to recall the fate of General Prchlik, of the students associated with Petr Uhl, of the journalists Jiri Lederer and Pavel Licka, the former partisan Ing. Kuba and the many others put on trial in the capital, regional and district centres.

The trials held this summer, however, have completely demasked the régime. People of various political views and public attitudes have been brought to court: communists, for instance, former Central Committee members Milan Hübl, Jaroslav Sabata, Alfred Cerny, members of regional Party committees Jaromir Litera, Zdenek Prikryl, Karel Kyncl, Antonin Rusek, MP for the Club of Committed Non-Party Members (KAN) Rudolf Battek, scholars Jan Tesar, Josef Belda, Karel Bartosek, J. Kalina, members of the Evangelical Church and Czech Brethren such as Father Dus, and philosopher Ladislav Hejdanek, student leaders Jiri Müller and Jaroslav Jira, Jaroslav Sabata's children and other students in Brno, officials of the Czech Socialist Party associated with Dr Silhan, workers, students, intellectuals, in short, a cross-section of Czechoslovak society.

All were put on trial because they had thought about the present state of Czechoslovak society. They saw Czechoslovakia living under conditions where her freedom of action in the national sense and as a state had been taken from her mainly by the intervention of Soviet troops in August 1968, conditions maintained by their continued presence. They saw a country whose political leadership had completely renounced any independent policies at home and abroad and had given in to Soviet pressure. This leadership of officials, imposed on the country, yet proclaiming that it was governing in the interests of the working class and was building socialism, did all in its power during the so-called normalisation process to prevent the people, and the workers in particular, from exerting any influence on government — it abolished the workers' councils when they had barely been established and took into its own hands again the management of industry and the fruits of its work, it drove the representatives of the working class from the trade unions, replacing them by compliant careerists. It abolished freedom of speech, the press and assembly. It expelled from the Communist Party and threw out of their jobs those who refused to recognise any such reality and would not submit. It crippled all Czechoslovak culture. Again it is organising sham elections. Czechoslovak society responds, for the most part, to this state of affairs by keeping silent, ignoring politics, retreating into private life, while the political, ideological, economic and moral crisis gets worse.

This situation led those convicted at the trials to the conclusion that it was not enough to reflect, it was also necessary to oppose the oppression and work for a change, or for a return to the previous course, to socialism with a human face. Consequently, they communicated their views on the current domestic and external political situation, on the elections, on tactical matters — by word of mouth or in writing — to their friends and acquaintances at home and abroad, to communists and members of the socialist left.

Such conduct, however, is a crime in Czechoslovakia today. Although the constitution formally guarantees to all citizens freedom of speech, of political opinion, of the press and assembly, citizens can be prosecuted under the law as it stands and is interpreted for venturing to think, to communicate their opinions and to discuss them. A citizen subverts the régime if he does not agree with the official policies, or if he fails to keep silent.

Those who faced the court were aware of this situation from the outset. They had made their decision, and they were ready to bear the consequences. They bore themselves with dignity during the investigation and in court, although many were held in pre-trial detention for up to nine months under conditions unworthy of the twentieth century. None sought to win their freedom by humiliating themselves, by confessing non-existent guilt or throwing the responsibility on others. Each chose his own course, in tune with his status, his possibilities, his situation and the case presented against him. But none felt themselves guilty, they did not desert their opinions, their public attitudes and their rights as citizens. The accused conducted themselves in court as communists or socialists, not despite the fact that they had not renounced their opposition to the Soviet intervention against the Czechoslovak attempt of 1968 to rehabilitate socialism, but for that very reason.

Yes, according to the law as it stands in Czechoslovakia today, and according to the currently valid interpretation of the law, the accused were guilty and were duly condemned, despite the fact

169

that, at times, the court had to use evidence of dubious value. These laws are not socialist, however, they are those of a totalitarian state and their purpose is to keep the present governing group in power. The legislation is directed against society as a whole, against workers, farmers and intellectuals. It contravenes both the natural law of man, and Marx's principles of socialist and communist society, not to mention being irreconcilably opposed to the principles of the Declaration of Human Rights which was officially approved by the Czechoslovak government. It must be stated that in Czechoslovakia, as elsewhere, the principle applies that to try cases under a law which conflicts with the people's interests and with their moral perception is a crime. Hence it is the right, indeed the duty, of citizens to behave in contravention of such laws, thereby contributing to their abolition.

Moreover, the political trials in Czechoslovakia are not held even in conditions comparable to those in Greece and Spain, not to mention the conditions under which Angela Davis was imprisoned and tried. The régime even infringes its own laws by excluding the public from the proceedings and not admitting the press. In pre-trial detention the prisoners are denied many basic rights — correspondence with their families is restricted, family visits are entirely banned, not to mention other visitors, the accused cannot receive material for study or books of their own choosing, they face considerable obstacles in the choice of defence counsel and in contact with them, they are held in cells with criminal offenders.

Despite all the harsh conditions, people in Czechoslovakia are not silent about the trials. Even with the entirely inadequate information available, despite the authorities' efforts to misinform the public, protests and dissent are to be heard. The attempt by some tens of people, including the former Deputy Minister of Foreign Affairs Dr Gertrude Sekaninova-Cakrtova, writer Pavel Kohout, philosopher Lubos Kohout, atomic physicist F. Janouch, to attend the trial of Milan Hübl evoked a warm response, as did the protests they addressed to the highest officers of state when they were refused admission to the courtroom. Solidarity with the families of the prisoners is notable. Nor do those who refrain from speaking out believe the information purveyed by the official press, radio and television.

The quality of the régime is amply demonstrated by the fact that it does not dare to tell our people the truth about the indignation which the Czechoslovak political trials have aroused abroad. Protests have come not only from left-wing and liberal intellectuals and

170

groups, but also strong condemnation has been voiced by the communist parties of Italy, France, Great Britain, Sweden, Belgium, Australia, Switzerland and others. The Italian Communist Party stated outright that it was the duty of every communist party to voice objections about the events in Czechoslovakia. Yet the Czechoslovak and Soviet newspapers write that protests about the trials come only from enemies of socialism or from a few misguided friends.

We express our solidarity with the actions and attitudes of the condemned fighters and comrades and we shall carry on their struggle to rehabilitate socialism with a human face. Our aim remains to build in Czechoslovakia a socialist society which will give citizens not less nor equal but more rights and freedoms than the most advanced capitalist countries provide, including freedom of speech, the press, assembly and organisation. We fight for a society in which the working people will genuinely manage the enterprises and firms, a society in a sovereign and free state in which personal life, culture and scholarship can develop freely. None of these demands detract in the slightest from the basic principles on which the socialist order should be founded and they affect the existing bonds of alliance only in so far as is necessary for the establishing of mutual equality.

The means and methods for conducting our struggle will depend on the concrete political conditions. It is not our intention to fight merely for the sake of fighting. We shall expose and criticise all measures directed against the interests of the Czechoslovak people. We support all positive measures by the régime to improve living standards, to remove civil, political and social discrimination, to revive life in the cultural and academic fields. The present political trials do not, however, set the course towards positive policies, they plunge our society into still deeper crisis.

We do not consider Czechoslovakia's fate to be predestined and unchangeable. Our struggle, in common with the struggle of all progressive forces in the world, will not be fruitless, though it may be long. In the present internal situation, Czechoslovakia lies like a boulder in the heart of Europe, and also for the leading group in the Soviet Union, whose invasion of August 1968 planted this boulder there, it is an obstacle to their efforts to get the European conference convened. Those with whom they want to reach agreement on European security keep reminding them — and now again very urgently in connection with the political trials in Czechoslovakia — that European security cannot be ensured by governments signing a pact not to attack each other, especially when the Soviet Union has infringed the principle, on several occasions, twice by open military intervention. European security can be founded solely on mutual understanding, frank discussion, exchange of views, ideas and experience, mutual trust and open international relations. The superiority of socialism cannot be ensured by closing frontiers, by prisons, camps, jamming foreign broadcasts, by ideological defensiveness and fear of information. The political leadership of any country, politicians who, regarding themselves as representatives of socialism, are afraid that they have nothing to offer in an open exchange of views and information, that they are incapable of taking the offensive in this area, cannot feel secure even after signing dozens of pacts. The state need have no cause for fear, and socialism can make sense only when it is not afraid of its informed citizens participating in the development of society. That was the type of state, and the type of socialism, for which those convicted in the Prague, Brno and Bratislava trials were working. We and many of our friends and comrades in the other socialist countries, including the Soviet Union, are working for the same thing today. The requirements for European security and the requirements of socialism, so grossly ignored in Czechoslovakia today, are constantly drawing closer in the European context. Therein lies our hope, and also our task and our responsibility.

Socialist Movement of Czechoslovak Citizens

8   Anna Sabatova's Appeal

[Anna Sabatova's letter to all the communist and socialist parties of the world belongs among the documents of the socialist opposition, for it proves that even police repression cannot stifle the voice of this opposition. The wife of the condemned communist official Jaroslav Sabata here takes over the task of speaking for someone whom prison had deprived of the possibility of speaking.

Jaroslav Sabata had previously been the party secretary of the Brno district. At the fourteenth party congress on 22 August 1968 he was elected to the central committee. Professor of Brno University and, following his demotion, a building worker, on 8 August 1972 he was sentenced to six and a half years' hard labour; his daughter Hana was sentenced to three and a half years, his elder son, Jan, to two and a half and his younger son, Vaclav, to two years. Thus five members of the Sabata family (including Jaroslav's daughter-in-law Ivanka) were arrested between 9 and 20 November 1971. Anna Sabatova alone remained outside; like half a million other communists she was excluded from the party and sacked from her work, and was obliged to earn her living washing dishes in a works canteen. Her appeal, however, is no "appeal for mercy" from a desperate wife and mother who begs on behalf of her husband and children. She demands "respect for democratic rights" for all, and poses a weighty question for the international workers' movement: how can one explain the contradiction that the communist parties, in countries where they are not in power, aim at allying themselves with socialists and other progressive forces, while in the countries where they have conquered power they present their former partners as "enemies" and treat them as such? This is a very serious question for anyone who is looking for a left alternative, and for all those socialists who believe that an alliance with communists is possible. And it is not a good sign when no answer comes to Anna Sabatova's appeal, with one exception (the Communist Party of Australia published it in January 1973 in their weekly journal *Tribune*). Anna Sabatova's children have been released from prison — first Vaclav, then, in December 1973, Jan and Hana, on account of their "good conduct". But Jaroslav Sabata remains in prison under severe conditions: likewise Milan Hübl, Jan Tesar, Jiri Müller and others, who were condemned along with him.

Therefore, and also for the fundamental reasons put forward in the letter, Anna Sabatova's appeal has unfortunately not lost any of its impact and currency in the three years since it appeared. Her desire for an answer to the theoretical and practical questions concerning the building of a socialist society demands a reply from the European left, especially the socialist and communist parties of the West to which she addressed herself. Most of them behave as if these questions were irrelevant. It would be tragic if she has to wait until, like the communist Jaroslav Sabata, she is standing in the dock before she gets an answer.]

To all Communist and Workers' Parties
Dear Comrades,

After careful consideration, I am starting to write this letter a few hours after the court passed sentence on the last member of my family, my twenty-one-year-old daughter Hana. She has been sentenced by the Regional Court in Brno to three-and-a-half years in prison. The sentences on my other children and on my husband are also unconditional terms of imprisonment.

It may, perhaps, seem strange that an individual Czechoslovak woman presumes to address such an important forum as the Central Committee and the memership of communist and workers' parties throughout the world.

I have decided on this step because, in my country, Czechoslovakia, there are no official quarters at the present time to grant me a hearing. The letter which I wrote to Dr Gustav Husak, First Secretary of the Communist Party of Czechoslovakia, about the arrest of all my family in December 1971 remained unanswered.

I, their mother, have seen all my children put in prison — the children to whose upbringing my husband and I sacrificed so much, children of pure, fine character who have earned the respect of all who know them. My youngest son is not yet twenty years old. I find myself as a mother in a unique and exceptional situation. Therefore, in these the most grievous moments of my personal life (I have experienced another terribly bitter moment — 21 August, 1968), I am guided in what I do by my maternal feelings, my honour as a citizen and by the firm conviction which has led me for twenty-five years to work for socialism in the ranks of the Communist Party of Czechoslovakia. I am, unfortunately, aware of the complications which may arise for me, despite all the proclamations about internationalism, as a result of this public statement. I risk the possibility that I, too, may suffer detention in consequence of this act. I have nothing to lose, however. To be able to move about outside the prison walls is not for me freedom.

Nor can I seek comfort in the work which I did for a number of years as a communist journalist. Nowadays, none of the expelled communists who differ from the official party view on the August act of so-called international aid are allowed to be employed in the media, anywhere in the cultural or scientific field, or in any responsible post of a similar nature. As stated by official quarters, this applies to half a million Czechoslovak citizens. That is not to mention socialist-minded people and citizens working for socialism who have had to leave their previous employment because of their support for the democratisation of public life along the lines embodied in the Action Programme which the CPCz adopted in the spring of 1968 and which it was pledged, before the whole nation, to implement. I myself have been deprived of the opportunity of earning my living in the employment I held since spring 1970 in Olomouc, seventy kilometres from where my family lived. The Brno firm Benzina refused to transfer me to work at a petrol station nearer home.

My husband, Dr Jaroslav Sabata, a communist from the age of nineteen, head of the Psychology Department at J. E. Purkyne University, Brno, until spring 1968, then until autumn 1968 secretary of the regional committee of the CPCz in Brno after regular election by the regional conference, later to his arrest on 20 November, 1971, employed as an iron worker with the firm Inzenyrsko-prumyslove Stavby, has been sentenced to six-and-a-half years in prison. This university teacher — a communist beloved by his students — who for thirteen years also lectured at the university on marxism-leninism and prepared many of his students for joining the Party, is now nine months in detention under conditions which, out of consideration for the present holders of power in Czechoslovakia, I will not describe in detail. I will say only that my husband, against doctor's orders (in 1964 he suffered from infarct myocardia, and as a result of sustained overwork he suffers from chronic inflammation of the stomach and duodenal ulcers), had up to his arrest to do heavy manual work because he could get no other job. In prison, in May 1972, he had a heart attack during which he was unconscious, and he is given food which causes him pain,

175

although I managed, after several weeks' effort, to send a medical certificate to the prison. In this letter, I would like to describe some of the circumstances of the court hearings which I attended personally. These were the trials of my sons Vaclav and Jan, the trial of seven Brno communists, all former party functionaries, and the trial at which my daughter was sentenced. I will confine myself to one of these — the trial at which my husband was condemned.

The building where the court sat was guarded as if the men on trial were a gang of hardened criminals. Relatives and friends had to show their identity cards both in the public corridors of the regional court and outside the building. The atmosphere around all the trials held in Prague and Brno in the summer months was marked by an endeavour to keep the proceedings as secret as possible, although they were officially announced as public trials.

That foreign journalists were not admitted will be known to you. But you probably do not know that admission to these public trials was granted to only one close relative of each defendant, and that by special permit from the regional court which was valid only on presenting one's identity card. You will certainly be interested to know that our penal code allows, in the case of trials held in camera for reasons of state, military or economic security, for each defendant to appoint two aides, their number being restricted only if the total should exceed six.

The only actual difference between these public hearings and proceedings in camera was that these trials in the summer were also attended by a few picked people, representatives of local government and the Party: here in Brno there were no more than ten. Others present in court were the defendants, their defence counsel, the members of the bench, the prosecutor, clerk, members of State Security and the police, and the uniformed guards who brought in the male defendants in chains. To be objective, I must add that the women were led in freely, the guards merely holding their arms. I should also add that close relatives, including grown-up children, could take turns in court, but never, at least not here in Brno, was a defendant allowed to have more than one member of the family present at the same time. In formal matters the bench followed the rules, the defendants could speak as they considered necessary.

All who have been on trial are sincere supporters of the socialist order in Czechoslovakia. From the localities where they lived and from their workplaces they were all described as publicly known, active citizens who had devotedly helped to build up this state.

As for the trial of the seven communists, former officials of the

176

regional party committee (one of a district committee) — the chairman of the bench, Dr Wolf, said in his speech stating the grounds for the verdict: "Neither the bench as a body, nor any individual member have formed the opinion that the men here convicted were enemies of socialism". That is to say, these communists were condemned for holding different political views which by word of mouth and in writing they made known among themselves and a few dozen others of similar political persuasion. These were mostly people known for many years to the defendants in party and public work. That the information may be as accurate as possible, I would mention here that in this way were circulated typewritten documents, and also publications issued abroad, such as *Listy* and *Svedectvi*, and also reports from the communist press (e.g. *Unità*, *Humanité*, *Rinascita*, etc.). Among documents presented as evidence by the prosecution was also the report of the proceedings of the Extraordinary Fourteenth Congress of the CPCz, which was not published in Czechoslovakia but was issued by party publishers in Italy. My husband himself wrote some theoretical documents, for instance, material for discussion known as the "Short Action Programme", in which he tried to find common ground between communists and those socialists who do not hold marxist views but support the socialist order in Czechoslovakia. I would also point out that the Short Action Programme expressly states that the action of nationalisation in February 1948 was a necessary and just act about which there can be no discussion. It is not true that my husband, or any of the convicted communists, favoured bourgeois democracy. All to a man are unequivocal supporters of socialist democracy based on the interests of the broadest masses and also controlled by the masses. My husband has always stressed as a matter of principle the need for control from below, that is, by the will of the people.

Many communist and similar parties of the Left, trade unions, and democratic anti-imperialist opinion throughout the world are, I believe, justifiably concerned about the series of trials in Czechoslovakia. I am convinced that the communist and workers' parties, individual communists and marxists, and all other advocates of socialism have an inalienable right to speak out on matters concerning convicted communists, socialists and other citizens. The same right belongs to democratic public opinion in the world concerned with upholding the basic human rights.

The international communist and workers' movement must find a common platform based on the substance and not on the superficial aspects of events in Czechoslovakia. In this connection one must ask: why is the armed entry by night of the allied troops on to the territory of Czechoslovakia denoted as international aid, while disagreement among many communist and left-wing parties is regarded by our authorities as interference in our internal affairs, that is, as distinct from "international aid", as something inappropriate and undesirable? Why can the Czechoslovak citizen learn nothing of these expressions of disagreement from the legal press in his country? And I put a further question as follows: why were the trials kept secret if they were justified?

It is noteworthy that my sons, the investigation of their case having been concluded on 2 March 1972, were brought to trial at the end of July, in the holiday period; that is, they had to spend over four months more in custody, while my husband's trial took place three days after the investigation was closed.

Finally, I would add: not only can the protests of communists and left-wing organisations, including democratic anti-imperialist public opinion, alter the hard fate of the Czechoslovak prisoners. I am profoundly convinced now more than ever before it is the task of the day to work out and clarify political questions on a higher theoretical level, within the communist and workers' movement itself. We need especially to clarify how the power won by the working class is to be implemented further in the socialist countries. In my view, it is not logical to argue that these are issues solely concerning the parties governing in countries where power has been won by the working class under the leadership of communist parties.

For it is essential that communist parties and their allies in countries where the bourgeoisie still rule should be given prospects that will make socialism attractive to other strata and groups of the population beside the working class. One cannot make use of allies only during the fight for power and the first phase of building socialist society. In the interests of the world communist movement they must be assured also for the later period, that is in the developed socialist society which we have, for example, in Czechoslovakia, all democratic rights. And this in such a manner that these rights will be genuinely, not merely formally, exercised.

Anna Sabatova, mother of three convicted children,
wife of the communist in opposition Dr Jaroslav Sabata

9   Petition by Czech Writers to the President of the Republic

[The collective action carried out by prominent Czech writers on behalf of political detainees in December 1972 is an example of the legal form of struggle for democratic rights and against police persecution. After the "Ten Point Manifesto" and the repeated protests of nuclear physicist Frantisek Janouch about the publications ban against scientists who had been expelled from the party and about the breaching of other laws too, this was a further example of those efforts which lay within the framework of the current laws and which aimed at maintaining these laws and abolishing arbitrary rule. By this action the Czech writers proved anew that they could be neither bribed nor intimidated, that they were not willing to be silent about the illegal persecution of people who had worked for socialism all their lives and had been condemned in the political trials of summer 1972.

In spite of the fact that the Czechoslovak constitution gives every citizen the right to present petitions to the president of the state, the official propagandists started up a libellous campaign against the authors of the petition and called them "enemies of socialism". In a report of the presidium meeting of the official so-called Writers' Union of 15 December 1973, there was talk of "a provocative petition, organised at the instigation of and with the support of foreign anti-communist centres"; the action was described as "an attack against the state by certain individuals who were compromised because of their active participation in preparations for a counter-revolutionary uprising in 1968". The occupation régime's official critic, Jiri Hajek, denounced the authors of the petitions (but without mentioning their names) as "a militant, right-wing oriented phalanx" (*Tvorba* no. 6, 7 February 1973).

The press campaign was of course joined in by the police, who interrogated Pavel Kohout, Ludvik Vaculik and Vaclav Havel and in various ways subjected the writers who had signed the petition to pressure, in order to make them withdraw their signatures. But only Jarmila Glazarova and Milan Jaris withdew; later the poet Miroslav Holub explained in a public self-criticism that he regretted having given his signature. The rest withstood the pressure and did not withdraw their signatures, in spite of the fact that they suffered further difficulties (most of those who signed are not permitted to publish in Czechoslovakia).

Neither the text of the petition nor the names of the authors were published in Czechoslovakia. This only serves to confirm that the régime knew very well that the majority of the population would have welcomed this humanitarian action and that, after the publication of so many well-known writers' names, it would not have been possible to speak about a "right-wing oriented phalanx", since in most cases they were old communists and socialists who were known not only for their literary but for their political activity.

The collective action of the Czech writers is yet another example of their civil courage and their closeness to the people; it is true that it did not produce a concrete result, but in its relation to international protest and solidarity actions it was certainly not without influence on the authorities' decision in December to release twelve political detainees from the group who were sentenced in summer 1972.]

Mr President,

The coming year will see the fifth anniversary of the event which has so strongly marked the life of our country and of us all. In the same period the world has achieved encouraging successes on the road to understanding, which promises in future to ease the lot of peoples and nations considerably.

At such a time we find all the more painful the knowledge that a number of people are held in prison in Czechoslovakia on political charges. Many of them are widely known to be socialists who have given of their best towards building up our society. Several are, in addition, seriously ill and others are suffering mentally owing to the fact that in our corrective establishments political prisoners are held together with criminal, morally debased elements.

However much we, the signatories, may differ in our views on various fundamental and particularised issues, we are agreed that magnanimity towards political prisoners cannot detract from the authority and prestige of state power, on the contrary, it demonstrates its humanity. Therefore we address ourselves to you, Mr President, at Christmas time, a time regarded in the greater part of the world as a festival of humanity, with the plea that you grant an amnesty for the political prisoners.

180

At the same time we ask you, Mr President, to arrange, irrespective of the above demand which may be subject to administrative delay, that the political prisoners receive the same concession as is allowed to other convicted people, namely, leave of absence, in this case for Christmas. The joy this will bring to their families will be the finest reward for you and for all who share in this matter, and it will redound to the credit of the entire republic.

With profound respect,
Adolf Branald, Jiri Brdecka, Josef Brukner, Lumir Civrny, Ladislav Dvorak, Jarmila Glazarova, Jiri Hanzelka, Vaclav Havel, Josef Hirsal, Adolf Hoffmeister, Miroslav Holub, Bohumil Hrabal, Milan Jaris, Zdenek Jirotka, Vasek Kana, Ivan Klima, Alexandr Kliment, Pavel Kohout, Jiri Kolar, Jan Kopecky, Karel Kosik, Frantisek Kozik, Vaclav Lacina, Jan Mares, Frantisek Pavlicek, Svatopluk Pekarek, Jiri R. Pick, Jarsolav Putik, Jarsolav Seifert, Jindriska Smetanova, Karel Siktanc, Jiri Sotola, Josef Topol, Zdenek Urbanek, Ludvik Vaculik.

Prague, 4 December 1972

10 Statement by the Socialist Movement of Czechoslovak Citizens

[The significance of this document lies above all in the fact that it proves how neither the political trials of summer 1972 (the purpose of which was to finish the socialist opposition off once and for all) nor the persecution which followed could liquidate the socialist opposition. This was also confirmed by the continued appearance of illegal handbills and publications, especially *Politicky mesicnik* and *Narodni noviny*, which since the middle of 1973 have again been coming out regularly every month, with precise information and commentaries.

This document, however, which appeared in August 1973 in the form of a leaflet distributed in Prague and other towns, also demonstrates the political continuity of the socialist opposition since the Manifesto of 28 October 1970. All the political positions so far adopted by the Socialist Movement of Czechoslovak Citizens show themselves here to have been correct, and to have remained as the fundamental purpose: the ending of occupation and of political repression, political and economic reforms, the extension of the influence of the population on political decision-making in all spheres, dialogue between leadership and opposition, overcoming of the consequences of 20 August 1968 through national reconciliation and the setting up of a leadership which could rely on the confidence of the population. What is new, however, is the development of an orientation towards international détente. The statement supports this tendency, including the accords signed between West Germany and the USSR and Czechoslovakia. This proves the mendacity of the official propagandists when they accuse the opposition of being against the strengthening of international co-operation and of maintaining cold war positions. At the same time, however, the statement correctly points out that the present situation of crisis in Czechoslovakia is a hindrance to the process of détente. What is especially remarkable is that part of the statement which is devoted to the relationship between Czechoslovakia and the USSR. It is not filled with hostility to the USSR, in spite of the fact that in the eyes of broad sectors of the people the relationship between the two countries has been very severely compromised. On the contrary, the statement aims at improving this relationship and at renewing it. Of course, the only way of achieving this is to get rid of the consequences of 21 August 1968 — and not through official self-criticism or declarations but by actions.

This is the same way of thinking as that which appears in Josef Smrkovsky's letter to Brezhnev in August 1973 and Alexander Dubcek's letter of 17 January 1974. These demands and appeals may appear utopian today; but they are not, if they are seen in the longer perspective of the next five years, with the possibility of an intensification of the conflict between the USSR and China and new crises in Eastern Europe, from which the USSR will have to find a way out. Furthermore, the statement once again confirms the realistic position of the Czechoslovak socialist opposition: it takes into consideration "useful compromises" and partial solutions, which may ease the life of the population at least momentarily. In this too, the interests and feelings of the majority of the population are reflected; it demonstrates the maturity and presence of mind of the Czechoslovak socialist opposition.]

Five years ago, on 21 August 1968, troops from the five Warsaw Pact countries entered our country. This military intervention was intended to halt the revival of Czechoslovak society which itself had stemmed from a realisation that general and comprehensive development was dependent on profound, albeit gradual, changes in many aspects of our communal life. Furthermore, such changes would be essential for Czechoslovakia, an advanced and cultural European country, to do no more than keep in step with the revolution in science, technology and culture, quite apart from the question of implementing the socialist and democratic programme which the majority of the Czechs and Slovaks supported. Most important of such changes were democratisation and the provision of legal guarantees of fundamental civil rights and freedom.

In recent years, the Socialist Movement of Czechoslovak Citizens has frequently stated its attitude to the August intervention and the effect this has had on our national life and on international relations. We have repeatedly condemned the crimes and the ignorance of the present régime, the dismissal and harassment of those whose political views fail to conform, the political trials, the systematic destruction of Czechoslovak culture and the paralysing of public life. Nothing has changed in our attitude to these political practices. Nor, alas, has there been any change for the better in our public and political life.

But the world has changed considerably during the past five years. The war in Vietnam has been halted as a result of negotiations between all the interested parties. New relationships are being created in Europe through the conclusion of treaties between the USSR, Poland and West Germany and the recognition by mutual agreement of the reality of two German states. A settlement between Czechoslovakia and West Germany, based on recognition of the nullity of the Munich Agreement, is being prepared. The visit of the General Secretary of the Soviet Communist Party to the United States has led to an improvement in the relations between the two strongest world powers. The many international negotiations, the successful opening of the conference on European security and co-operation and on the reduction of nuclear forces in Central Europe are all clear indications of a turn away from cold war towards the easing of tension and peaceful co-existence. A system of guarantees is being built up in Europe which should in future exclude any method of solving conflicts other than negotiation. This policy is in the interests of the Czechoslovak people, whose existence as a nation and as a state has always been entirely dependent on good international relations — it may indeed be said that Czechoslovakia lies at the centre of European problems.

If no genuine solution is found for the Czechoslovak question, Czechoslovakia will by its stagnation and the paralysis of its internal development constantly poison the atmosphere in Europe and throughout the world. It will constitute an obstacle to confidence among the countries of Europe and the world powers. The Czechoslovak question will continue to divide the international communist movement and will contribute to the division of anti-imperialist forces.

Opportunities and change

The Czechoslovak problem can, of course, be solved or left unsolved; it can be relegated *ad acta.* Today all issues are global and interconnected. Five years is sufficient time for reason to replace passion, for a sober attitude to supersede recrimination, for responsibility to replace mere concern for prestige, for arguments about the causes and the consequences of past events, about what would have happened "if . . .", to be halted in favour of practical, patient efforts to make good the damage caused by recent years to the internal life of Czechoslovakia and her relations with other countries, especially with the Soviet Union and the other socialist countries.

Three years ago, in a statement of policy by the Socialist Movement of Czechoslovak Citizens, we declared good neighbourly relations and alliance with the Soviet Union, our biggest neighbour and a world power of first rank, to be essential.

It is still true that it will be necessary to overcome the negative and undiscriminating attitude of the majority of our people to the USSR. The reasons for this attitude are understandable, but being purely emotional and hence unconstructive, it cannot lead to a positive solution. Moreover, it is an attitude to a certain line of Soviet policy as it was manifested five years ago. But we cannot change this attitude.

However, a gradual change can be brought about if the Soviet leadership shows in some way, in the spirit of its present policy — perhaps less in words and more in deeds — that it wishes, and also considers it beneficial for itself, to make good the consequences of 21 August 1968.

In the new international situation, this alternative is entirely possible. Within the socialist camp the leading representatives of the forces holding back the advance of peaceful policies are now out of political life — people like Shelest, Ulbricht, Gomulka. Only in Czechoslovakia is a group composed, for the most part, of those who masked their own bankruptcy and inability to adapt to change by declaring socialism to be threatened, clinging desperately to power. It is also common knowledge that these people have tried hard, and are still trying, to hold back any positive changes at home and in Europe; even so important a step as the settlement of relations with Federal Germany had to be forced through against their will.

New international atmosphere
However, the new international atmosphere strengthens the awareness that good neighbourly relations and alliance cannot be ensured by military presence nor by a handful of unprincipled protégés trying to deceive themselves, their allies and the world at large. We repeat that such relations can be assured only by a society of free and aware citizens, who can have no other interest than this.

In this new atmosphere, then, it is essential that an end be put to the situation where hundreds of thousands in our country are second- or third-class citizens who, to the detriment of the entire community, do not possess the right to work according to their abilities and their knowledge, who are humiliated and harassed by the power of the state and whose children have no right to full education. Their return by degrees to full participation in the economic, scientific, cultural and political life of Czechoslovakia would be of enormous benefit to our country. This by no means implies that all those who have taken their places would have to leave, that revenge would be taken and the vicious circle of persecution and recrimination start anew. All posts must be filled by those best equipped to benefit their fellow citizens, their country and socialism.

Such a policy could not, however, win confidence and support while people jailed merely for criticising the present régime remain in prison. Czechoslovakia must not be listed with Spain, Portugal and Greece as a country where communists, socialists and democrats are imprisoned.

It is also necessary to deal with the serious problems confronting the Czechoslovak economy. Today we are still reaping the fruits of the wave of investment during the second half of the 1960s. Beneath the seemingly healthy surface, the consequences of a technological lag are already becoming apparent. The main reason for this is the exclusion of tens of thousands of skilled specialists and the suppression of all initiative except that imposed from above. Investment in projects with no future and the return to the outdated system of command management of the entire economy are other factors.

The crisis in sales of consumer durables — cars, refrigerators, television and radio sets etc., which are also being ousted from the home market by products from other socialist countries, usually manufactured under licence from the West, is a forewarning of troubles throughout the economy. Before losses reach enormous proportions, it is necessary to speedily renew the search for methods of management suited to Czechoslovak conditions and to the level of our economic development, and to use all mechanisms which can help towards progress.

Economic integration
Economic integration is an essential factor in economic development today. To oppose this trend at a time when the USSR and the USA are planning joint projects for industrial enterprises in the interest of both countries would be an outdated anachronism. A course needs to be followed, however, which ensures that no country should suffer and that the benefits of economic association should be felt by the public both as producers and consumers.

Moreover, Czechoslovakia must be in a position, as the other socialist countries are today, to join in economic and scientific co-operation with the advanced capitalist countries in the interests of her own economy and of developing co-operation in Europe.

We are aware that the problems that have accumulated over the years cannot be solved at a stroke. We repudiate those who want to solve nothing because, apart from persecuting others, they are capable of nothing. But neither can we agree with those who set maximalistic demands, who want everything at once and who see useful compromises as the betrayal of ideals. We are convinced that any solution, even a partial one, of our problems is better than none, in so far, of course, as it is not an end in itself but a means towards creating a better atmosphere of mutual understanding and appreciation of the problems of others. When changes are seen in this way, the solving of one problem must lead to solving others.

But the events of 1968 and everything that has followed, have left too deep a scar on the political and moral consciousness of our people. To heal it, neither words nor any superficial measures will suffice. What is required is a genuine attempt to tackle all the fundamental problems. Failing this, the internal disruption of our society will persist, and will paralyse the efforts of all who wish to work to this end.

Czechoslovakia, a land of highly developed culture, could within a few years be a community of satisfied citizens whose aim would not be mere consumption; she could be a modern socialist society. But in the meantime she presents a picture of a country which is lagging more and more behind the rest of the world, including the socialist countries, in industry, science and culture. This country of deep-rooted democratic traditions which could stand in the first rank of progressive European countries with a democracy carried into socialist practice and with human freedom, presents a gloomy picture of silent, apathetic people, intimidated by the arrogance of power, which despises their opinions, a society under police despotism and with its prisons full.

The future
Just as the programme of peaceful relations between the two leading world blocs has been brought into being against the will of many opponents on both sides, so it is possible and necessary today to solve the remaining problems, including that of Czechoslovakia.

Concrete and practical steps, taking into account the customs

187

and traditions of our country, are not alien to those who, in 1968, in an entirely different time and a different world, were misunderstood in so many quarters — sometimes involuntarily, sometimes intentionally. One of the causes of this misunderstanding, perhaps, was that, overloaded with the work of modernising their own country, they tended to underestimate the importance of clearly stating their plans in the context of international relations.

All interested parties, all who have an interest and good will, wherever they may have stood in the past, should participate in solving Czechoslovakia's problems. The greater the share, however, in preparing and implementing a positive programme that is taken by those representatives of the Czechoslovak people who enjoy the confidence of the people, the more profound and lasting the results that could be achieved, the more rapid the advance and, consequently, the smaller the risk that would have to be faced.

Such a course would have the spontaneous support of the Czech and Slovak nations, and also of all peace-loving, democratic and socialist forces in Europe and all over the world. It would also be a significant contribution towards furthering the advances so far made in reducing tension in Europe and the world, and this is today the most essential prerequisite for any social progress.

Socialist Movement of Czechoslovak Citizens

21 August 1973

11 Letter from Jaroslav Sabata to the Central Committee of the CPCz

[Jaroslav Sabata's letter, which on 14 July 1973 he addressed from prison to the central committee and to its secretary Gustav Husak and which is published here for the first time in full, is one of the most interesting documents of the socialist opposition. This is perhaps the first time in postwar Europe that a communist condemned to a long prison sentence has addressed himself to the central committee of the party not as a pleader for mercy nor with self-criticism and submission, but as a conscious political partner who knows that he represents an important current in the communist movement and who proposes a political dialogue between the party leadership and the socialist opposition.

The main themes of the dialogue, according to Sabata, are the questions of civil rights and "unity in diversity" within the socialist states and the communist movement. He goes on to say that the socialist opposition bases itself on socialist ideology and that it therefore has the right to offer opinions that differ from the official conception. Sabata correctly asks why autonomous socialist groupings should not work in a socialist society, and why such a dialogue should lead to a weakening of socialism. He poses here the problem of the meaning of socialism as a society which ought to give its citizens more real freedoms than the bourgeois parliamentary system, and not as a society in which the persecution of people such as Sabata in Czechoslovakia and Grigorenko in the USSR can take place.

Sabata, who knows the heart of the bureaucratic élite very well and who clashed with Husak at the central committee session of 31 August 1968, has no illusions about his proposal being accepted. This shows itself in the fact that at the same time as sending it to the central committee he also wrote to the secretary of the Communist Party of Great Britain, John Gollan, asking him to intervene in the quarrel, which affected the whole international workers' movement. In this note Sabata stresses that "the appeal for a dialogue is not an abject appeal for mercy but an expression of revolutionary thought and a conscious political act". He defended

189

the "January policy" of 1968 as "a constituent part of the great political and ideological struggle for renewal, which the Twentieth Party Congress of the CPSU instigated" and which is in progress in all the communist parties and on the left as a whole.

For many reasons which limit the autonomy of the other communist parties in relation to the CPSU (even a non-stalinist party such as the British one), Sabata's proposals for intercession were not accepted. Excerpts from Sabata's letter were presented in the Labour left weekly *Tribune* on 9 November 1973 by Marian Sling, widow of the executed Czechoslovak communist Otto Sling.

Jaroslav Sabata got no answer from the central committee of the Czech party either — except that as a punishment he was removed from Bory prison and sent to Leitmeritz, where he is even more strictly isolated from the surrounding world. It is difficult to say whether the party leadership had changed its opinion under the influence of a changed world situation (the military putsch in Chile and the Middle East war), or whether the visit by two representatives from the ministry of the interior in May 1973, whom Sabata refers to, was from the outset merely aimed at finding out if he was prepared to make a self-criticism and dissuade his friends in the opposition to cease their activity, thus paving the way for a possible Moscow-type "Yakir-Krasin" operation in Czechoslovakia.

However, Sabata's demand for dialogue exists. It is a proud testimony to the opposition's determination to continue the struggle even from behind prison walls, and to Sabata's axiom to the effect that "the people do not beg for their inalienable rights, they fight for them" (letter to John Gollan). It heralds a future in which dialogue between the ruling group and the opposition over conceptions and forms of socialist construction will be something completely normal in the socialist countries. It is already a fact, today, that there are many roads to socialism. The point is now to recognise this.]

Jaroslav Sabata
Section 5/1
Plzen — Bory

Central Committee
Communist Party of Czechoslovakia
For the attention of the General Secretary, Dr Gustav Husak

Dear Comrades,

In the first half of May I expressed the wish to meet responsible people in order to discuss the possibility of finding a political solution to the differences which divide us and set us against each other.

The preliminary exploratory talk held on 17 May 1973, indicated that a dialogue between the ruling party and the left-orientated part of the opposition is, in principle, possible. The outcome of this exploratory talk met with a lively response from my comrades and friends. Their agreement and confidence encourage me to develop the idea of a dialogue and to formulate it in the binding form of this letter to the highest organ of the party.

Under no circumstances do we see the purpose of the dialogue to be our speedy release from prison. That is not our reason for wanting to negotiate. Naturally, the question of our trials exists and our attitude to them is clear. But we do not place this issue in the forefront, it is a subsidiary and not the main question. It would not exist if it were not for the more general question — that of civil rights. The prologue to our trials and convictions was the severe restriction of these rights, which explains why we could be publicly labelled as enemies of socialism without any opportunity to defend ourselves in a dignified and effective manner. The organs of security and the judiciary which accused and convicted us of allegedly hostile activity and hostility to socialism were merely completing what had been initiated in the political field. The complex of political and legal problems linked, directly or indirectly, with our cases is far from being a matter which we might put aside in favour of more immediate concerns and more tangible results. And it would, in any case, be short-sighted to do so. In the present state of affairs recurrences of political conflicts and of the use of repressive measures are unavoidable. Of course, there is the so-called state security prevention, but that, at the best, can merely contain the situation or conceal it from public view; it cannot prevent anything.

We do not want to look on passively at all this. Therefore we propose a dialogue, and therefore we pose as the prime question that of civil rights.

Some people might possibly see our posing of this question as being motivated by a desire to obtain better conditions for subversion, or even for subverting the socialist order of society and the state, as the Penal Code has it. To that we reply — we stand firmly on the soil of this order, and we know well what this declaration implies and to what it binds us. Our disagreement and our criticisms do not concern the essence of socialism, but the concrete forms and methods of governmental and political administration, which have long since been deeply infected by the bureaucratic disease. In this we see the barrier to the full and free unfolding of all the potentialities and advantages of socialism, here, too, we see the true inner cause of the crisis we experienced at the close of the 1960s. We are convinced that the advent of a new epoch will compel change in these forms and methods and we are equally convinced that these changes will not mean the destruction of socialism but its advance. That is to say, in envisaging structural changes in socialism, we are in no way departing from socialist ideology.

Our political view does not derive from abstract speculation; it draws on many years of experience among the wide masses of the people. Our desire is to state this experience rationally and constructively; we do not want to draw destructive conclusions from it, nor to contribute to any facile dramatisation.

You may respond by saying that everything of substance which needed to be stated politically was included in the line adopted by the Fourteenth Congress of the CPCz, or is contained in your resolutions, and that it is, therefore, unnecessary for anyone else to put forward a special political platform. We would venture, in this connection, to refer to one of the leading ideas of the Fourteenth Congress. We have in mind the rejection of any kind of "skipping" stages or "overestimating" levels of development, and especially any unrealistic assessment of the moral and political unity of the people. We recall that precisely this approach expresses most profoundly and critically the attitude to the pre-January 1968 party line, especially to the last two congresses before 1968 (in 1962 and 1966).

We are fully justified in asking — is it out of the question for autonomous socialist trends, political trends going beyond the line of the ruling party, to exist and make themselves felt in our society? Is that impossible at our level of development? Is it something unnatural? Is it not, on the contrary, understandable that, following the grave conflict in our Communist Party, there should be such trends?

As we see it, one of the main reasons why these trends are viewed with alarm is the fear that, at the moment when it was admitted that the opposition trends, too, are "to some extent" right, doubt would be thrown on the entire normalisation and consolidation of political life, and the consequences — a new crisis — would soon be felt. We have no intention of making light of these fears. All the more so, since, in our view, many of the causes of the crisis have been overcome only superficially, they were not handled in depth, in fact — the causes of crisis have not been overcome. The fears could prove justified and would certainly be borne out if the policy of dialogue were to be in the hands of indecisive and unstable liberal forces.

As for us — ours is not a liberal position. We reject liberalism both in its "bureaucratic" (or "technocratic") and its "anti-bureaucratic" guises. We are not liberals or petty-bourgeois democrats adopting the stance of the revolutionary working-class movement. We firmly believe that it is precisely the revolutionary democratic stand of the working class which represents the main driving force in all the socialist and democratic changes witnessed, and yet to be witnessed, in this century. For this reason alone we cannot be indifferent to anything that has been accomplished on the basis of the revolutionary, democratic and socialist movement throughout the *entire* postwar period in our country. We agree with you that the positive results of socialist construction are superior to that which deserves to be condemned or is simply negative. We also agree when you say that Czechoslovakia is a consolidated state. Under normal circumstances, we shall — if you so wish — stand with you to defend the principles on which this state was founded, by which it maintains itself and develops.

Thus the policy of dialogue would not play the part which those who see the defence of socialist principles as a defensive and purely propagandist matter might, perhaps, like to ascribe to it. It is not intended to play into the hands of what is usually termed "ideological diversion"; on the contrary, it is a contribution to an offensive by the forces of socialism in the coming (qualitatively new) stage of peaceful confrontation between socialism and capitalism.

Finally — why should a dialogue between different views lead to weakening socialism, if those engaged in it are socialists? Why should the unity of the people be weakened by a positive relationship among forces which undoubtedly voice trends which are undoubtedly present among the people? A well-considered policy of dialogue can certainly contribute more to the unity of socialist society than any policy which ignores the actual state of affairs in the society and, in particular, ignores the fact that socialist unity will, for a long time to come, remain "unity in diversity" — not because somebody or other wishes it, but for the simple reason that it is so.

We may put yet a sharper point on our arguments — to ignore the actual conditions does not pay. And to suppress socialist opposition by declaring it to be anti-socialist amounts to that. What is more, it also involves ignoring propositions which can lead to further progress, and that can only prepare the ground for renewed upheavals. So, to sum up, we may say that the best way to start a new crisis is to refuse a dialogue. While the policy of dialogue, of settling differences in a political manner, is the best "preventive" against a recurrence of crisis, it is the road to removing the numerous sources of chronic crisis, the symptoms of which should not be ignored. In its more profound sense, it is also the road to the full development of democratic socialist conditions without which a transition to the free, self-administering society of the future is inconceivable.

We are aware of the price of struggle. We are radical, but we do not go to extremes. We welcome every step forward in the relations between us, every step which does not conflict with the spirit of dialogue. We shall not be discouraged if our offer is refused. We are sure about our undertaking, and we are resolved to make whatever sacrifice may be required of us to carry it through. In the event that your answer is positive, we shall not be so retrograde as to see it as a sign of weakness. We shall regard it as demonstrating the inner strength of the socialist state which, as the first in history, seeks its one and only progressive support in the awareness of its people and not in the old instruments of power.

We have faith in the strength of socialism, and it would be strange were we to assume anything else in your case. That is why we are writing this letter and this invitation. Let us speak in a new way, let us awake new hopes. Hopes which will not be illusory. Not only our people, but all friends of socialist Czechoslovakia would welcome that.

Yours fraternally,

Jarsolav Sabata

Bory, 14 July 1973

Other communists, and non-communists, tried and sentenced last year, join me in signing; they are: Jan Tesar, Milan Silhan, Jaroslav Meznik, Zdenek Vasicek.

P.S. The number of signatories is limited, mainly for technical reasons, because the extreme isolation in which the prisoners are held has made it impossible for them to read the documents. I would point out that this isolation contravenes the law on the serving of sentences in the first corrective group.

J.S.

12   Jiri Müller's Complaint against Prison Conditions

[Jiri Müller, born in 1943, was condemned to a term of punishment in prison during the political trials of summer 1972. He is one of the most interesting figures from the Prague Spring and represents its radical current, which is not very well known to the outside world. He belongs neither to the party officials who opposed Novotny and formed Dubcek's main support nor to the writers and intellectuals who came to the public attention because of their fight against censorship and for liberalisation. He belongs among those representatives of the younger generation who had been fighting for the idea of a democratic socialism since long before January 1968 and who had been persecuted for that reason.

As a representative of the progressive students, Jiri Müller had already begun to fight against the bureaucracy's monopoly of power and for the right for civil initiatives during the 1964-65 period. His appearance at the conference of the official youth organisation (the CSM) in December 1965, at which he demanded autonomy for the youth and student organisations in relation to the party, his interest in the Chinese cultural revolution and in the existence of the Sino-Soviet quarrel, his attempt to build an alliance with the workers: all this led not only to his having a great influence among students, but also to sanctions. He was excluded from the CSM, expelled from university and called up into the army. Rehabilitated in 1968, Müller became one of the recognised student leaders, one of the new men in the political life of Czechoslovakia. The characteristic feature of his activity was that he did not defend the particular interests of the students but concerned himself with the closest possible co-operation between students and workers. It was he who initiated the accords between the Students' Association and the Metalworkers' Union, which became a model for similar agreements between the students and other trade unions. In these agreements, which were made just after the Soviet invasion, they rejected the retreats and compromises of the leadership, supported workers' self-management and demanded the mobilisation of the masses in a struggle against the advance of

196

the conservative forces.

When the Students' Assocation was banned in June 1969, after Husak's takeover of power, Jiri Müller was one of the first victims of the gathering repression. In Spring 1970 he was expelled from the university for a second time and was forced to go and work as a salesman. However, he continued his political activity; in November 1971 he was arrested and accused of having taken part in the distribution of leaflets before the so-called elections (see document no. 4). On 21 July 1972 he was condemned to five and a half years' imprisonment at a political trial by the Prague state court.

During the interrogation and in court Müller behaved courageously, in spite of the fact that he was brutally treated in order to make him give false testimony. In his final speech at the end of the proceedings in front of the supreme court, on 13 September 1972, he said: "I would like to bring to the attention of the bench the methods by which I was forced to speak in Bohunice prison . . . when I refused to give the statement required of me, I was punched round the ears, grabbed by the hair and my head was banged against the wall . . ."

Like the others, Jiri Müller was condemned for "anti-socialist intrigues". To the court he denied these accusations as decisively as possible: "My activity was not anti-socialist. It was based on socialist positions and was directed against a régime which has emanated from the occupation of the state territory of Czechoslovak Soviet Socialist Republic by foreign armies, and which is based not on the consensus of the most important layers of society but on a system of enforced loyalty. I am deeply convinced that this policy will be rejected, and with it this political trial and those trials which are to follow. It goes without saying where my place will be in future developments."

The letter published here demonstrates that Jiri Müller has not been reduced to silence in prison, although his health has deteriorated so much that he is repeatedly in the prison hospital. His letter is not a personal complaint but a valuable document which reveals what lies behind the so-called normalisation process in Czechoslovakia.]

To The Federal Assembly of the Czechoslovak Republic
Re: Jiri Müller: complaint concerning the violation of Law No.

59/65 of the Penal Code Relating to conditions in prison.

I hereby lodge a complaint against the introduction of special prison routines, which I regard as unlawful both in principle and in practice. Denial of the right to consult my lawyer or to study the text of the pertinent law has considerably aggravated the difficulty of lodging a complaint.

The complaint is based on the following grounds:

Security
I have been put in the special section in Block 5 of Plzen Prison. I am kept in a locked cell with the window closed all day (minimum two persons, maximum four persons). The cell also serves as our workshop. Communication with persons other than the inmates of the cell is punishable. I may leave the cell only if granted special permission and must be accompanied by a warder. I may look only in a permitted direction. When I fall ill, I am not transferred to the infirmary but solitary confinement. Maximum security measures are applied in the special section — comparable to conditions when on remand. This degree of isolation does not apply to the other sections of the prison where the inmates are allowed to move about freely in the blocks and exercise yards.

Work
The law stipulates that prisoners should be provided with work commensurate to their state of health and abilities, and that working conditions must be comparable to those outside. The job I have been allotted — fixing pins and hairclips onto cards — corresponds neither to my abilities nor my state of health. The job is determined by the limited types of work possible in an isolated cell. In other sections work is not performed in isolated cells. This kind of work is exceptionally tiring on the eyes. Atrophied vision, dim artificial light and confinement in the limited space of the cell all day inevitably cause painful inflammation of the eyes, fatigue, headaches and deterioration of sight. No signal is given to announce the beginning and end of working hours and the lunch break. Non-fulfilment of the hard work norms is punishable by a reduction in the food ration and other penalties, and compels me to work overtime. In the first quarter of 1973 it took me ten-and-a-half to twelve hours a day of monotonous mechanical work to fulfil the norm. Interruption of work during the shift because of eye strain or stiffness is punished, irrespective of the fact that I am fulfilling the norm.

During the first quarter of 1973 I fulfilled the norm by 105 per cent on an average, and my gross earnings amounted to 440 crowns (2.42 crowns an hour on average), which is less than half the earnings in other prison workshops. This sum amounts to about one fifth of the average wage of Czechoslovakia, and eighty-five per cent of it is deducted for prison expenses. Time lost through no fault of the prisoner is not paid for. The legal provision for prisoners' participation in ensuring safe and healthy working conditions is not observed.

Social rights
The special section is located in an area where the atmosphere is highly polluted. I am affected by this during essential airing of the cell and during the exercise break. The sheets are filthy within four or five days and dirt is already washed into the ones we are given. I may use hot water once a week for about fifteen minutes, whereas in the other sections the prisoners may wash in hot water at any time. Skin infections are not infrequent under such unhygienic conditions.

The law provides for a minimum of one hour of exercise and fresh air a day. Inmates of other sections may walk about freely for at least two or three hours of their spare time a day including Saturday and Sunday. The special prisoners are taken out for exercise only five times a week under maximum security. If the prescribed "cultural programme" occurs in the morning, the exercise break is cancelled. We get less than the minimal time for exercise provided by the law. If we protest, our watches are taken from us.

During March 1973 I managed to make a list of the names of the prison warders responsible for my category and the length of the exercise they allowed. This showed on average that it was one-third shorter than the legal minimum. On 15 March the list was confiscated during a body search.

Apart from 15 minutes' drill during the exercise break (the drill was introduced on 4 April 1973, five months after the section was established) any kind of physical training in spare time is forbidden. (First Lieutenant Hruby informed us of this decision by the Chief Warder of Block 5, Captain Tvrdlik, on 4 April 1973). The other sections may play basketball or table tennis etc.

The work schedule in the special section reduces our total spare time, including one hour's exercise, to three hours.

Intellectual activity is systematically restricted. On 9 January

199

1973 an order was given that the special section would not be allowed to have their own books on specialised subjects or language textbooks. Classical books on Marxism-Leninism in the library would not be accessible to us (order conveyed by First Lieutenant Hruby). Written notes (notes on books etc.) would be destroyed during cell searches.

Legal provisions on the extension of educational facilities allow other prisoners to have their own foreign language textbooks and to attend language courses. The special section are even forbidden to learn foreign words. On 2 April 1973 my Russian vocabulary notebook was confiscated and on 4 April I was told by Hruby that any kind of vocabulary would be destroyed, in conformity with a decision taken by Captain Tvrdlik, Chief Warder of Block 5, Major Tous, "re-education" officer for the section and First Lieutenant Hruby.

Another example of deprivation of intellectual stimulus is that my parents were forbidden to copy out poems in their letters to me. The monotonous mechanical nature of my job, the long hours, continual isolation, the conflicts produced by the application of the regulations, unhygienic conditions, lack of exercise, light and air, and intellectual activity, combined with the general conditions, do not ensure regeneration of mental and physical powers.

Health care
According to the law, health care for prisoners should be governed by the same considerations as for the rest of the population. In fact, the aim is not to preserve mental and physical health. A sick prisoner of the special section is not transferred to the infirmary but to the "medical observation room". This is the official title for solitary confinement in a cell which is furnished in the same way as the others, but where — unlike the infirmary — doctors are not in attendance. Work is allocated with regard to the prisoner's isolation but not his state of health.

If a prisoner complains of eye ache the doctor automatically prescribes stronger glasses. Inflammation then occurs though it is obvious that this is caused by the nature of the work and working conditions. Yet ten different types of job are available in the prison.

The administration of the prison medical service enables the prisoners' needs to be neglected. For example when I started to serve my sentence, Dr Chvojka, the doctor who examined me, recommended a diet for gall stones. The head physician, Dr Sadilek, rejected the recommendation on the ground that I had not been

X-rayed in prison; he also rejected my application for an X-ray. After two months, during which I was treated for problems resulting from food other than that prescribed in the diet, I managed to get my gall bladder X-rayed. The X-ray confirmed the gall stones. The head physician rejected Dr Chvojka's new recommendation without giving any reason. I sent him a written request for an explanation on 7 January 1973, to which he did not reply. I have not yet received an answer to my letter of 8 March, addressed to the prison Governor Major Jezek, requesting him to put the matter to rights.

Legal position of prisoners in the special section
When attention is drawn to violation of the law, the prison officials usually respond: "The law can be interpreted in many ways; you have to go by the prison regulations". These regulations take precedence over Law No. 59/65 of the Penal Code, although they come under the law and are supposed to be based on its articles. The prison officials with whom I have come in contact refuse to discuss either the law or observation or violation of its articles. Any appeal to the law is countered by a reference to the prison regulations. Thus, when I complained to the Prison Governor that permission to consult my lawyer had been unlawfully refused, he informed me "as far as legal representation is concerned, you must abide by the regulations". The prison regulations contain no reference at all to legal representation whereas the law guarantees it. The prison regulations are in direct violation of legal requirements: Article 2, Section 3 authorises destruction of prisoners' mail; Article 8, Section 3 stipulates exercise only on weekdays.

Prison officials, obliged by law to observe prisoners' rights, ignore the right to participation in the running of the prison as stipulated by law. They flout the law which lays down that prisoners in the first offenders' category shall not be punished by solitary confinement. The prison officials violate the provisions of the law on legal guarantees for the protection of prisoners.

On 11 December 1972, I was threatened and prevented from consulting my lawyer, and on 14 March 1973 my letter applying for legal advice on composing a complaint about prison conditions was withheld. The complaint about unlawful restriction of my rights which I submitted to the Governor Major Jezek, was dealt with by Captain Tvrdlik, the Chief Warder of Block 5, who informed me: "A lawyer has no right to deal with matters related to prison conditions".

Besides obvious violations of the law, distorted interpretations of the law also occur. The prison regulations which should mirror the practical application of the law reflect only one of its aspects. Article 16 — joint measures for the protection of health — contains only four sections on *prisoners' duties*. The same applies to the three sections of Article 11 — fulfilment of work duties. Prisoners' rights in daily life have been omitted from the prison regulations.

In practice such situations as the following arise: Article 10, Section 11 stipulates that "prisoners are required to attend to their personal hygiene", but my written request to wash my socks in warm water was not granted. Application of the regulation "the prisoner may keep in his cell only things for which he has been given permission" results, for example, in the destruction of prisoners' written notes (notes on books etc.). Also the unlawful restriction of his civil rights.

I have been denied a copy of Law No. 59/65 of the Penal Code, governing prison conditions. I have been in the special section of Block 5 since 23 October 1972. During November I asked for the loan of a copy of the law. First Lieutenant Hruby informed me that no copies were available, also that it was not desirable that I should become acquainted with the content of the law and that permission would not be granted. A month later Captain Tvrdlik gave permission for my lawyer to provide me with a copy of the law. But the copy sent by my lawyer was not handed over to me. Instead, I was permitted to glance through it twice in the presence of a warder, but I was forbidden to make any notes. I was forbidden even to note down the numbers of the articles because that "could lead to your using them". On 25 December 1972 I lodged a complaint with the Prison Governor describing the prison officials' conduct as an attempt to prevent me drawing a comparison between the law and the existing prison conditions.

While examining my complaint, Captain Tvrdlik threatened to punish me if I were to make any accusations against the prison administration and its personnel. I asked whether I would be allowed to keep a copy of the law; he said I would not. First Lieutenant Hruby put it more explicitly the following day, saying: "You'll never see the law again." On 14 March 1973 I was informed that my letter to my lawyer describing my attempts to obtain a copy of the law had been confiscated. On 15 March 1973, First Lieutenant Hruby told me — and wrote down in his report on his talk with prisoner Jiri Müller of 14 March 1973 — that a copy of Law No. 59/65 of the Penal Code would be sent to me as soon as it reached the prison library. On 14 March I asked for the copy from my lawyer, which had been put away with my bundle of personal effects. This was refused. First Lieutenant Hruby told me I might "read the text of the law but only from a copy belonging to the prison". On 5 April I asked whether the prison had obtained a copy of Law No. 59/65 and was told by First Lieutenant Hruby: "That's not so easy. We can't get hold of one here and no one has been to Prague yet."

The last stipulation of the prison regulations in Block 5 says: "When due for release or parole the prisoner is required to sign a pledge of silence."

Penal re-education

A characteristic feature of penal re-education is the disparity between duties imposed on the prisoners and the fulfilment of everyday duties towards prisoners. For example, the regulations insist that certain clothing shall be worn to the bathroom, yet the use of hot water is restricted. The conditions authorised in the special section and the knowledge that the special section was established as a more extreme form of repression for a certain type of prisoner affects the way the warders treat the prisoners. An unequal relationship, fraught with tension, can be overcome only by correct behaviour on both sides. The warders' arrogance, harassment, and the arbitrary nature of their orders lead the prisoners to defend themselves and this evokes further repressive measures. It is difficult to describe the atmosphere in which seeming trifles may cause inhuman humiliation and loss of dignity — the announcement that a seriously ill prisoner can wait for medical attention for as long as fifteen hours (Lieutenant Besta, 17 January 1973) — lights put out in free time on the grounds that we are not working; reading and letter writing made impossible (ordered by Sergeant Nemec, 3 February 1973, First Lieutenant Chemlik, 11 February 1973) — being told that I must guess the intervals at which to take antibiotics (Lieutenant Besta) — the reply "I'll decide how long you can be there" as a response to my observation that according to an announcement by the Chief Warder of Block 5, twenty minutes was allowed for bathing (First Lieutenant Chemlik, 23 December 1972) — mode of address during exercise break: "Wipe that grin off your face and keep your bins where I bloody well tell you" (Sergeant Nemec, 15 March 1973).

The main prop of the penal system is discipline. Discipline is not interpreted as fulfilment if duties by prisoners combined with respect for their rights — stipulated by law — but as total submission by the prisoners ("You're here to obey orders" — Sergeant Sulc, 6 February 1973). Penal re-education in the special block has no interest in the prisoners and their problems — the prerequisite of both education and human relations — it often becomes an instrument for destroying human dignity.

Re-education categories

The law recognises only three re-educational categories. These are differentiated by the scope of the prisoners' rights, the extent to which they are restricted, the type of re-educational programme, the permitted degree of participation in the running of the prison and the types of security measures.

The court classified me in the first category — the mildest. The prison officials try to explain the difference between Block 5 and the other categories as "internal differentiation", which they claim is a legal differentiation permitted by the law.

But the routine in the special section in Block 5 is tougher than the other blocks and also than the second and third categories. My position is not more favourable than that of prisoners in the second and third categories. This is obvious from the lack of social rights, legal guarantees etc.

Penalties are inflicted which are forbidden in the first category, cultural facilities are worse than in the second category (on average a cultural programme is one to one-and-a-half hours in isolation twice a month). It is impossible to speak about the extent of participation in the prison administration because no form of such participation has been set up, despite the fact that the law provides for this in all prison categories. Security measures and the isolation arising from them are more rigorous than in the third category. The special section is an extraordinary feature of the penal system, outside the penal forms stipulated by law.

Further circumstances confirm this. About twenty men sentenced for subversion in the seven trials held in July and August 1971 have gradually been transferred from custody to the special section. Also some prisoners sentenced earlier under Part 1 [dealing with political crimes—trs.] of the Penal Code, who had been serving their sentences in the normal blocks of Plzen Prison have been transferred to the special section. The special section was not established by an order of the judiciary but by State executive organs — it was proposed at the highest level of the Ministry of Justice and approved by the Prosecutor General (according to information given by First Lieutenant Hruby). The section came into being on 20 October 1972 when Dr Alfred Cerny (tried with Dr Jaroslav Sabata et al) and Karel Koutny (tried with Dr Tesarova et al) were transferred from custody in Brno to Plzen Prison.

Confinement in isolation and subjection of physical and mental persecution are typical of the extraordinary penal system. It is true that the STB did not discover anything they wanted to know from the above-mentioned trials; but this does not authorise them to maintain the same routine after conviction as on remand. It is true that the men for whom the special section was established are members of the various groups comprising the socialist opposition in Czechoslovakia. But this does not give the authorities the right to introduce a routine which does not fail to ensure the prisoners' physical and mental health, but systematically undermines it to the point of inflicting permanent damage.

Conclusion

In my opinion the above facts demonstrate that the conditions under which I am forced to serve my sentence constitute a system for which there is no legal or political justification. Officials and warders act upon orders issued by their superiors on the prison staff.

I do not know the goals of which the extraordinary penal system is one example. However it is undoubtedly a reflection of the official attitude to the existence of a socialist opposition in Czechoslovakia. As I understood from the Chief Warder of Block 5, Captain Tvrdlik, the decision to establish a special section in Block 5 of Plzen Prison is an aspect of the class struggle against members of the political opposition who have been sentenced to imprisonment.

Higher level political decisions, as well as the consequences arising from them, should not conflict with the existing laws in a country where the law is respected.

Prisoner Jiri Müller No. 11175
2, Block 5/2, Labour Camp, Plzen 1
16.4.73

13   Against the Terror in Chile — and Elsewhere

[The following article appeared in the illegal opposition monthly *Narodni noviny* in October 1973. It is an interesting example of how the socialist opposition reacted to the terror in Chile (it issued several protests and statements of solidarity), and at the same time it reveals the hypocrisy of the Czechoslovak régime on this question. To the Western reader, a comparison between the military coup in Chile and the occupation of Czechoslovakia may seem exaggerated or misplaced. Many will object that however regrettable the situation in Czechoslovakia may be, this country and indeed the USSR are "socialist states" and therefore cannot be compared with the capitalist system.

Certainly there are distinctions, but in the reverse sense. It is a bigger tragedy if a state which calls itself socialist treads human rights into the ground than if this is done by a military junta which does not claim to be socialist. All those people who believe in socialism as a more just kind of social order at least must grasp this.

In a series of documents the socialist opposition had declared its solidarity with the Polish workers (in the winter of 1970-71) and with the opposition in the USSR, as it did with the struggle of progressive democratic forces against totalitarian dictatorships throughout the world, from South Vietnam to Greece, Spain, Iran, Brazil and Chile. Thus it demonstrated that it was inspired by the spirit of international solidarity and that its criticism of the great power politics of the current Soviet leadership had nothing to do with anti-socialism or anti-Sovietism.

The left in the West must be clearly informed that solidarity does not go only in one direction. One cannot protest against the suppression of freedom and human rights in Greece, Spain, Brazil and many capitalist countries while keeping silent or even approving when the same thing happens in countries which call themselves socialist, on the pretext that this kind of criticism "is playing into the hands of reaction". The suppression of human and civil rights in the socialist countries is in itself the worst anti-socialist propaganda there can be, and it is in the interests of everyone who believes in socialism to take up an open and principled position against it.]

AGAINST THE TERROR IN CHILE — AND ELSEWHERE!
Since 11 September fascist terror has raged in Chile, with all that
goes with it: raids, arrests, executions, killings "while attempting
to escape", the destruction of basic civic freedoms, the return
of land to the landowners and of the nationalised enterprises to
capitalist owners. This kind of violence is being denounced all over
the world. Even in the Czechoslovakian newspapers, space is freely
granted to protests. (There are certain exceptions of course, such
as Pavel Kohout: he announced his criticism in a letter to the
Minister of Culture, Klusak, and explained why his protest had
also been published abroad.) Those who are delighted that someone somewhere managed to kick the communists around are short-
sighted. For one thing, it is not only the communists who are
affected in Chile at the moment, and secondly, no true democrat
can be really delighted when freedom is strangled somewhere.

There were more democratic rights and freedoms in Chile under
Present Allende than under the military junta, simply because
Allende ruled in a democratic way. Of that there can be no doubt.
Because he answered the opposition without violence and within
the law, Allende greatly helped the military rebels to carry out
their plans. Certainly mistakes, perhaps even serious ones, were
made. The government of Popular Unity certainly failed to deal
with some of the basic needs of the people during the three years
of its existence. However, nothing can change the fact that as a
government it was more representative of the people than the junta
is.

The decisive problem of supplies (which arose when the transport workers declared their destructive strike) could have been
solved with aid from the socialist countries, if they had been prepared to give it. A loan of twenty "Antonov" transport aircraft
could have been fixed in a few hours, even if they would have had
to take a complicated route (after all, the USSR managed this very
well with military equipment to Egypt). The aircraft, together
with a supply of lorries, could have helped considerably to solve
a problem which ultimately caused indifference to the fate of
Allende's régime. The socialist countries did not give this sort
of help though they were probably prepared to help in certain
other areas (the running of state security etc.).

However paradoxical it sounds, the USSR was in fact content,
in spite of its formal protests, with what happened in Chile (so was
the USA of course). The meticulous preservation of democratic
processes in the process of building a socialist society were a thorn

in the flesh of the Soviet Union. They were afraid that yet another kind of socialism, a Chilean kind, with a human face, would be added to the four already existing (Soviet, Chinese, Yugoslav and Cuban — not to mention what the Italian or Spanish communists imagine socialism to be). Soon the Moscow centre would no longer be a centre but just one of the provinces, as Lenin in fact predicted. Brezhnev could never support such a course. It would have been difficult for the countries of the Warsaw Pact to invade Chile, but other people took care of that.

President Allende, the Chilean equivalent of Dubcek, is dead. But what has followed his death is — except for the killings (but the Soviet armies contributed to that in our country as well) — so similar to Czechoslovakia that it must be obvious. The methods of putschists are the same, whether they come from a Russian steppe or South America.

On 23 October 1973, *Rude Pravo* was upset when a West German CDU deputy spoke of the putsch as an "intervention" (as if one could mention such words in Czechoslovakia!). Perhaps the word should be "entry", or better still "brotherly international aid"? Moreover, Chile is yet one more proof that the USSR does not grant aid where it is needed. Let us see what else upsets the normalised Czechoslovak press. Local committees were broken up (as were workers' committees in our country). The junta banned lessons in Marxism at universities (in our country all departments of Marxism-Leninism were banned after August). Freedom of assembly, association, written and verbal expression no longer exists (just try a reunion of the Club of Committed Non-Communists, or call a demonstration in one of the smaller squares of Prague, or try to write what you think in a newspaper. Such a notion is ludicrous in present-day Czechoslovakia, and in the Soviet Union they lock people up in lunatic asylums for making such demands). In Chile, as under Hitler, the junta burns books which are inconvenient or written by authors whom they do not appreciate (in our country they are not burned in public— but if you know anyone working in a public library, just ask him to show you the list of books which have been thrown away, taken out of circulation or destroyed. The number of titles runs into thousands). In Chile, infringements of privacy are an everyday affair (but how many Czech homes have been broken into by STB agents without a court order, how many of our flats have been fitted with bugging devices such as the one which Professor Kaline mentions in his appeal against his two-year sentence?). "Thousands of Chileans from

208

ordinary people to well-known personalities like Dr Asenjo, the 1973 Nobel Prize winner, have been expelled from their place of work, their only 'crime' being that they support progressive ideas". (In this respect, the junta has been behaving clumsily. Where else but in Czechoslovakia were hundreds of thousands of people, from internationally famous artists to journalists, students and ordinary workers, expelled from their posts for the same thing?) The "new rulers introduced complete control over television and radio" (and what is it like in our country? Compare what the television and radio were like in 1968 and 1969 with what they are like now). The junta ordered "work shifts for the nation" (an analogy so perfect that even the title corresponds). It banned the left-wing press (a long list of journals were banned under Husak — let us simply remember three which stood out: *Zitrek, Reporter* and even the communist *Politika*). It has abolished trade union rights (perhaps it would be worthwhile asking Karel Hoffman, a "noted representative of the working class" who has never worked in a factory, to list the rights of our trade unionists. A few seconds would suffice).

Yes, we must agre with our press: what is happening in Chile is indeed fascism. But fascism is still fascism, wherever it takes place and with whatever jargon it is camouflaged. Fascism is simply fascism, no matter under which label it operates, whether it rages in Chile or Czechoslovakia. That is why we are united with the Chilean people and that is why we should protest, not only against the threat to the life of Luis Corvalan (who, by the way, approved of the occupation of our country in 1968), but against the threat to the lives of hundreds of other people. We must also protest against the sacking of people from work, against censorship, against infringements of privacy, against the ban on freedom of association, against the ban on certain books, against the abolition of trade-union rights. All this must feature in our protests. We must underline that we are against it, no matter where in the world it is happening, and we must fight against it.

14   Alexander Dubcek's Letter on the Occasion of Josef Smrkovsky's Death

[Alexander Dubcek's letter of 18 January 1974 was his first public utterance since September 1969, when the official press failed to publish his last speech to a meeting of the Central Committee before his exclusion from the party. This letter too was not officially published in Czechoslovakia, but was circulated in duplicated form and printed in the illegal monthly *Narodni noviny* in April 1974. It is cast in the form of a private communication, but Dubcek clearly intended to make it known both abroad and inside Czechoslovakia, so that he could present his views on the current situation and on the possibilities of further developments. This is demonstrated by the conditions under which the letter was written. Dubcek received the telegram informing him of Smrkovsky's burial too late (which was obviously intentional), and could therefore not take part in it personally. The following weekend, however, accompanied as always by agents of the secret police, he went from Bratislava to Prague to convey his sympathies to Katrin Smrkovska, the dead man's widow. He would have left it at this gesture, but he wanted to leave behind a testimony to what he thought; and so he handed Mrs Smrkovska the letter which he had written in Bratislava. Dubcek's letter was published on 13 March in the Italian communist weekly *Giorni — Vie Nuove,* which two years previously had published an interview with Josef Smrkovsky. The thanks for this was due above all to the editor of this journal, the writer Davide Laiolo, a member of the central committee of the Italian Communist Party, which had made no secret of its sympathies for the Prague Spring and its representatives.

As a result of this letter, in April 1974 Dubcek was sharply attacked by Husak and then interrogated by the state police. They wanted to know who had "inspired" him to write the letter, who he had spoken with and who had taken it out of the country. Dubcek confessed to having written the letter on his own initiative, but he strictly refused to discuss its content with the police. Certainly, the letter expresses the personal view of Alexander Dubcek and can therefore not be regarded as an official document of the socialist opposition. In spite of this, however, it occupies an important place in the development of the opposition. The significance of the letter can be summed up in three main points:

1. Not even five years of pressure, bullying and isolation by the police could force Dubcek to make a "self-criticism" or to say or do anything that would have hepled to legitimate or justify the occupation of August 1968 and the ensuing "normalisation". On the contrary, in this letter Dubcek defends openly the socialist character of the 1968 policies, which are characterised by the current régime as "anti-socialist" and "counter-revolutionary".

2. With his criticism of Husak's behaviour, Dubcek reveals the shameful nature of his theory of "the lesser evil" which has to be supported or at least accepted because the other alternatives are even worse (this is an argument which the western press even takes over). It may be asked why Dubcek does not criticise the well-known dogmatists such as Bilak, Indra, Kapek, Jakes, Hoffman etc. He had good reason: Bilak and the rest had been so discredited in August 1968 that they were not in a position to upset the unity between the party and the people. The "dismantling" of this unity could only be carried out by one man, who was acquainted with the ideas of the Prague Spring, who had pledged his trust to Dubcek, and who had the halo of being a former victim of stalinist terror. That man was Husak, and therefore the main responsibility for the current situation falls upon his shoulders.

3. One of the most interesting but also one of the most debatable points of the letter is the part in which Dubcek gives his view of the way out of the current crisis. Here there is a certain distinction between the concept and above all the formulation of Dubcek on the one hand, and of the socialist opposition on the other, as there is in some of the previous documents. While the socialist opposition has come to the conclusion that the military invasion of August 1968 was the logical consequence of the anxiety of the bureaucrats in power in Moscow, Berlin, Warsaw and Sofia about the "democratic contagion", and that it could only have been prevented by adopting a firm attitude, mobilising the population and the army and working out a compromise on this basis, Dubcek in his letter poses the question of whether the allies were sent "false information".

This does not mean, however, that in Dubcek's opinion it was simply sufficient for the Soviet leadership to have been better informed, and everything would have turned out differently. He knows better than anyone how much trouble was spent in sending

211

correct information — but in vain. His formulation of the question should not be seen as political naïveté but as a conscious tactic, which can only be understood by someone with experience of the party apparatus and of reading between the lines. Dubcek knew that his letter would reach the hands of the Soviet leadership and that they would grasp what he was saying. His formulation of the event as a "mistake" is a hand offered to Brezhnev or his successor: if the latter wants to escape from the situation in which Czechoslovakia is an open wound in the world communist movement and a hindrance to collaboration between communists and socialists, then he only needs to say that he was "wrongly informed" and he is excused. Dubcek relies not only on the exigencies of Brezhnev's *Westpolitik* and the pressures from the Chinese, but also on the fact that three of the most adamant partisans of military intervention in 1968 — Shelest, Gomulka and Ulbricht — were no longer on the political scene.

This tactic has several catches. It assumes that the Soviet leadership needs a positive "tidying-up" of the Czechoslovak situation, whereas in fact it is quite possible that it sees the situation as normal — especially since it is now essentially indistinguishable from the other East European countries. And it assumes that as a result of growing pressure from China or even in the case of a conflict with China, Moscow will seek to relax the East European régimes, so as to play along with the populations of these countries; whereas the anxiety which is always felt in relation to external danger may well have precisely the opposite effect. Finally, one must not underestimate the influence and the resistance of the givers of "false information" in the party, state and security apparatus, who form the essential basis of the current régimes in Eastern Europe, who after the events of 1968 in Czechoslovakia and 1970-71 in Poland are not going to give up their positions, and who see "counterrevolution" behind any reform.

Precisely because of all these questions about future developments — which are of great significance not only to Czechoslovakia and Eastern Europe but also to the whole of the western left — Dubcek's letter is an important document, and a contribution to the discussion which is being conducted in the socialist and democratic opposition: not only in Czechoslovakia but also in the USSR (see, for instance, the debate between Roy Medvedev and Academician Sakharov). The fact that Dubcek felt it necessary to break his silence is proof of his view that one should not remain passive but actively contribute.]

Dear Comrade Smrkovska,

I heard of Josef Smrkovsky's death only the day before yester-day, reported by a Vienna news agency. And only this morning have I received the telegram informing me that the funeral is today at five. The news shocked me deeply, all the more so since Josef was only sixty-three years old. Until just now I didn't even know where and when his funeral was to be. And, with so little time left, I sent just a brief telegram. I hope you got it.

Now perhaps I may express at somewhat greater length my profound sympathy at the loss of Comrade Smrkovsky, a man who devoted himself throughout his hard and stormy life to the Party, the working class, the people, to the fight for the victory of the socialist revolution and the building of socialism.

We all have our faults, and he, being only human, had his too. But I want on this occasion to speak about him as a man who was above all a communist — that was the prime fact guiding his entire life and work. When he died, he had been stripped of his party membership, but he was always a communist.

His life was given above all else to a determined and selfless fight against the bourgeoisie, for the liberation of our country from the fascist occupation and for indissoluble friendship with the Soviet Union. He proved this to the full as one of the leading members of the underground Czech National Council, actively engaged in pre-paring and directing the Prague Rising. Not by chance did he join in this fight, but with the absolute conviction of a man who had clearly chosen his goals at the moment when he joined the Communist Party of Czechoslovakia during the days of the bour-geois republic.

A progressive worker, a proletarian, he found his rightful place in the party ranks. And faithful to the purpose which both his feel-ing and reason had prompted him to choose, he joined the working class fight against the bourgeoisie for national and social emancipa-tion. Equally, in the period of building socialism, he knew where he was needed. He worked tirelessly both as a rank-and-file fighter and as a responsible member of government bodies. Nor did his faith in the Party and in socialism waver even in the fifties, when he too fell victim to the violation of party principles and socia-list legality.

Later, thanks to the good sense and strength of the Party, it was possible to surmount this tragic chapter in his life and in the party's history. Again he took his place in government, at the difficult time when the mounting crisis in the party and in society as a whole required to be solved, at the time of struggle to implement to the full the principles of inner-party democracy and to accomplish what are commonly termed "the policies of the Prague Spring". At that time Smrkovsky was a notable representative of Party and state.

The tragedy which subsequently befell him was — if possible — heightened by the circumstance that it was his old friend and colleague of the "spring" 1968 days, Gustav Husak, who in April 1969 came out against him, and by the deliberate use of slanders and employing personal power, advanced the accusations which resulted in his expulsion once more from the Party. Thus it was not given to Smrkovsky to retain that which had been the meaning of his whole life — his membership of the Party. And once more he was labelled as an enemy of the working class, of internationalism and the republic. The tragedy was not his alone . . .

Yes, when he died he was not a member of the Party, but he had certainly not become an enemy of the people. I know that he was and always remained a communist.

I can well imagine the difficulties you have had about the funeral. They were certainly the same as I faced eighteen months ago when my mother died — shortly after she had been expelled from the Party. Her great sin was that she was unable to agree with the views and the accusations fabricated against me, accusations concerning my alleged anti-Party activity.

The Party rejected my mother even after death. The League of Antifascist Fighters showed not the slightest interest in her funeral, nor did the Women's Union express sympathy with us; as for the Church, my mother did not really belong to it. . . . So we were sincerely grateful only to the nightwatchman at the undertakers', who accompanied her on her last journey to the Bratislava Crematorium. When I wished to bury the urn with her ashes in her birthplace, Urhovec, I was requested to do so secretly and without attendance by the public. I carried her urn to the cemetery early one morning, accompanied by my son Peter. And that, too, maybe has caused me to write you this lengthier letter with reflections about the life of Josef Smrkovsky.

I am convinced that he wanted above all else not "to open the door to the return of capitalism", but to achieve complete and unrestricted inner-party democracy, a strengthening of confidence among the people and the working class, transforming this into revolutionary and creative strength of the Party and making the

Party more attractive to the youth. He was well aware of and never lost sight of the importance of our country's ties of friendship. He gave proof of that throughout his life.

Our real problem was to implement the principles of marxism-leninism in a more realistic and less mechanical manner in a situation requiring that we build a mature socialist society without losing sight in so doing of the general principles which make the building of socialism possible. At the same time we persistently underlined the need to respect the particular conditions in each country — the level of development, the mentality and the historical background of our nations . . .

You know, in common with thousands of other party members, and Comrade Smrkovsky knew too, that in January 1968 and in the following months, the Central Committee had to tackle very many difficult and complicated problems which had accumulated in the Party and throughout our society. We were justified in recognising the objective necessity of avoiding any repetition of the "Hungarian events". The problems could not be solved in a vacuum. Hence it was no accident, nor due to carelessness on our part, but in accord with the laws determining matters independently of the will of individuals, that in this great, healthy, irresistible movement of revival in the Party which is commonly referred to as the "Prague Spring" and was supported by almost the entire Central Committee, the Party leadership and the overwhelming majority of Party members and the public, there emerged voices and trends hostile to the party and the people. But, since the Party leadership never betrayed the interests of the CPCz, the people, the alliance and internationalism, thanks, too, to Comrade Smrkovsky — and it is true they never betrayed, because the sole criterion is the truth of the matter, of its essence, and not the labels employed — so hostile forces would, in any case, have had no hope of success and no practical opportunity for asserting themselves.

To this day I am unable to grasp how our allies could accept at their face value the patently unobjective and distorted reports about the way we intended to tackle the internal problems of the CPCz and our society, about the actual balance of forces, which evolved during the Prague Spring in favour of the Central Committee, the Party and state leadership. The same goes for information concerning the party leadership and especially its individual members. Yet it was precisely such information which aroused suspicion and fears as to whether we were really capable of solving our problems with our own internal resources. Evidently contri-

215

buting to painting a false picture of the situation were all those who were incapable of abandoning sectarian methods alien to genuine party work, those who were losing, or had already lost, the ability to do a job and were anxious about their personal positions, they did this because their entire view of what was happening was coloured by the fear of losing their leading role in the Party. Unhappily, it is much easier for many party officials to confuse the bureaucratic commands with the Party's leading role; their attitude is encouraged by the psychosis of immediate and blind obedience that comes with power. Their aims — and it was not a matter merely of "return" to the situation prior to the "spring" — were purely visions worthy of a Potyemkin. They behaved as if the very foundations of society were under attack. An atmosphere of that kind can be very dangerous and careerists can easily exploit it. Now the system of personal power has been restored, from top to bottom, with different people, but often with the same men. Evidently the problem for many of them was not to improve the Party's policies and work, to offer creative ideas — they confined themselves, rather, to substituting one man for another in official posts and to doing so without upsetting things in the Party, in mass organisations, in cultural and economic life, and without having to undertake any reform measures.

This meant losing what is most precious to a party of the Lenin type, the confidence of the masses in the party, confidence won by policies to which each individual, and the masses, had made significant contribution through their initiative and activity and which was directed towards the complex development of socialist society. That cannot be achieved except on the basis of free agreement, belief in and support for Party policy on the part of the population at large.

That was the chief problem for us and for Comrade Smrkovsky — to make the Party's leading role more effective, not to deprive the working class of this vital instrument in the socialist revolution and the building of socialism, as the official document "Lessons" pretends . . .

I have written this kind of letter because it is addressed to you, who have lived and grown with the Party for many long years. I have written in the hope that I may help to alleviate your suffering and grief in your hardest hour, when Comrade Smrkovsky has departed from you — and he departed without a sign of recognition from the Party to which he devoted his whole life. I want, by this letter, to tell you that he did not live in vain.

Remain firm in your conviction that he did not die a traitor to the Party, but as a communist. Please accept condolences from myself and my wife. As you can imagine, my wife's life beside me is no easier than mine. We are reviled and defenceless. And that, I feel, is the most tragic aspect of these events. My wife, too, has been expelled from the party. But we bear no ill will against the party, the movement nor against its ideals. They are far stronger than the obstacles placed on the road which leads ever forward. We have not allowed ourselves to be discouraged. All honour to the memory of Comrade Smrkovsky.

Alexander Dubcek

INDEX

219

Some other titles in the MOTIVE series

Michel Raptis
Revolution and Counter-Revolution in Chile

Henri Lefebvre
The Survival of Capitalism

Franz Jakubowski
Ideology and Superstructure in Historical Materialism

Agnes Heller
The Theory of Need in Marx

Mihaly Vajda
Fascism as a Mass Movement

Hilda Scott
Women and Socialism — Experiences from Eastern Europe

Andras Hegedus
Socialism and Bureaucracy

Andras Hegedus, Agnes Heller, Maria Markus, Mihaly Vajda
The Humanisation of Socialism

Bill Lomax
Hungary 1956

Henri Laborit
Decoding the Human Message

222

C1